ALIEN TONGUES

Also by Elizabeth Klosty Beaujour:

*The Invisible Land: A Study of the Artistic
Imagination of Iurii Olesha*

Alien Tongues

BILINGUAL RUSSIAN WRITERS OF THE "FIRST" EMIGRATION

Elizabeth Klosty Beaujour

Studies of the Harriman Institute

Cornell University Press

Ithaca and London

First published 1989 by Cornell University Press.

International Standard Book Number 0–8014–2251–5
Library of Congress Catalog Card Number 88–43287
Printed in the United States of America
*Librarians: Library of Congress cataloging information
appears on the last page of the book.*

*The paper in this book is acid-free and meets the guidelines for
permanence and durability of the Committee on Production Guidelines
for Book Longevity of the Council on Library Resources.*

The Estate of Vladimir Nabokov has granted permission to quote from: *Bend Sinister*, 1947, *The Annotated Lolita*, 1970, *Poems and Problems*, 1970, *Strong Opinions*, 1973, and *Look at the Harlequins!* 1974, published by McGraw-Hill Book Co.; *Pale Fire*, 1962, *The Gift*, 1963, and *Speak, Memory: An Autobiography Revisited*, 1966, published by G. P. Putnam's Sons; *The Real Life of Sebastian Knight*, 1941, published by New Directions Publishing Corp.; *Dar*, 1952, and *Drugie berega*, 1954, published by Ardis Publishers; *The Nabokov–Wilson Letters*, edited by Simon Karlinsky, 1980, published by Harper & Row Publishers; and the Russian version of *Lolita*, 1967, published by Phaedra Inc., Publishers.

For Tom, who brought bilingualism home

Studies of the Harriman Institute
Columbia University

The W. Averell Harriman Institute for Advanced Study of the Soviet Union, Columbia University, sponsors the Studies of the Harriman Institute in the belief that their publication contributes to scholarly research and public understanding. In this way the Institute, while not necessarily endorsing their conclusions, is pleased to make available the results of some of the research conducted under its auspices. A list of the Studies appears at the back of the book.

Contents

Tempt not alien tongues,
rather try to forget them

[Ne iskushai chuzhikh narechii,
no postaraisia ikh zabyt']
—Osip Mandel'shtam

Preface

Because this is a book about writing in more than one language, it seems necessary to provide readers with the writers' words in their original tongue as well as in an English translation. Titles are cited first in the original, but for ease of reading, given the variety of languages involved, quotations are presented first in English and then in the source language. The chief exception to this practice is the Appendix, for Samuel Beckett not only wrote in both French and English but also systematically self-translated his works from the language in which he had first written them into the other. Always citing Beckett in English first would obscure the very process under discussion. Quotations in the Appendix are therefore given first in the language of the work's composition and then in the one into which Beckett translated it. In general, translations of texts that the authors have not themselves put into English are mine; when they are not, the translation is credited. Out of old habit and an aversion to diacritical marks, I have used the Library of Congress system of transliteration from Russian into English, except for the names of writers who have adopted a specific Western spelling and for direct quotes from works written in English in which other transliterations are used.

When one ventures beyond the borders of one's home discipline, it is a pleasure and a relief to find encouragement from colleagues who are specialists in other areas. I thank Stanley Novak, Gerald Turkowitz, and Martin Chodorow for their patience with a neophyte. I am especially grateful to Loraine K. Obler for her willingness to share bibliography and for her suggestions (gentle, but firm) for curbing my occasional unscientific flights of extrapolation. Fellow Slavists Richard Sheldon and Maurice Friedberg were kind enough to read all or part of the manuscript and to make detailed suggestions. I am particularly indebted to Simon Karlinsky, without whose ground-breaking work on Marina Tsvetaeva and Boris Poplavskii a good part of Chapter 5 would have been impossible. My thanks also go to Michel Apel-Muller, Nina Berberova, Raymond Federman, Vladimir Pozner, Zinaïda Schakovskoy, Leo Vroman, and Vasily Yanovsky for their willingness to answer questions.

I owe a special debt to my former students Diane Manthei and Lilit Gampel, who, working from heavily corrected yellow pads, typed various versions of this book with intelligence and great good humor—sometimes, I fear, even at the expense of their own work.

The preparation of the final version of the manuscript was supported in part by a George N. Shuster Faculty Fellowship award.

Most of Chapter 3 was previously published as "The Bilingualism of Elsa Triolet," *Comparative Literature Studies* 20, no.3 (Fall 1983), 317–328, Pennsylvania State University Press, University Park, Pa. Portions of Chapters 1, 2, 3, and 4 appeared in "Prolegomena to a Study of Russian Bilingual Writers," *Slavic and East European Journal* 21, no. 1 (Spring 1984), 58–75.

Grateful acknowledgment is made to the following for permission to quote previously published material: Editions d'Art Albert Skira, for *La mise en mots*, by Elsa Triolet, © 1969 Editions d'Art Albert Skira, Geneva; Editions Denoël for *Du bilinguisme*, edited by Abdelkebir Khatibi, 1985; Oxford University Press for *After Babel*, by George Steiner, 1975; Harcourt Brace Jovanovich, Inc., and Jonathan Cape Limited for the English translation of *Letters, Summer 1926* by Boris Pasternak, Marina Tsvetaeva, and Rainer Maria Rilke, edited by Yevgeny and Yelena Pasternak and Konstantin M. Azadovsky and translated by Margaret Wittlin and Walter Arndt, 1985; Editions Robert Laffont for the introduction to *Les Oeuvres romanesques croisées*, by Elsa Triolet, 1964; Les Presses de la cité for *Lumières et ombres*, 1964, and *Une manière de vivre*, 1965, by Zinaïda Schakovskoy; Editions Littéraires et Artistiques, La Différence, for *Le langage et son double*, by Julien Green, 1985; Insel Verlag for permission to quote from letters between Rainer Maria

Rilke and Marina Tsvetaeva included in *Rilke und Russland: Briefe Erinnerungen Gedichte*, edited by K. M. Asadowski, 1986.

ELIZABETH KLOSTY BEAUJOUR

New York City

Bibliographic Abbreviations

RLSK   Vladimir Nabokov, *The Real Life of Sebastian Knight* (New York: New Directions, 1941).

SM   Vladimir Nabokov, *Speak, Memory: An Autobiography Revisited* (New York: G. P. Putnam, Wideview/Perigee, 1966).

SO   Vladimir Nabokov, *Strong Opinions* (New York: McGraw-Hill, 1973).

Summer Letters   Boris Pasternak, Marina Tsvetaeva, and Rainer Maria Rilke, *Letters, Summer 1926*, ed. Yevgeny Pasternak, Yelena Pasternak, and Konstantin M. Azadovsky; trans. Margaret Wittlen and Walter Arndt (New York: Harcourt Brace Jovanovich, 1985).

Tsvetaeva—WWP   Simon Karlinsky, *Marina Tsvetaeva—The Woman, Her World, and Her Poetry* (Cambridge: Cambridge University Press, 1985).

ALIEN TONGUES

Introduction:
Bilingual Trajectories

Elsa Triolet once exclaimed that, having written in both Russian and French, she had been condemned to a *mi-destin*, a half-destiny.[1] She was justified in complaining, for the achievements of modern bilingual writers are rarely considered "whole." We usually know only the books in one of a writer's two languages. At best, we may have read some of the others in translation, but we still miss the relations between the languages, and our monocular vision reduces these writers' potentially double destiny to a kind of artistic "half-life."

Bilingual and polyglot writers must be seen in their linguistic complexity.[2] Not merely the sum of two (or more) monolinguals, bilingual writers are in many ways intrinsically different from their monolingual fellows. In fact, bilingual writers may have more in common with bilingual writers in other languages than they do with monoglots writing in any one of the languages they use. To demonstrate this contention, I attempt a kind of disciplinary diglossia, combining the insights of literary criticism with those of neurolinguistics. For, as I try to show, the bilingual writer's difference begins on the level of his or her cerebral organization for language and reflects the broader variety of linguistic processing strategies available to bilinguals.

Such an interdisciplinary synthesis runs the risk of itself being doomed to a "half-destiny." Although it is true that some of the following chapters can be read more or less independently of others, the cross-fertilization attempted by the book as a whole is potentially useful both to neurolinguistics and to literary studies. I have tried to make the introduction to the neurolinguistics of bilingualism informative, yet as painless as possible—a kind of "neurolinguistics for poets"—in the hope that those readers who may be primarily concerned with Nabokov or other individual authors will come to agree that the neurolinguistics of bilingualism is interesting in itself and that it sheds new light on some of the significant particularities of bilingual writers *as writers*. Neurolinguists may find that a knowledge of the artistic trajectories of specific bilingual writers is of more than anecdotal value in today's neurolinguistic and neuropsychological disputes about the nature and consequences of bilingualism—especially because so little of the now voluminous neurolinguistic research into these matters deals with what I call "cultivated bilingualism," and almost nothing has been said about bilingual writing per se. Since what I propose is an integrative study of phenomena that are usually interpreted through the professional methodological vocabularies of two quite disparate disciplines, I have tried to keep the language as commonsensical and unmarked as possible, so that readers whose training is primarily in one discipline or the other will find fewer obstacles on the path to disciplinary polyglotism.

For mechanical reasons, my notes are placed at the end. Many of them are, however, substantive, and without them *Alien Tongues* is a *demi-livre*. Readers will, I hope, find these notes rewarding rather than anticlimactic.

Bilingualism is problematical for all the disciplines that should take it into account because it invariably introduces messy methodological complications. Nevertheless, there is no reason to assume that knowledge of more than one language is an exceptional human condition. In fact, a very large proportion of the world's population is polyglot. The daily use of several languages in different contexts is and has been the norm in many societies. Twentieth-century disruptions have encouraged bilingualism, and we all know native speakers of German, Russian, Chinese, or "minor" languages who have had to learn to "express themselves" in languages other than their "mother tongues." There are even fairly large numbers of people who have become *writers* in a language other than their first. Joseph Conrad is the usual example, but many other nineteenth- and twentieth-century authors would do just as well.[3] Still, such authors, while bi- or multilingual, are not usually polyglot *as writers*. And although we know and easily accept the fact that in previous centuries, before the myth of Romantic "self-expression," people wrote in Latin as well as in their vernacular languages, and although we do not object too strongly to the bilingual practice of literary criticism, there seems to be something disturbing and anomalous in the case of a modern poet or novelist who has defined himself as a writer in one language and has then either switched entirely to another or has continued to alternate with some regularity between the two.

Until recently, literary critics and linguists have avoided the phenomenon of the modern bilingual writer, the major exception being Leonard Forster's interesting and wide-ranging *The Poet's Tongues*.[4] Even an article with a title as promising as "Widespread Bilingualism and the Creative Writer" immediately excludes the possibility of most interest to us, declaring that it is "not concerned . . . with the bilingualism of cultured individuals, or small cultured groups in unilingual societies."[5] Věroboj Vildomec's classic *Multilingualism* does consider cultured polyglots, but, aside from a few comments on Conrad, he does not actually discuss writers who are bilingual or polyglot.[6] André Martinet, in his preface to Uriel Weinreich's *Languages in Contact*, justifies Weinreich's failure to consider bilingual writers by declaring that "the clash, in the same individual, of two languages of comparable social and cultural value, both spoken by multitudes of monolinguals, may be psychologically most spectacular, but, unless we have to do with a literary genius, the permanent linguistic traces of such a clash will be nil."[7] Martinet has been led astray by the sociolinguist's methodological concentration on the spoken language. It would seem obvious that bilingual writers of talent and some reputation (even if they are not "geniuses") do leave traces in the *written* language, some of which then become part of the spoken language. The example of Pushkin is particularly relevant here, but one could also make a strong case for the influence on both the written and spoken language of such twentieth-century polyglots as Joyce, Nabokov, and Beckett.

Linguists who should have known better, including Vildomec, have maintained that active multilingualism inevitably hampers literary expression.[8] Among neurolinguists, Macdonald Critchley has gone so far as to state flatly that no bilingual has ever achieved fame as a poet or a prose writer in both his languages.[9] Martin Albert and Loraine Obler, in their generally even-handed review of neurolinguistic studies of bilingualism, *The Bilingual Brain*, declare that Critchley is wrong in this regard because "his argument is contradicted in other cultures, for example the Islamic"; but even they do not acknowledge that there exist in modern Western culture writers who have achieved renown in more than one language and that such writers are more numerous than one might suppose, among them several of the most important writers of the twentieth century.[10] Somewhat belatedly, François Grosjean has recognized that Samuel Beckett and Vladimir Nabokov are "proof" that "one person can write literature in two different languages," but surely this is damning with faint praise.[11]

My primary sample for study is provided by the bilingual Russian writers of the "first," post-1917 emigration. The Russians of the "first" emigration make up a relatively homogeneous group, part of a sudden, more or less simultaneous, and involuntary displacement en masse of much of a cultured community. One might have expected that there would already have been many bilingual Russian writers in the nineteenth century, when Russian-French bilingualism was commonplace among literate Russians. Some Russian authors, among them Pushkin and Turgenev (and in a sense, Tolstoi), as well as Viacheslav Ivanov, did try writing in French, but none of them produced a major literary corpus in a language other than Russian. Somewhat surprisingly, it was only after the 1917 Revolution that a number of Russian writers, finding themselves in exile, successfully made the transition to writing in a second language. Still other writers of the first emigration might have opted to become bilingual writers—the purely linguistic capacity was there—but, as we shall see, they ultimately took Osip Mandel'shtam's advice and refused to "tempt alien tongues."[12]

For the Russians of the first emigration, "balanced bilingualism," or anything even approaching it, was no longer the norm. While many members of the first emigration did have some childhood acquaintance with the second language in which they would ultimately write, Russian was, except perhaps for Nabokov, clearly their dominant early tongue. Most of them retained heavy accents in other languages throughout their adult lives and would never have been taken for "native speakers" of their second language. But one does not need to be a native speaker to become a bilingual writer. Bilingual writers are rarely "balanced." What characterizes them is that they have committed themselves to working extensively, though not necessarily exclusively, in a language other than the one in which they first defined themselves as artists.[13]

The trajectories of writers such as Vladimir Nabokov, Elsa Triolet, Zinaïda Schakovskoy, and Vasily Yanovsky who did commit themselves to writing in a language other than Russian, thus compounding their exile, are complex, apparently tortuous, and in many ways idiosyncratic. Yet they all passed through a similar process; and while it is happily not possible to predict with any certainty what the consequences will be for writers who commit themselves to active bilingualism, and while their works differ in many ways, when one considers the complete careers of the bilingual Russian writers of the first emigration, certain patterns do emerge.

Some of the writers of the most recent, "third" Russian emigration have also begun to experiment with writing in English or French or Hebrew. The outstanding poet among them, Joseph Brodsky, is already struggling with the sense of being "less than one."[14] But all these writers are still in the early stages of the process of their bilingual evolution, and I therefore do not consider them in detail. Nor do I analyze the works of those Soviet writers who, while writing primarily in Russian, sometimes also write in the languages of their native national republics. I leave them aside in part because they are still active and their trajectories are incomplete, but also because their situation is so fundamentally different from that of our primary sample of exiles.

I therefore propose to begin by outlining those findings of neurolinguistics which are relevant to bilingual writing. Then, because scientists have done relatively little interviewing (as opposed to *testing*) of bilinguals, I follow this discussion of the "hardwiring" of bilingualism—if "hardwiring" it proves to be—with a consideration of how bilingual writers *feel* about their practice, and I attempt to see how this affect may correlate with the cerebral structures and the range of processing strategies available to "bilingual brains."

While Vladimir Nabokov is necessarily a central figure in any consideration of bilingual writers, other bilingual members of the first Russian emigration are also worthy of attention in their own right. The central chapters of this study, therefore, consider Nabokov, Triolet, Schakovskoy, and Yanovsky, as well as some bilingual Russian writers such as Vladimir Pozner and Il'ia Zdanevich who are less well known or whose work is less completely bilingual, as well as two writers who might—perhaps in some sense *should*—have become bilingual writers but declined to do so: Marina Tsvetaeva and Boris Poplavskii. Because it is important to see whether the patterns that emerge among these writers are exclusive to them, or whether they are independent of the purely Russian aspects of their linguistic situation, it is useful to have a "control." For this purpose, I provide an appendix that considers the bilingual aspects of the writings of Samuel Beckett, the only bilingual writer of Nabokov's generation who could challenge his supremacy. Beckett's trajectory makes an informative contrast to those of the Russians, yet it supports my general argument.

Although the process of their linguistic metamorphosis was often exquisitely painful for Russian bilingual writers while they were undergoing it, many of them eventually came to realize that what at first seemed a sacrifice, a treason, almost a self-murder, was in fact merely a step in a much more complex process that, over the long run, was not destructive or subtractive but, on the contrary, generative and positive. As we shall see, these writers ultimately came to realize that they were not either Russian *or* (say) French writers; nor were they Russian *and* (say) French writers. They were something else entirely, something that was not necessarily *more* or *less*, but that was definitely *different*.

CHAPTER ONE

The Neurolinguistic Substrate
of Bilingual Writing

It is extremely difficult for a monoglot to disassociate thought from words, but he who can express his ideas in two languages is emancipated.

—S. J. Evans

Although the weight of the evidence proves that humans are not rational animals, they are certainly (*pace* Nim and Koko) language animals. All human beings are "wired" for language. Since Paul Broca's discovery some one hundred twenty years ago that injuries to certain parts of the left cerebral hemisphere caused aphasia, there has been a daunting amount of research on brain and language and, in recent years, a seemingly exponential increase of studies of the ways in which the brains of active bilinguals may be differently organized for language than those of monolinguals.[1] For, as Robert Zatorre has observed, it is in fact remarkable that a person should be able to learn and use more than one language,[2] and neurolinguistics must try to understand how the cerebral mechanisms that are specialized in language processing manage to keep these systems separate and yet also allow them to mix voluntarily. Many fundamental questions have been investigated over the past twenty years: Are the brains of bilinguals and polyglots really differently organized for language processing than the brains of monolinguals? If so, does this difference in organization manifest itself in different patterns of cerebral dominance for language? Do bilinguals process and store information and speak and write their

7

two languages by means of one system or two? Or are there some functions for which the languages share a system and others for which they are separate? Is it possible that the learning of a second or third language influences previously established patterns of cerebral development and dominance? May learning a new language affect the way in which the *first* language is processed? Does bilingualism have any effect—positive or negative—on intelligence or creativity?[3]

Neurolinguistic and psycholinguistic answers to such questions cannot entirely explain, and still less explain away, the bilingual literary creativity that so commonly astonishes the readers of someone like Nabokov; yet, if one is going to study bilingual writers, it is essential to have some idea of the (possibly) anomalous neuropsychological substrate that underlies bilingual writing and that may, in its turn, be affected by it. Let us begin with the accumulated evidence that the brain is much more flexible for language than had previously been assumed, that individual human brains are more idiosyncratically organized for language than had been thought, and that patterns of hemispheric participation in the same adult individual may vary at different stages of life and of new-language acquisition.

Cerebral Lateralization for Language

It has long been established that much of the neocortex of the left hemisphere of the "normal" human brain is specialized for language and that the left cerebral hemisphere is the one that is generally "dominant" for language functions.[4] But there is also evidence that significant groups are statistically less left-lateralized for language processing than are the adult, right-handed, monolingual males without a family history of left-handedness who are considered to constitute the norm.[5] Many tests and studies of aphasic patients have shown that the left-handed (even those for whom the left hemisphere is dominant for language), women, children, and *bilinguals* (irrespective of sex and handedness) are frequently less lateralized for language than the norm.[6] In recent years, studies have reported considerable right-hemisphere involvement in language processing even for right-handed males, particularly during the learning of a second language if it is acquired after the first language has been firmly established.[7] The *manner* in which the second language is learned may also be an important factor in the extent to which the right hemisphere participates, particularly in the earlier stages of acquisition.[8] Jyotsna Vaid has observed that young adults who have acquired a second language informally are more likely to show more right-hemisphere participation in second-language processing, whereas those who have learned in a formal context involving writing are likely to show even greater left-hemisphere participation in the second language than in the first.[9] Some studies suggest that right-hemisphere involvement in second-language processing may in some cases persist in proficient bilinguals, even after the learning stages have passed; others, however, have not found such differences in lateral dominance for most language tasks, regardless of when the second language was learned, how long it was used, or how well it was known, although they do not rule out right-hemisphere participation in semantic processing.[10]

In the face of such apparently contradictory results, many neurolinguists have come to the position that (in part because of problems in the methodologies used to determine whether lateralization for one of a bilingual's languages is different from lateralization for another) there is no way to answer these questions of differential lateralization for all bilinguals, since one cannot assume that the results of any given study, even one that has been properly conducted, will be true for *all* bilinguals —or even for a majority of bilinguals.[11] For our purposes, what we need to retain from the inconclusive literature on lateralization is that evidently not all brains are organized for language in exactly the same way, that there is a broad range of patterns of hemispheric participation in language processing, and that a considerable variation of hemispheric representation of certain language functions may and does exist in individual bilinguals. Furthermore, not only may language be differentially represented in the hemispheres of different people, but participation of the right hemisphere in language processing may be different in a single individual at different periods of his developing bilingualism or polyglotism, depending on situation, levels of competence, and different patterns of language use.

It is also important to realize that, quite aside from whether the bilingual's languages are differentially lateralized, they are often differentially represented even within the dominant left hemisphere. As George Ojemann and Harry Whitaker and Whitaker, Daniel Bub, and Susan Leventer have shown, although the range of possible left/right variations in language laterality is impressive, the range of possible variations in intra-hemispheric localization is even more so.[12] Their studies of several bilingual brains have shown that usually the two languages only partly overlap. The weaker language tends to be represented more diffusely around and beyond the central language zone of the left hemisphere. There are sites at which one or the other language is represented exclusively as well as sites at which both languages are represented, though not necessarily to the same degree. Whitaker and colleagues note that up to 50 percent of the cortex of the left hemisphere may be available to be occupied by language. Thus, there is probably a "spatially flexible (plastic if you will) range of cortex that may be recruited for language functions within the hemisphere, as well as a flexible distribution of processing strategies to allocate between the two hemispheres."[13] They observe that this is a situation one would expect if the localization and representation of language behavior in a nervous system were determined more by experience than by genetics, and that the specific location of cortical representation of language in given cases may be the result of a variety of experiential factors. Thus it would seem that cortical organization for language in the adult brain is to some degree flexible and that there are areas in the dominant-language hemisphere that *may* be committed to language but that *will* be so committed only if the individual becomes bilingual or polyglot.[14]

These studies are particularly significant for our purposes. Not only do they show partial overlap and partial separation of the languages of bilinguals in the cortex, but they also insist on the idiosyncratic nature of the physical organization of language in each bilingual, noting in conclusion that it is in fact remarkable that there "is as much consistency in localization as has been demonstrated in the literature of lateralization."[15] It is evident, then, that the brains of adult polyglots will be differently organized than they would have been if they had remained monolingual, and it is therefore fair to maintain that the fact of bilingualism per se may have neurophysiological consequences.

Specialized Cognitive Functioning of the
Right and Left Cerebral Hemispheres

As more complex views of laterality and language processing have developed, the kinds of questions asked by neurolinguists have changed and are being formulated less in terms of "where" language is (or in the case of polyglots, languages are) located than in terms of *which aspects* of the language system(s) are being accessed or tested.[16] As Harold Gordon, Robert Weide, and others argue, language is in some sense an epiphenomenon, dependent for expression on the specialized cognitive functions of a variety of brain areas. Determining the contribution of the specialized functions of the left and right hemispheres to second-language learning and processing is therefore not a simple matter of "locating" language in one area or another of the left or right hemisphere, for comprehension and production of language draw on many basic brain functions (e.g., pattern perception, visual and auditory memory, and temporal analysis and production) that are not purely linguistic in nature.[17] As Jyotsna Vaid, Fred Genesee, and Linda Galloway remark, if language consists in an aggregate of perceptual and mnemonic processes, some of which are better served by the left hemisphere and others by the right, then both hemispheres must be understood as contributing to language processing.[18] It is therefore probably more important to understand the specialized cognitive functioning of the left and right hemispheres than to understand "lateralization" per se, if one wants to comprehend the complexities of second-language acquisition and use.

There is considerable evidence that the hemispheres may differ more significantly in their *manner* of processing linguistic and other kinds of stimuli than in the *kind* of stimuli they treat.[19] Many studies have shown that each hemisphere processes stimuli according to its inherent processing mode.[20] The left hemisphere therefore proceeds more analytically and serially while the right hemisphere processes information in a more simultaneous, associative manner.[21] Thus it is likely that if a task favors a sequential, analytic, phonetic processing strategy, the left hemisphere will dominate. If, however, the task favors pattern recognition or memory, the right hemisphere with its capacity for holistic, parallel, and imaginal processing is likely to dominate. Consequently, tests purporting to show differences in hemispheric lateralization for language may in fact be reflecting different ways of processing which are accessed by different tasks.[22]

As I have already mentioned, whether or not (and how much) the right hemisphere is involved in second-language learning has been a question hotly disputed among researchers over the past few years.[23] If one regards this quarrel in terms of varieties of processing strategies, it is possible to reconcile the apparently contradictory experimental data. Depending on the way in which a second language is learned—with stress on formal, traditional use of reading and grammar or in an "acquisition situation"—*tasks* may be different and, therefore, hemispheric participation may also differ.[24] One can expect greater left-hemisphere dominance for languages learned via the analytic and written modes, and greater right-hemisphere involvement in "interactive" contexts.[25] Many studies also show that a major right-hemisphere role in language processing lies in the social and expressive functions of language, and Eta Schneiderman and Chantal Desmarais see evidence of a relationship between second-language learning talent in adults and a more bilateral pattern of representation for language.[26] It is also more than likely that studies have noticed more right-hemisphere participation in some language-learning situations because of the right hemisphere's critical role in the apprehension of novel stimuli, its preponderance of inter-areal connections, and the greater proportion of associative cortex in the right hemisphere.[27] As Schneiderman remarks: "It seems plausible to suppose that the processing of a given linguistic unit by a linguistically mature native speaker who recognizes it as an element of complex syntactic and semantic systems in which it can have multiple meanings is probably quite different from the processing of that same word as a novel stimulus by an acquirer who lacks such systems in the target language and may simply perceive the stimulus as an undifferentiated string of sounds."[28] Obler and colleagues observe that we may find, as some suspect, that the right hemisphere contributes such cognitive abilities as effort and specialization for novel stimuli, which, while not *simply* linguistic may be necessary or at least linked to linguistic processing.[29] The right hemisphere may also mediate in the interpretation and expression of emotion.[30]

There would seem, then, to be a growing tendency among researchers on bilingualism to argue that even if the right hemisphere does not participate in a differential way in the *representation* of language in a bilingual, the increased participation of the right hemisphere in the language *processing* of many bilinguals can be explained in terms of their use of more global, nonanalytic, and nonsequential strategies in their treatment of certain linguistic elements than is the case with monolinguals.[31]

Particularly interesting in this connection is the work of Beverly Wulfeck, Larry Juarez, Elizabeth Bates, and Kerry Kilborn.[32] Citing Bates and MacWhinney's 1981 pilot study, which showed that bilinguals tended either to transfer their first language strategies to sentences in the other language or to adopt different strategies for each language corresponding to those of monolingual speakers, Wulfeck and colleagues demonstrate the use by a group of Spanish-English bilinguals of a *third* kind of strategy.[33] Instead of engaging in separate modes of processing in each of their two languages, these bilinguals seem to possess a unitary system that adopts clues from each language and operates in the same fashion for both languages. However, while each subject had created a unitary system for processing sentences in both languages, not all subjects in the study had chosen the *same* clues and not all processed sentences in the same way.[34] If these studies are replicated, they will provide an important confirmation of the theory that bilinguals have *more* processing strategies available to them than do monolinguals, and that some of these strategies may also be qualitatively different from *any* of the strategies available to monolinguals.

Cognitive Flexibility

The most significant findings of neurophysiological research for a study of bilingual writers are those which indicate that bilinguals have available to them a wider range of strategies for processing both linguistic and nonlinguistic information than do monolinguals. Although early and frequently chauvinistic studies of bilinguals assumed that polyglotism could not but be disadvantageous to intellectual growth, many recent studies (particularly those of Elizabeth Peal and Wallace Lambert; Sandra Ben-Zeev; and Loraine Obler, Martin Albert, and Sandra Lozowick) indicate that bilingualism may in fact be accompanied by certain cognitive advantages.[35]

Peal and Lambert were the first researchers to present persuasive data indicating that balanced bilinguals demonstrated greater cognitive flexibility than monolinguals in a variety of areas. In their landmark study of bilingual ten-year-olds in Montreal, the results of which have been confirmed by Lambert's own later work and by many other studies of middle-class bilingual children, Peal and Lambert found that their subjects' experiences in two languages and two cultures had given them advantages that monolinguals did not enjoy.[36] Their experience with two language systems appears to have contributed to a superiority in concept formation and to superior performance on tests requiring a certain mental or symbolic flexibility. In short, bilingualism was associated with a more diversified set of mental abilities: "Bilingual young people relative to monolingual controls show definite cognitive and linguistic advantages as these are reflected on measures of 'cognitive flexibility,' 'creativity,' 'divergent thought' [which focused on such aspects of cognitive functioning as fluency, flexibility, and originality], 'problem solving,' etc."[37] In contrast, the monolingual appears to have a more unitary structure of intelligence that he must use for all types of intellectual tasks. Lambert speculates: "Perhaps it is a matter of bilinguals being better able to store information; perhaps it is the greater separation of linguistic symbols from their referents or the ability to separate word meaning from word sound; perhaps it is the contrasts of linguistic systems that bilinguals continually make that aids them in the development of general conceptual thought. My own working hypothesis is that bilingualism provides a person with a comparative, three dimensional insight into language, a type of stereolinguistic optic on communication that the monolingual rarely experiences."[38]

Other researchers have also noted that bilingual children's enhanced ability to separate form and meaning results in greater metalinguistic awareness and more flexibility in performing cognitive operations.[39] Schneiderman and Desmarais observe that "the child, when faced at an early age with the necessity of setting up alternative neural pathways and processing strategies for incoming language data may be generally less inclined to rely on more fixed or rigid strategies for a number of cognitive tasks."[40] Similarly, Ben-Zeev found that "bilingual children showed more advanced processing of verbal material, more discriminating perceptual distinctions, more propensity to search for structure in perceptual situations, and more capacity to reorganize their perceptions in response to feedback."[41] The patterns bilingual children seek are primarily linguistic, but this process also operates with visual patterns: for example, their aptness at isolating the dimensions of a matrix.[42] It is important to emphasize that not only do bilingual children (predictably) perform better on tests that measure metalinguistic awareness, but they also demonstrate superiority on such tests as the widely used Raven's nonverbal progressive matrices, the Lavoie-Laurendeau nonverbal IQ test, and on "divergent thinking" tasks.[43] Bruce Bain and Agnes Yu have also found positive cognitive consequences of bilingualism for such participative nonverbal tasks as portrait-emotion recognition, which they consider to "dramatically emphasize the cognitive flexibility accruing from bilingual experience."[44]

In his *Mirror of Language*, Kenji Hakuta observes that these recent studies suggest the following conclusion: "Take any group of bilinguals who are approximately equivalent in their first and second language abilities and match them with a monolingual group for age, socio-economic levels, and whatever other variables you think might confound your results. Now, choose a measure of cognitive flexibility and administer it to both groups. The bilinguals will do better."[45] But Hakuta has doubts about the causal nature of the relationship, declaring that because of the cross-sectional nature of the studies, we are unable to infer the direction of cause and effect.[46] For the purposes of my analysis of bilingual writers, where examples are drawn from a population of émigrés, all of at least middle-class origin and usually from families where learning a second language was normal and additive, it does not matter whether the causal arrow moves from the acquisition of the second language toward cognitive flexibility or whether the reverse is true. What is important and almost indisputable is that there exists a clear relationship, causal or not, between fluency in more than one language and superior indices of cognitive flexibility.

Some researchers who do accept the causal relationship between cognitive enhancement and bilingualism in children consider that the advantages conferred are temporary, involving what is essentially a more precocious recognition of the inherent separability of sign and referent, rather than a permanent or absolute difference. It would seem, however, that insofar as adult cognitive structure in any individual is the result of patterns and parameters laid down over time on the basis of individual linguistic and other experience, the trace patterns and strategic preferences of adults who were pre-pubertal bilinguals will have developed differently than they would have if the individual had remained monolingual or become bilingual later.

If, as it appears, the neural substrate for language changes throughout a person's lifespan in response to a variety of influences, including not only affective attitudes, education, and situations of language acquisition, but also varying patterns and periods of language use, then one would expect bilingualism to have significant influence on cognitive functioning not only in childhood, but through adulthood and into old age.[47] While, for obvious methodological reasons, there has been considerably less research on adult bilinguals than on children, numerous recent studies strongly suggest that bilingualism confers a continuing advantage for tasks involving metalinguistic awareness, or separating word sounds from word meaning, generating synonyms, being sensitive to communicative needs, and perceiving new sounds.[48] In tests of divergent thinking or cognitive flexibility, bilinguals have rather consistently been found to outperform monolinguals in the ability to generate original uses, and recent studies have shown bilinguals to be ahead in both divergent and convergent thinking tasks.[49] Bilinguals themselves frequently mention a greater awareness of the relativity of things and a more critical approach to life as advantages of their linguistic status.[50] The advantages of bilingualism even appear to remain evident among healthy elderly bilinguals. Although for the most part the performance of elderly, fluent bilinguals in their second learned language is comparable to that of their monolingual counterparts, Obler, Albert, and Lozowick have recently published a study of aging bilinguals wherein the investigators report that—contrary to their general expectations and on a number of measures—elderly bilinguals performed better than their monolingual counterparts. These results suggest that, by virtue of being bilingual, one actually develops exceptional language-production skills, especially labeling skills, that last throughout the bilingual's life.[51]

Talent in Second-Language Learning

It has been proposed that bilingualism can have very positive effects on individuals' cognitive flexibility by making available a greater range of processing strategies for a variety of cognitive tasks, among them some that are not exclusively linguistic. But the reverse can also be argued. In a recent article, Schneiderman and Desmarais propose a *neuropsychological basis* for talent in adult second-language learning whereby the "talented language learner would possess greater neurocognitive flexibility that would permit him or her to avoid processing second-language input via the cognitive pathways which have been established for the first language."[52] (That most second-language learners will at first attempt to process second-language input as if it were part of the first-language system, and that untalented learners will continue to do so, is a phenomenon only too well known to practicing language teachers.)

Neurocognitively flexible individuals are not obliged to rely on a single set of predominant pathways for language-related processing, but instead use a variety of processing strategies and associated neural pathways. "Talented" adult language learners sometimes also appear to adopt unconventional strategies in carrying out a variety of language-related tasks. They are "likely to use more concrete or intuitive modes of operation rather than relying on more formal, superordinate types of organization, have superior memory for unfamiliar items, and show advantages in verbal over non-verbal or visio-spatial skills." Predictably, given the structural difference between the two hemispheres, those flexible individuals who rely less on left-hemisphere strategies for the processing of descriptive systems such as language will appear less lateralized for language than is "normal."[53] Talented language learners also frequently rely on verbal strategies to perform *non*verbal tasks. There may, however, also be some cognitive disabilities (in particular involving certain skills normally associated with the right hemisphere) linked with *extraordinary* skill in adult language learning that it is important at least to mention here.[54] For example, there may be mild to severe visio-spatial disabilities, particularly with respect to mental rotation of figures, figure-ground relationships, and orientation in space.[55]

There remains one other important point to be made in regard to "talented" adult second-language and third-language learners. Usually, when one speaks of people who are "talented" for language, one is thinking of individuals who have learned to use a second or third language, or even more, without production errors—in particular, people who speak these languages without a telltale foreign accent. It is estimated that only some 5 percent of language learners achieve "native" status in all respects including accent, and this is especially true for people who have learned a language after puberty.[56] Yet, many adult learners of a foreign language may acquire grammatical speech, a wide vocabulary, and complete fluency in their second language.[57]

While it is understandable that phonologists and neurolinguists who study speech production should argue whether there is a cerebral or muscular plasticity that disappears with the onset of adolescence, making it unusual for adult learners of a language to acquire accent-free speech, by other standards of linguistic functioning, accent is a minor problem.[58] The practice of Russian (and other) bilingual writers confirms a plethora of evidence that it is perfectly possible for bilinguals to function in both their languages fluently, creatively, and at a higher level than most monolinguals—aside from the vexed question of accent. It is also striking that many Russians of the first emigration, even writers who learned their second language *before* puberty, had strong accents in their second language and made no effort to correct them. They cherished the telltale accent of their mother tongue and, sometimes, even flaunted it (witness the old joke that Roman Jakobson, the linguist and theoretician of literature, spoke Russian in sixteen languages). As we shall see, bilingual writers are usually aware of their emotional need to keep an accent when they speak in their second or third language. In fact, speaking a second language with an accent would seem to be an essential psychic pledge (at least for the Russians of the first post-1917 emigration) that permits bilingual authors to *write* their second language *without* an accent. If it is true, as Schneiderman and Desmarais maintain, that "ego-permeability" is an important prerequisite for acquiring a nativelike accent in a second or third language, then perhaps we may take the inability or refusal of otherwise competent bilingual writers to acquire such an accent as a sign of a certain ego-*im*permeability that allows them to appease their feelings of guilt at having "betrayed" their mother tongue and still maintain an unshaken sense of self.[59] But this is rightfully the

matter of a later chapter. What is important to observe here is t
the same person may exhibit a heavy accent together with a m...
tery of all other aspects of oral and written production—except
perhaps for translation.

Many fluent bilinguals have trouble translating, and it is usual
for them to express themselves more easily—on almost any subject,
in any context—in either of their two languages than it is for them
to translate from one to the other. Michel Paradis argues persuasively that the processes underlying translation are very different
from those which underlie speaking, understanding, reading, or
writing different languages. He has, for example, recorded extraordinary cases of aphasic bilingual patients who had lost the ability to
speak in a language but could translate into it when told something
in their other language.[60] That translation appears to be an activity
apart from speaking or writing fluently in second or third languages is of considerable importance in a study of bilingual writers,
whose relationship to translation is usually passionate and turbulent. Particularly crucial are the problems bilinguals face in *self*-
translation, which is usually the activity that forces writers who
have been considering writing in another language, tentatively experimenting with it, finally to commit themselves to writing in their
second language.

But before I discuss the epic internal struggles with self-
translation waged by writers such as Vladimir Nabokov and Elsa
Triolet, there is one more large problem of neuro- and psycholinguistics to consider. At issue is the crucial matter of how bilinguals
(and, still more complexly, polyglots) keep their languages separate—or whether indeed they do.

Access, Storage, and Interaction of Languages in Bilinguals

How do bilinguals keep their languages apart or allow themselves
to code-switch? Does each language entail a system of its own, with
separate trace patterns, or are they compounded in some respects?
Do bilinguals have a single lexicon, or two (and polyglots three or
four)?[61] Is there some kind of switch in the brain that regulate-
schoice of language? A monitor system? How is incoming linguistic
material processed? Do bilinguals store items or concepts indepen-

dently of the language of input in a supra- or sublinguistic form, or in the language of input, or in both?

These matters are still the subject of considerable controversy, in part because of the methodological problems that inevitably afflict neuro- and psycholinguistic research.[62] On the question of lexical storage, for instance, François Grosjean notes that different tasks tap different aspects and levels of the language system; therefore, different tests give results that may appear ambivalent. In such tasks as short-term recall of bilingual lists of words, subjects concentrate on the form and on the language of the words; but in other tasks, such as category-instance judgments and long-term memory tasks, they concentrate on the semantic characteristics of the words.[63] Furthermore, as Paradis observes, most studies of lexical storage in bilinguals have not distinguished between a conceptual memory store, which is independent of language(s), and a linguistically constrained semantic store (or, for bilinguals, *stores*).[64]

The results of bilingual Stroop tests suggest that linguistic input is processed for meaning in each language used by the subject, regardless of the language in which the information is tendered.[65] On tests where the subject focused on the content of visually presented sentences, "subjects seem to process language input (both words and sentences) at some semantic level beyond the language-specific."[66] (This will turn out to be a very important piece of evidence for our purposes.) There is also a strong possibility that bilinguals build a unitary system for perception and maintain two separate output systems.[67] Certainly, as Paradis asserts, to the extent that a bilingual speaks two languages like a native, he *cannot* possess a single, basic internal dictionary in which words in both languages are pooled, for each aspect of a word—morphological, phonological, graphemic—is bound to be stored separately from that aspect in the other language. "Only to the extent that the meanings of the words are connected to a sufficient number of the same nonlinguistic conceptual features (i.e., refer to similar mental representations) can they be considered equivalent."[68]

At any rate, as Loraine Obler observes, it is obvious that the lexical system of the bilingual is complex, combining both independent and interdependent aspects.[69] As early as 1968, Paul Kolers had speculated that neither the common-storage nor the separate-storage hypothesis was adequate to the complexity of the actual tasks performed by bilinguals. Because some information can be stored in such a way that it is readily accessible in either of two languages, whereas other kinds are closely bound in terms of access to the language in which they are stored, a third arrangement combining features of the other two was required.[70] Currently, the most plausible hypothesis would seem to be Paradis's three-store proposal: "One store, corresponding to the bilingual's experiential and conceptual information, contains representations of things and events, properties, qualities and functions of objects; in a word, what is known about the world. Then the bilingual has a store for each of his two languages, each of which is differentially connected to the conceptual store."[71]

The three-store solution is a bilingual variant of what is called the "dual coding" approach to language and cognition. It assumes that language behavior is mediated by two independent, but partially interconnected, cognitive systems. One, the "image system," is specialized for dealing with information about nonverbal objects and events; the "verbal system" is specialized for dealing with linguistic information. The image system organizes information in a synchronous or spatial manner, combining visual, auditory, kinesthetic, and other sensory components of nonverbal information into integrated wholes so that different components of a complex thing or scene are available at the same time in memory. In contrast, verbal information is organized sequentially into higher-order structures. Although these systems are independent, they are interconnected, and one symbolic system can initiate activity in the other.[72] A bilingual, however, would appear to need two linguistic stores. As Allan Paivio and Ian Begg also note, bilinguals' verbal codes would appear to be separate insofar as they are capable of functioning independently with little interference. At the semantic or conceptual level, though, the two languages appear to share an underlying system to a substantial degree, and there is evidence that this commonality applies more to concrete than to abstract material (this is consistent with the "dual coding" idea that what is shared is knowledge of the world or experience in imagery).[73]

It is nonetheless important to stress, as does Paradis, that the conceptual store is *differentially* organized, depending on which language is used to verbalize an idea, feeling, or experience, because "units of meaning in each language group together conceptual features in different ways. . . . Some units of meaning [in both languages] (e.g., English: ball / French: *balle* and *ballon*) share most of their features. Others share only a few."[74] Thus, while the two languages share a number of basic cognitive and language-processing operations, they also have language-specific operations and strategies.[75]

The three-store solution is a more sophisticated answer to a question that had initially been posed too simply (one store or two). As Paradis has observed, no simple model will account for any complex situation.[76] I will not discuss here a crucial additional element of complexification—the fact that parts of the linguistic system other than those at the level of meaning may also be blended, subordinated, or coexist in varied proportions.[77] If one recalls that any individual bilingual may exhibit elements of language mixing, compounding and subordination within each stratal system, that he may exhibit different configurations for encoding and decoding (to say nothing of *written* encoding or decoding), and that he may change his various interlingual stratal relationships over time in the course of his linguistic development and experience,[78] and if one then considers that hundreds of millions of human beings speak and sometimes read and also write *more* than two languages, then the problems of linguistic storage and access in bilinguals and polyglots become truly mind-boggling in their complexity.

How bilinguals and polyglots can either keep their languages separate or code-switch at will is only a slightly less complicated question. Recent research on code-switching would seem to indicate that a simple "on/off switch" model cannot account for all aspects of both the independence and interdependence of languages. Take, for example, the ease and rapidity with which skilled readers of two languages can, in reading silently, rapidly comprehend a passage no matter to what extent words from several languages are mixed (even in violation of the normal grammatical rules for code-switching).[79] Obler and Albert propose instead of an on/off input switch a flexible, continuously operating monitor system, sensitive to changes in the linguistic and nonlinguistic environment, that will never entirely switch one language off but that channels efforts, scanning for clues in order to allow the bilingual listener to process language efficiently.[80] This would seem much more satisfactory than a simple switch and, in fact, even more parsimonious. Otherwise, one would have to visualize polyglots like Jakobson as having the equivalent of a whole panel of switches somewhere inside the head.[81]

In the face of such complexity, it is tempting to accept Paradis's belief that there is no need to posit an anatomical localization or even a specific functional organization, a switching mechanism or a monitor system: "The decision to speak in English or Russian is surely of the same order as the decision to speak at all or remain silent or the decision to wiggle one's little finger or to keep it still." Equally appealing is his compromise solution to the question of where and how languages are stored in the brain.[82] Although both (three? four?) languages may be stored in identical ways in a single extended system, Paradis thinks that the elements of each language probably form separate networks of subsystems within the layer system. If the "subset" hypothesis is correct, "bilinguals have two subsets of neural connections, one for each language (and each can be activated or inhibited independently because of the strong associations between elements) while at the same time they possess one larger set from which they are able to draw elements of either language at any time."[83]

This model is particularly attractive because it recognizes that while it is perfectly possible for bilinguals to behave as though their second language is not there (at least for production tasks—one cannot refuse to understand information proffered in a language that one knows but does not feel like using for the moment), they may choose to mix elements from both languages for a variety of reasons. If they like, they may even process materials from one language with strategies more appropriate to the other. For human beings do not always choose the simplest and most parsimonious route to anything. The Underground Man already knew that. Deliberate choice, whim, and the reasons for such choices in a wide range of linguistic matters constitute an annoying wild card in neurolinguistic studies and limit what those studies can tell us. Paradis to some extent acknowledges this in his comments about the unlikelihood of the existence of a simple switch mechanism,[84] and Hakuta has also remarked, in a discussion of how test procedures may influence results, that to the extent that the results are malleable, observed differences between individuals can be seen as choices they are making between alternatives—for various reasons, which may include trivial ones. In fact, Hakuta opines that there is reason to suspect that the kind of *test* procedure involved may influence whether subjects behave as though their two languages are independent or interdependent, and whether they function as coordinate or compound systems. He concludes that "it is more a matter of choice than of rigid determinism. It would be well for cognitive approaches to bilingualism to keep in mind the mental flexibility of human beings."[85] I would add the cussedness and playfulness of human beings, and the pleasures of redundancy and linguistic choice, when such choice has as its motivation not concrete, empirical, communicative utility but the manifestation of "one's own sweet will."[86]

"One's own sweet will" is only the most intractable of a variety of factors that make bilingualism, particularly "cultivated" bilingualism, in many ways resistant to purely scientific study. In this chapter, I have reviewed those findings of psycho- and neurolinguistics which explain the physiological substrate of "cultured bilingualism." This background is essential to any serious attempt to understand how bilingual writers actually function, and many of the findings of neurolinguistics are in fact very helpful in analyzing the practice of bilingual writers. But as the most sophisticated neuro- and psycholinguistic researchers admit, there are often methodological problems with scientific research on bilinguals because of the daunting array of significant variables which may influence differential cerebral organization for languages and even the cerebral localization of languages. The large number of such variables in the history of any given bilingual—when the second (third, fourth) language was acquired and at what age; under what circumstances (formal or informal); in what context (whether the second language was culturally dominant or an "outside" language, whether it was a part of the individual's personally and socially atypical heritage); with what affective elements the languages are charged, etc., etc.; to say nothing of "one's own sweet will"—go a long way toward explaining why psycho- and sociolinguistics have found bilingualism so frustrating to deal with.[87]

Although neurolinguistics can make some very useful generalizations about the physiological substrate of bilingualism, each bilingual is a specific case, and the variables are important and almost impossible to measure or compare statistically. This has led some researchers to insist on the scientific value of studying "interesting cases," while it has led others to attempt to reduce the extremes in an effort to establish some norms. The latter researchers have frequently been obliged to generalize in ways that may jeopardize the validity of their findings. Consider, for instance, the (real) case of a brilliant young researcher working on the bilingual processing of category information among an English- and Slavic-speaking population. His "monolingual" controls, who supposedly spoke only a Slavic language, turned out in fact to be persons who had lived in the United States for a number of years and did indeed know some English, although they had not been exposed to it before the fatidic age of twelve, after which some researchers believe one cannot become "really" bilingual.

Even Wallace Lambert, whose extremely interesting research on bilinguals in Montreal I have cited frequently, has admitted: "We have also noted that the linguistic backgrounds of actual bilinguals are often too complex for experimental studies. As a consequence, we have been forced often to *restate certain bilingual problems in a more general form* so that they can be investigated with experimental methods *that only approximate the real bilingual case*"[88] (emphasis added). Uriel Weinreich, in his *Languages in Contact*, also admits that the factors which determine the relative "dominance" of language in bilinguals are multifarious and unmeasurable, and he takes the usual and unfortunate solution of simplification: "The number of individuals whose speech and life histories would have to be examined in order to correlate each factor separately may be prohibitive; it may not even be possible to find enough different individuals in a single contact situation to isolate all of the factors. *In practice there can therefore be no objection* to correlating types of interference with groups of dominance factors, as long as the complexity of the configurations is borne in mind at all times, and only individuals with similar configurations are considered together"[89] (emphasis added). Of course, there can, and probably *should* be, objections, since the "complexity of configurations" is not and cannot be "borne in mind at all times," either when one is looking for relationships that can be formulated statistically or, even more so, when one is looking for "first principles."

In their effort to generalize from the inevitably messy data on actual bilingualism, researchers also illuminate the reasons why theoretical linguistics, in particular transformational-generative linguistics, avoids taking account of bilingualism or treats it as merely another case of style switching. The Chomskyans would argue that the complex phenomena of the real world (in this case, bi- and multilingualism) are just too complicated to enable one to learn anything about "first principles." They would consider it necessary to study "pure," or radically simplified (in this instance, monolingual) cases if one hopes to arrive at binding principles of linguistic theory.

For all these reasons, one has no choice but to take sides in the quarrel of the linguists over whether one should study "interesting" complex cases or, rather, proceed on the basis of purified experiments. Beyond the essential and basic information to which I have devoted this first chapter, only the careful analysis of particular cases can add significantly to our knowledge of the practice of bilingual writers. So idiosyncratic in their acquisition and their use of their second (or third) language are the writers of even my relatively homogeneous sample of Russians (all more or less of an age, all facing the choice of whether or not to write in a language other than Russian as they remade their lives abroad after the Revolution) that studying them will certainly not be useful in the attempt of transformational-generative linguistics to establish "first principles." But this is not to say that it may not be useful in other ways and for other purposes. Particular and complicated as each of these writers is, together they form a significant sample of an interesting subset among bilinguals. It is therefore important, both from the literary and from the linguistic point of view, to study them individually, and still more important to study them individually *as bilinguals*. For in their idiosyncrasies they illustrate in important ways François Grosjean's and Carlos Soares's contention that

> bilinguals should be studied as such and not always in comparison with monolinguals. Instead of being the sum of two monolinguals, bilinguals are competent "native-speaker-hearers" of a different type; their knowledge of two languages makes up an integrated whole that cannot easily be decomposed into two separate parts. In addition, bilingual language processing will often be different from that of the monolingual; one language is rarely totally deactivated when speaking or listening to the other (even in completely monolingual situations) and in a mixed language mode, where the two languages interact si-

multaneously, bilinguals have to use specific operations and strategies rarely, if ever, needed by the monolingual.[90]

The distinction made by Grosjean and Soares is crucial. Bilinguals *are* " 'competent native speaker-hearers' [and, I would add, writers] of a different type" than monolinguals. A chemical analogy may be helpful: language in a bilingual may be conceived of as a molecule of water—a new organization that results from the combination in certain specific proportions of atoms of hydrogen and oxygen. But although this analogy is better than that of "addition and subtraction," it too holds only up to a point. Under the proper conditions, you always get water. There are no proper conditions for bilinguals, especially for bilingual writers. Each one conducts a lengthy and frequently painful series of experiments on himself, varying the proportions of the two languages, balancing, weighing, separating, mixing. Sometimes—in fact, frequently—at the end of a period of experimentation that may last most of a lifetime, the bilingual writer understands and accepts this difference. The way the writer naturally uses each language is different from what it would have been had he learned only one. And although a bilingual can *act as if* his two languages were entirely independent if he so desires, and although given *utterances* in either of the languages may seem entirely comparable to those of a monolingual, this is not an accurate reflection of the complexity of the bilingual's linguistic system. As we shall see, most modern bilingual writers, after passing through a phase of obsession about maintaining the linguistic purity of their first language (and attaining linguistic purity in their second language), will ultimately choose not to prevent the mutually complexifying and enriching interference of their languages. By the end of their careers, the greatest of them accept the fact that a polylinguistic matrix is basic to their life and art[91] and that their languages function in a kind of creative tension, the literary results of which are frequently startling and always unique.

CHAPTER TWO

The Mental Geology
of Bilingual Writing

I don't think in any language. I think in images.

—Vladimir Nabokov

Listening to you, one would think that bilingualism is only a source of pain. It *also* enables you to play, doesn't it?

[A vous écouter, on dirait que le bilinguisme n'a engendré que des blessures. Il sert aussi à jouer, non?]

—Nicole Chaperon, at a conference
of bilingual writers.

The neurolinguistic evidence amply warrants François Grosjean's conclusion that a bilingual is not merely the sum of two complete or incomplete monolinguals, but rather a unique and specific linguistic configuration.[1] Yet my contention that a bilingual writer is a special kind of literary animal who should be considered *whole* is not based on neurolinguistics alone. As Kenji Hakuta has observed, one should avoid the temptation to believe that "the neurological evidence is somehow a truer reflection of reality than the psychological level."[2] It is to the "folk-psychological level" of the experience of bilingual writers that this chapter turns, for it is at least as important to know how bilingual writers live their condition of difference (in particular, how they "feel" about it) as it is to know about the neurolinguistic substrate of their conscious psychic experiences.

Because cultivated bilingualism is associated with various measures of cognitive enhancement and may actually have positive intellectual consequences, one would expect that bilinguals would be pleased with their situation. Even though they are unaware of the neurolinguistic underpinnings of their bilingualism, and although they do not consider themselves to be intrinsically different from monolinguals, most cultivated adult bilinguals recognize the advantages of their bilingualism and view it in a positive light.[3] Very few consider their bilingualism to be in any way a handicap or even an inconvenience.[4] Bilingual writers are, of course, particularly aware of the benefits of bilingualism; unlike most bilinguals, however, they are not entirely grateful for them. Bilingual writers do feel fundamentally different from monolinguals, and they are uncomfortable with their singularity. In fact, when they speak or write about their bilingualism, it is usually to complain. They frequently sound as though Macdonald Critchley and Uriel Weinreich were correct in maintaining that bilingualism hinders literary creativity, despite the existence, quantity, and quality of their own bilingual writing which itself disproves this contention. We are therefore faced with a paradox: bilingual writers whose work is conclusive evidence that bilingualism is not merely "additive" but even "multiplicative" at times *feel* as though their bilingualism were unnatural and negative—a curse or a dread disease. We must therefore address this apparent contradiction between the recent findings of neuro- and psycholinguistics, on the one hand, and the subjective emotions and attitudes of bilingual writers, on the other, while at the same time considering the more numerous areas where the subjective psychological experiences of bilingual writers seem to confirm the neurolinguistic evidence.

The bilingual Russian writers of the "first" emigration, who constitute the primary sample for detailed analysis in my central chapters, have particularly ambivalent and *slozhnye*, or "complex," attitudes toward their bilingual situations. Their psychic dilemmas are, however, widely shared by bilingual writers of other nationalities. In order to support my contention that bilingual writers form, if not a breed or a nation, at least a significant category apart, I will also cite the comments of contemporary non-Russian bilingual writers when their experience correlates with and replicates that of the Russians.

Mental Geologists

Current neurolinguistic science provides a physiological analogue, if not a justification, for some of the observations that bilingual and polyglot writers frequently make about their relations with their languages. To begin with, bilingual writers feel that their languages have volume, that they take up space, and that there is a physical distance in their heads between the languages that they master (or that, occasionally, appear to master them).[5] The evidence presented by George Ojemann, Harry Whitaker, and others that language is more widely represented in the cerebral cortex of the linguistically dominant hemisphere in bilinguals than it is in monolinguals, and that there are sites where only one language is represented and not the other,[6] would seem to support the bilingual's impression of an internal linguistic geography. Bilingual writers who feel that they are thus inhabited by "linguistic space" tend to use geographical and geological imagery to express their sense of the physical distance between the languages inside their heads. Take, for example, Vadim Vadimich, the hero of Vladimir Nabokov's *Look at the Harlequins!* and himself an elderly bilingual writer in English and Russian. Vadim Vadimich has an internal map and declares, "Russian and English had existed for years in my mind as two worlds detached from one another. (It is only today that some interspatial contact has been established.) . . . I was acutely aware of the syntactic gulf separating their sentence structures."[7] Or Jacques Hassoun, who attempts to describe in French the situation of his now-little-used native Hebrew and Arabic by evoking a ravine between two dunes: "An amateur archaeologist, trying to understand what this geological depression hides, would discover that it is the conjugation of two rivers, which although dead, still mark the landscape with their single conjunctural flow"[8] [Un archéologue amateur . . . essaierait de comprendre ce que cache cette dépression géologique. Il découvrirait alors que cette dépression est une conjugaison de deux rivières, qui, pour être mortes ne marquent pas moins le paysage de cette unique coulée conjoncturelle]. Hassoun's metaphors of a lava flow (in this case, already hardened or petrified) or, further on, language rivers gone underground are typical of the images used by bilingual writers to describe the behavior of their languages, which they often feel to be *moving through them*, laying down long-term patterns and traces, independent of their will.

Bilingual writers also speak of their languages shifting and folding over and under each other in irregular layers through their cerebral space. As George Steiner (himself a thoroughgoing polyglot with "native" fluency in three languages) recognizes, in certain bilingual situations, such as a return to a country or a set of circumstances where a language other than the one he has been recently using is primary, the latter will shortly shift "both horizontally and in regard to centrality."[9] Steiner observes that the conditions of "the external world" reach in "to touch and regroup the layers of our speech." He then qualifies his geological metaphor by complexifying it: " 'Layers' is, of course, a piece of crass shorthand. It may mean nothing. The spatial organization, contiguities, insulations, synaptic branchings between, which account for the arrangement of different languages in the brain of the polyglot, and especially of the native bilingual, must be of an order of topological intricacy beyond any that we can picture" (*AB*, 292). Still, many polyglots do need to *picture* their languages, and, despite his caveat, Steiner himself indulges in an extraordinary, extended series of metaphors of complex linguistic space in an attempt to visualize the relations among his own languages: "What manifold space contains their coexistence? Does one imagine them as a continuum on some kind of Moebius strip, intersecting itself, yet preserving the distinctive mappings of its surface?" (p. 117). Or, proposes Steiner, turning again to one of those geological images with which bilinguals particularly like to describe their languages: "Ought one, rather, to picture the dynamic foldings and interpenetration of geological strata in a terrain that has evolved under multiple stress?" (p. 117).

But the image of continental drift, of slowly sliding tectonic plates and occasional violent breaks, is in fact far too regular to mirror the constant shifting of language that occurs in bilingual mental activity, and Steiner also attempts to give a sense of this heightened internal movement: "Do the languages I speak, after they diverge to separate identity from a common centre and upward thrust, combine and recombine in an interleaved set, each idiom being, as it were, in horizontal contact with the others, yet remaining itself continuous and unbroken? Such infolding would, presumably, be a constant mechanism. . . . With each linguistic shift or 'new folding,' the underlying stratification has, in some measure, altered. With each transfer of energy to the articulate surface, the most recently used plane of language must be traversed or enfolded and the most recent 'crust' broken" (*AB*, 117–118).

It is interesting that Steiner's "layering" sensation corresponds rather closely to Gordon Rattray Taylor's comment: "There are six layers in the cortex, and even six such networks have fantastic discriminatory and integrative powers, as Von Foerster has shown. But in each of the six layers are many cells ranged above one another. We should probably think, therefore, not of regular layers but of numerous folia dissolving into one another. And as the connections and thresholds shift, functional networks will appear, expand, contract, join up, separate and vanish within the structural network."[10] To some extent, of course, the bilingual's sense of *vertical* movement is comparable to the sensation some monolinguals also have of an upward movement from thought to language, and this sensation may itself be related to the fact that the cortex contains tiny columns of nerve cells that run through the thickness of the cortex, perpendicular to the surface. But for the bilingual or polyglot with his double (triple? quadruple?) linguistic systems, all moving somehow to the surface, the upward movement is much more convoluted and usually involves not merely a sense of complex layers, but also of a *common core* from which the various vertical paths emerge. Therefore, Steiner's complex and active description also includes the image of a "common centre" below the point at which the various languages diverge as they move up to begin their intricate dance in the upper levels of the mind. It leads Steiner farther down toward the internal source of his languages. This is, in fact, the goal of his metaphysical spelunking operation, as he attempts to elucidate for himself whether there is in his head a *Muttersprache* buried vertically deeper than his two other native languages—a question of major psychological importance for early bilinguals and polyglots who often need to feel "rooted." And "if there is a common centre, what geological or topological simile can provide a model? During the first eighteen to twenty-six months of my life, did French, English, and German constitute a semantic magma, a wholly undifferentiated agglomerate of linguistic competence? At some deep level of energized consciousness, or, rather, preconsciousness, do they still? Does the linguistic core, to continue the image, stay 'molten,' and do the three relevant language streams intermingle completely, though 'nearer the surface' they crystallize into distinct formations?" (*AB*, 118).

The "molten core" is a crucial but ambiguous image. Does the "core" represent the domain of those linguistic universals which the transformational-generative linguists claim underlie language per se? Or does the core suggest Walter Benjamin's "pure" language, which is "imprisoned" in all actual languages?[11] Is the "core" the unreachable seat of the Ur-language, the inaccessibility of which so frustrated Mallarmé? Possibly, but writers who refer to the "ultimate language" can as easily place it above as below existing languages, thus violating the geological metaphor. Witness Marina Tsvetaeva's lines, which Joseph Brodsky says may be "the most significant parentheses in the history of Russian poetry": "(though German is more native than Russian / For me the most native is Angelic!)" [(pust' russkogo rodnei nemetskii / Mne vsekh angel'skii rodnei!)].[12]

What Steiner himself seems to have in mind is a mixture of the elements of the actual languages he spoke as a child (and if the core remains "molten," that mixture will include all the languages he will subsequently speak, as well). It is most likely, therefore, that Steiner's "core" ultimately corresponds to the findings of neurolinguistic studies such as L. Doob's, which suggest that bilinguals process language input, words as well as sentences, at some unnamed semantic level beyond or below the language-specific, a level that is common to both (or all) languages.[13] Perhaps what Steiner senses and tries to express through the geological metaphor of the molten core is not something linguistic at all, but is rather the existence of the conceptual store, proposed by Paradis, to which separate languages are differentially connected.[14]

Paradis's and Kirsner's work would also seem to provide the neurolinguistic and physiological basis for a related impression reported by bilinguals.[15] Not only do they feel that their languages are physically located in distinct places in their heads and that some may be farther down than others, they also sense a physical distance between thought and expression in any language—that is, the existence of *meaning* somewhere beyond or below the words in which it is formulated in any of their languages.[16] Gordon Rattray Taylor observes something we all know instinctively, that at some stage "thought is neither words nor images, but feelings. . . . Words and images can be employed to pin down these feelings, or to supplement them."[17] This experience of thought *before* formulation in words is especially frequent among bilinguals. When Elsa Triolet in her artistic self-portrait *La mise en mots* [Putting into words] asks the rhetorical question "Is it not true that the journey from thought to words is shorter for me in Russian than in French?"[18] [N'est-ce pas que le passage de la pensée aux mots est pour moi plus court en russe qu'en français?], this is not merely a metaphorical way of saying that she finds it easier to write and speak Russian than French. In fact, for her, the contrary is sometimes true, and the "distance" is longer in Russian.

The extent of the distance depends on a variety of circumstances, but distance between thought and language, any language, there always is. And while many bilinguals reply "both"[19] when they are asked in what language they think (usually meaning that they will sometimes use one, sometimes the other language, depending on a variety of variables), Nabokov, who understands the process better and who realizes that there is a level where thought is not always dependent on one language or the other, replies: "I don't think in any language. I think in images. I don't believe that people think in languages. . . . No, I think in images, and now and then a Russian phrase or an English phrase will form with the foam of the brainwave, but that's about all."[20]

The image of language(s) as sea foam, almost chance variables, the surface by-products of a deep movement of great primordial forces (from which, certainly, entrancing creatures are sometimes formed), is nicely Nabokovian, a seeming *boutade*, simultaneously serious and outrageous. But what Nabokov says of himself has also been said by Albert Einstein, by Julien Green, by and about Yvan Goll (whom Leonard Forster calls "that rare thing, a truly equilingual poet") and others.[21] Goll was able to make himself at home on both sides of shifting national frontiers, in part because "below the rhetoric can be discerned the elements in which Goll really thinks— he thinks in images. . . . As his basic means of expression lay below the threshold of language, he was able to formulate it either in French or in German, or indeed, after his emigration to the United States in 1940, even with some degree of success in English."[22]

Of course, monolingual writers may also "think in images" (as, if the "dual coding" theory is correct, do we all),[23] but bilinguals and polyglots are more acutely aware of the process because of the heightened sensibility to the separability of referent and word conferred on them by their option of traveling the "distance" from "thought" to "words" in more than one direction. Nabokov's comment is misleading insofar as it implies that images are only visual. This, of course, is not true, and Nabokov in particular insists on his capacity for *audition colorée*: seeing letters in colors intimately linked to sound.[24] Nabokov also frequently thinks in "literary images" that are both visually and linguistically couched. He is perfectly aware of this, and gives to Vadim Vadimich (a bilingual writer constantly tormented by being taken for another, greater author, the titles of whose books curiously parallel his own) a meditation on the relationship of "images" and "words" in his currently used second language. Vadim Vadimich's comments are another, more careful metaphorical explanation of the creative process to which Nabokov referred in his interview:

> But I have managed to transcend the rack and the wrench of literary metamorphosis.
>
> We think in images, not in words; all right; when, however, we compose, recall, or refashion at midnight in our brain something we wish to say in tomorrow's sermon, or have said to Dolly in a recent dream . . . the images we think in are, of course, verbal—and even audible if we happen to be lonely and old. We do not usually think in words, since most of life is mimodrama, but we certainly do imagine words when we need them. . . . The book in my mind appeared at first, under my right cheek (I sleep on my non-cardial side), as a varicolored procession with a head and a tail, winding in a general western direction through an attentive town. . . . I then saw the show in full detail with every scene in its place, every trapeze in the stars. Yet it was not a masque, not a circus, but a bound book, a short novel in a tongue as far removed as Thracian or Pahlavi from the fatamorganic prose that I had willed into being in the desert of exile. An upsurge of nausea overcame me at the thought of imagining a hundred-thousand adequate words and I switched on the light . . . [*LATH*, 122–123)]

In this instance, Vadim Vadimich's as yet nonverbal "show" has already emerged from words—the future book's title, which came to him in his second language: "As was also to happen in regard to my next English books (including the present sketch), the title of

my first one came to me at the moment of impregnation, long before actual birth and growth. Holding that name to the light, I distinguished the entire contents of the semi-transparent capsule" (pp.
120–121). Other (flesh-and-blood) bilingual writers do not always
"see" the "semi-transparent capsule" of the "words" of the title;
sometimes they begin a work with a phrase internally "heard."[25]
The language in which they "hear" the phrase or sentence determines the language of the work. In these cases, the process begins
higher up in the clearly felt stratification, which would seem to reflect the traditional, pre-Derridean hierarchy of "thought," imitated
by "voice," imitated by "writing."

The parallel spatial verticality of the hierarchy from "meaning"
through the languages at their command is sensed particularly
clearly by writers who are also translators. Translators often report
that they do not feel their movement between the source and target
languages to be *lateral*, as laymen might expect. Rather, it involves a
plunge *below* both languages, as though one were to get from one
side of a pool to the other by diving in, swimming deep underwa-
ter, and reemerging on the other side. For example, François Cheng,
discussing his apprenticeship as a translator of poetry from Western languages into Chinese and vice versa, speaks of having being
able to establish a system of subterranean mental canals that free
him from the imprisoning mirrors of the languages, mirrors that
impeded his work.[26] One is tempted to see in these busy underground passageways from one language to the next an image of the
corpus callosum, the heavily traveled bundles of fibers running beneath the cortex, which enables each hemisphere to transmit information to the other and which is particularly heavily used for
language purposes in bilinguals, especially for writing.

Steiner, too, resorts to the image of a parabolic linguistic journey
between languages: "The polyglot mind undercuts the lines of division between languages by reaching inward, to the symbiotic core.
In a genuinely multilingual matrix, the motion of spirit performed
in the act of alternate choice—or translation—is parabolic rather
than horizontal. Translation is inward-directed discourse, a descent,
at least partial, down Montaigne's 'spiral staircase of the self' "
(*AB*, 119–120).[27] Insofar as one finds within oneself the "intention"
that underlies each language but that can only be realized by the
totality of the intentions of all available languages "supplementing

each other,"[28] this downward progress enables one to reverse the Tower of Babel: "In contrast to Babel, which engendered confusion, the bilingual writer builds a kind of underground Babel from one language to another, as though he were digging, not to find the original language, but rather the knowledge of a secret unity hibernating beneath centuries of incomprehension"[29] [Et par opposition avec la Babel ayant engendré la confusion, l'écrivain bilingue construit d'une langue à l'autre une sorte de Babel souterraine, comme s'il creusait pour retrouver non pas la langue d'origine, mais la conscience d'une unité secrète endormie sous des siècles d'incompréhension]. The descent is especially perilous—and even more necessary—in *self*-translation. As we shall see, self-translation is frequently the rite of passage, the traditional, heroic, psychic journey into the depths of the self (a version of Sigmund Freud's self-analysis or Joseph Campbell's archetypal voyage) that is a necessary prelude to true self-knowledge and its accompanying powers.[30] Only when (and if) they have negotiated the hell of self-translation can bilingual writers proceed through the purgatory of the first years of writing in a second language and fully realize their bilingual potential.

The Pleasures and Perils of "Option"

Before bilingual writers arrive at and successfully traverse the hell of self-translation, they must pass through other preliminary trials. As we have seen, neurolinguistic studies (in particular those of Sandra Ben-Zeev, Elizabeth Peal, Wallace Lambert, James Cummins, Loraine Obler, Martin Albert, and colleagues) have found that bilinguals often show cognitive and linguistic advantages over monolingual controls in a variety of areas such as "cognitive flexibility," "creativity," and "divergent thought." In practice, this means, among other things, that they probably have alternative neural pathways available for some tasks, that they are therefore less inclined to rely on rigid and unvarying strategies, and that they tend to process linguistic material in a more open-ended way. They are particularly good at seeking out patterns in information proffered to them, and they frequently favor intuitive strategies of organization.

The presence of alternative strategies for processing languages is happily unparsimonious. While it may aid efficiency in some tasks, its primary service to bilingual writers is to offer them the pleasures of redundancy and of play, fostered by their awareness of the inherent separability of sign and referent and their tolerance for certain kinds of ambiguity. Otherwise dissimilar writers such as Nabokov and Beckett are connoisseurs of the pleasures of stereolinguistic optics and of the redundancy resulting from having two languages at their artistic disposal (even though, in Beckett's case, the two systems are used to doubly insist that there is nothing to be said and nothing with which to say it).[31]

That these writers' characteristic angles of vision are directly related to the fact that bilinguals have available to them a wider variety of processing strategies than do monolinguals obviously cannot be *proven*. Nor is it possible to determine objectively *why* a bilingual uses one linguistic processing strategy rather than another, but it is evident that the variety of processing strategies available to bilinguals provides them with neurolinguistic *options*, which set them apart from monolinguals. These processing options are paralleled on the conscious level by the bilingual's choice of which language to use. And while it is true that bilinguals frequently shift languages without making a conscious decision to do so, polyglot and bilingual *writers* must deliberately decide which language to use in a given instance.

The conscious awareness of option is both the greatest blessing that bilingualism provides the writer and the greatest curse. The monolingual writer is unaware, happily ignorant, the bond servant of the patterns and structures of his only language. The bilingual writer, constantly conscious of the relativity of his symbolic systems, is always in what might be termed the "anthropological stance," distanced in his use of language to communicate with the outside world, and, even more important, in internal conversation with himself.[32] Bilingual writers must, like all writers, produce the "best words in the best order"; but, in addition, they are often tempted by possibilities from a competing system, theirs to use if they but would. All bilinguals who write in two languages know the frustration of being stuck in a sentence in one language, casting about for alternatives, and having the perfect phrasing come to mind—except that the sentence is in the "wrong" language! Thus, bilingual writers must eliminate those paradigmatic options which are not from the language they are using at any given time. This problem is, of course, greatly exacerbated when one is writing in one language about things culturally associated with another.

There may be any number of reasons why a bilingual writer chooses one or the other language for a particular use at any given moment. Many extra-literary factors (accidents of visas granted or refused, the cultural context in which one currently finds oneself, whom one marries, the presence or absence of a large readership in one or the other language, "the desire to please a shadow,"[33] or even financial opportunity) may determine the choice, as may the writer's professional judgment concerning the "literary appropriateness" of one language or the other for a specific work. As Nabokov once remarked, "an old Rolls-Royce is not always preferable to a plain Jeep" (*SO*, 106). Sometimes, retrospectively, the writer may even decide that he has made a mistake and that a work has been written in the "wrong" language, as in the case of Elsa Triolet's third novel *Zashchitnyi tsvet* [Camouflage].

Nina Berberova has remarked that a work is "not infrequently written in a language other than the one in which, as it were, it should have been written," but that this is not important because "there exists in the world a minimum of five languages in which one can in our time express what he wants to the entire Western world. In which one of these this is done is then not so essential."[34] Objectively this may make sense, but most bilingual writers, even most of those who subsequently translate themselves, do not think so. For most bilingual writers, at the time, the decision as to which language to use seems crucial (particularly in the earlier years of their ambilingual careers). The average reader would agree. For although we may, albeit reluctantly, accept the idea that a work, at least a work of prose, can be more or less adequately translated into another language, we balk at the notion that it could, indifferently, have been written in a language other than the original one. The bilingual writer's initial horror and revulsion (the words are barely too strong) at the idea of self-translation stems from this source, which is why making his peace with self-translation is often a major factor in the bilingual writer's ability ultimately to come to terms with his special gift and the cursed obligation of choice that accompanies it. Whatever the idiosyncratic solutions worked out by individual writers, however, they all share the consciousness of linguistic option, and it is the fact of the choosing, not the particular choice, that is determinant.

To say that most bilingual writers are uncomfortable with the possibility to choose the language in which they will write would be to understate the case. At certain moments of their careers, many bilingual writers would willingly give up greater cognitive flexibility (alternative neural pathways and all) so as *not* to have several languages from which to have to choose. It would be a mistake to dismiss this discomfort as merely mechanical. It is true that at first, or even in the long term, a bilingual writer may experience more resistance in one language than another. But this is not the point. All writers accept with good or bad grace, as a given of their trade, the fact of the struggle with language. The real problem with having two languages is neither technical nor neurophysiological; it is not linguistic interference but, rather, emotional interference. Even Nabokov, who complained long, loud, and vociferously about being obliged to "abandon my natural language, my natural idiom, my rich, infinitely rich and docile Russian tongue, for a second-rate brand of English" (*SO*, 15), also admitted on occasion, "I had spoken English with the same ease as Russian, since my earliest infancy. I had already written one English novel in Europe besides translating in the thirties two of my Russian books. *Linguistically, though perhaps not emotionally, the transition was endurable*" (pp. 189–190, emphasis added).

The real obstacle, the emotional one, is at least partially due to the feeling shared by many bilingual writers that it is somehow *abnormal* to be able to write in two languages. Elsa Triolet is a case in point. At the end of her life, she still wrote of her bilingualism as a disease or an affliction: "It's like an illness: I'm sick with bilingualism" [On dirait une maladie: Je suis atteinte de bilinguisme] (*M en m,* 54). Jacques Hassoun also chooses the image of disease, filtered through the terminology of painting, to describe the mingling of languages within bilinguals: "We are all 'infected' by language"[35] [Nous sommes tous des "infectés" de la langue]. An accent in a second language may be considered a "hump."[36] Using a second language may create a kind of mortal fatigue. On the other hand, if the first language is unused for some time, the bilingual fears that it may atrophy like a limb that has fallen asleep too long.[37]

Yet the metaphor of illness is inadequate by itself, because an illness is something that happens *to* you; in most cases, becoming ill does not entail a moral choice. *Deciding* to become a bilingual writer, on the other hand, involves the assumption of what Zinaïda Schakovskoy called a "nightmarish freedom" [kakaia-to koshmarnaia svoboda] and is initially felt not as a phenomenon of growth, but as a loss—worse yet, as the breaking of a sacred tie.[38] It is peculiar, in a time when so much that used to be considered "sinful" is now considered merely an "alternative lifestyle," that writing in a second language should still be severely sanctioned by the author's psyche as if it were a primal crime, but it is certain that many bilingual writers do feel that what they are doing is, in the strong sense, *illegitimate*.[39] Depending on who they are, on the circumstances of their relations to their various languages, and in what period of their careers they find themselves, bilingual writers may express their linguistic situation in terms of bigamy, adultery, or incest.[40] To give but one example here, Triolet, abandoning the image of disease as insufficient to express both the anguish of her position and her sense of guilt, declared: "I am a bigamist. It's a crime in the eyes of the law. As many lovers as you please; two legal husbands—impossible" [Je suis bigame. Un crime devant la loi. Des amants, tant qu'on veut; deux maris enregistrés, non] (*M en m*, 54). To have a husband and a lover (lovers, "as many as you please") may be complementary, additive, helping to create a whole, if turbulent, emotional life. Even marriage, divorce, and remarriage, while painful, are acceptable and may imply some kind of internal development or growth. But in Western cultures, bigamy is, by definition, divisive: when two marriages claim simultaneous *legitimate* status, there is no hierarchy, no subordination; there is no center to hold. As Triolet put it, "To be bilingual is a bit like being a bigamist: but to which one am I being unfaithful?" [Etre bilingue, c'est un peu comme d'être bigame: mais quel est celui que je trompe?] (p. 84).

Triolet's marriage metaphor, her self-accusation of bigamy, brings us closer to the crux of the emotional problem of bilingual writers than does the usual, almost automatic, image of the "mother tongue."[41] To write is an adult activity, and comparable in the imagery of both Triolet and Nabokov to post-Oedipal sexual activity. To choose as an adult to write in a tongue other than the *Muttersprache* is a fairly frequent occurrence and does not seem to cause insurmountable difficulties, always supposing reasonable fluency. But *to have once written* in a language and then to choose, under whatever pressures, to contract oneself as a writer to another tongue is an altogether different matter. If the modern writer gives up writing in the first language (abandons the first husband or wife), he or she may experience the pangs of infidelity and guilt, as well as a sense of self-mutilation. In his "K Rossii" [To Russia] quoted here in his own translation, Nabokov cries: "I'm prepared . . . to be drained of my blood, to be crippled, / to have done with the books I most love, / for the first available idiom / to exchange all I have: my own tongue"[42] [Ia gotov . . . obeskrovit' sebia, iskalechit', / ne kasat'sia liubimeishikh knig, / promeniat' na liuboe narech'e / vsë, chto est' u menia,—moi iazyk].

As Julien Green observes, their language is almost all that exiles have: "a man's language is so very much his own property that he almost identifies himself with it. . . . We are inclined to consider that what belongs to us and what we cherish most is somehow a part of ourselves. Our worth, our moral value, depend largely on the value of that very thing which we wish to make our own."[43] In Nabokov's lines, language is not only *property*, but *body*, ultimately self. By abandoning his language, Nabokov feels that he risks his physical and spiritual wholeness and integrity. He does this consciously and in full knowledge of the consequences. Although he could, like so many of his compatriots in exile, continue to write in Russian, his bilingualism also allows him the option of voluntarily betraying his last tie to Russia—the language that has embodied his already established self as a writer. Osip Mandel'shtam, for one, was categorical about the consequences of such a switch: "Language alone can be acknowledged as the criterion of unity for the literature of a given people, of its conditional unity, all other criteria being secondary, transitory, and arbitarary" [Takim kriteriem edinstva literatury dannogo naroda, edinstva uslovnogo, mozhet byt' priznan tol'ko iazyk naroda, ibo vse ostal'nye kriterii sami uslovny, prekhodiashchi i proizvol'ny].[44] For accepting the option of this intimate betrayal, Nabokov must hold himself alone morally responsible.

In the difficult situation of linguistic infidelity, the only external support for the bilingual writer frequently comes from his or her "human" spouse. It is curious that, at least among the Russians of the first emigration, it is those who were the most monogamous (in the usual sense), and particularly those married to Russians, who most successfully negotiated the perils of linguistic treason—not those, as one might have expected, who married native speakers of the second language. Marital fidelity to Russia seems frequently to have provided at least a partial shield against the psychic disintegration that threatens bilingual writers, particularly if they are, as so many of them have been in this century, in exile.

The bilingual writer, especially in exile, may feel traitorous, amputated, and divided, not so much the bearer of a *bi-destin*, a "double destiny," as Triolet and Roman Jakobson put it, but of a *mi-destin*, a "half-destiny."[45] All the advantages that neuro- and psycholinguistics see as inhering in bilingualism (the range of strategic options, the greater flexibility of symbolization, the heightened sense of "relativity") may become psychic disadvantages to a writer who is in involuntary exile from his homeland. Exile and bilingual writing are inextricably related in obvious ways in the lives and careers not only of Russian and East European émigrés, but also of most of the other bilingual writers currently or recently practicing. But themes of loss or psychic division are plentiful even in the works of exiles who continued to write in their first language. Such themes were present in the works of both Triolet and Nabokov even before their change of language. These themes may be ascribed to exile, or to bilingualism per se, or to some combination of both, but it would not be accurate to attribute such preoccupations exclusively to the professional abandonment of the mother tongue. Yet the sense of having a *mi-destin* rather than a *bi-destin*, the sense of a profound, irreducible psychic split, is clearly exacerbated by the internal conflicts leading to and following on the decision to change literary languages. And while exiled writers *may* feel that they have only a half-destiny, even if they remain loyal to their first language, most writers who change languages in midcourse *do* feel mortally split and even in danger of psychic disintegration, at least during the period immediately following their apostasy.

Split

I am still inhabited and constrained by this uncertainty of my being and this drama of duality.

[cette incertitude de l'être personnel et cette dramaturgie du dédoublement qui n'ont pas fini de m'habiter, de me contraindre.]

—Claude Esteban

Silence and madness seemed to me to rise above the horizon of unbridled polyphony, and they oppressed me.

[Le silence et la folie m'ont paru surgir à l'horizon de la polyphonie démesurée et je les ai trouvés oppressants.]

—Tzvetan Todorov

Although most successfully bilingual writers seem ultimately to achieve a certain serenity about their practice, this peace of mind and conscience is usually the result of a lengthy and difficult internal struggle. During periods of psychic stress caused by changing their languages, bilingual writers feel themselves to be not merely "monstrous" or Janus-faced, but split or even schizophrenic—as indeed they should, according to those linguists and psychologists who consider bilingualism to be an abnormal state. In 1977, M. Adler took the strong position on this question, in effect maintaining that bilinguals may actually *be* split personalities: "Often bilinguals have split minds. . . . All the particularities which language conveys, historical, geographical, cultural are re-embodied in a bilingual twice: he is neither here nor there; he is a marginal man. . . . Bilingualism can lead to a split personality and, at worst, to schizophrenia."[46] Grosjean, taking a more reassuring position, observes that to *his* knowledge bilinguals are no more likely to become clinically psychotic than are monolinguals. Recognizing that some bilinguals feel they change personality when they change languages, he quite reasonably suggests that "what is seen as a change in personality is simply a shift in attitudes and behaviors corresponding to a shift in situation or context, independent of language."[47]

Other neuro- and psycholinguists also play down the internal psychic consequences of switching languages and attribute the mental shift that occurs when a bilingual changes languages more to the influence of the external situation that brings about the change of language than to the change of language itself. Einar Haugen, himself a bilingual, observes: "The popular impression that a man alters his personality when speaking another tongue is far from ill-grounded. When I speak German to Germans, I *automatically shift my orientation as a social being*" (emphasis added).[48] These are commonsensical remarks that certainly pertain to utilitarian uses of bilingualism, particularly to bilingual speech. They may even on occasion pertain to bilingual writers in their nonliterary linguistic functioning, but they are totally inadequate to describe the experience of bilingual writers functioning as writers, particularly in the early stages of their careers. In the latter circumstances, the sense that bilingual writers have of being two separate personalities is not a function of a context "independent of language." When they actually sit down to write, and *choose* one language rather than another, nothing is "independent of language" anymore. Using language in its literary mode is not merely a behavior among others; it determines and defines most other behaviors, and frequently the language chosen is itself a large part of what the bilingual writer is talking about.

The choice of a language in which to write obviously depends much less on the constraints of the external context than does the choice of a language for any given utilitarian speech utterance. There are even fairly frequent instances when a bilingual writer will choose the language in which he writes a work *against* the logic of subject matter and context. Take, for example, the decisions of several bilingual Russians to write their childhood memoirs first in a language other than their mother tongue, even at periods when they were actively using Russian for other literary purposes.[49] Or consider Julien Green, who wrote novels drawn from his American experience in French, whereas he wrote a book about his French childhood in English. It is true that he had begun what was to become *Memories of Happy Days* in French and then switched to English after about twenty pages because, living in America during World War II, he despaired of finding a French publisher and felt it would be more "natural" to write in English in an American context, even though the subject was French. But what is curious about Green's experience with *Memories* is that when he compared the beginnings written in French and in English, he saw that they were significantly different, not because the subject was different or because his intended audience was not the same, but because the languages were different:

So I laid aside what I had written and decided to begin the book again, this time in English, my intention being to use practically the same words, or, if you wish, to translate my own sentences into English.

At this point, something quite unexpected happened. With a very definite idea as to what I wanted to say, I began my book, wrote about a page and a half and, on rereading what I had written, realized that I was writing another book, a book so different in tone from the French that a whole aspect of the subject must of necessity be altered. It was as if, writing in English, I had become another person. I went on. New trains of thought were started in my mind, new associations of ideas were formed. There was so little resemblance between what I wrote in English and what I had already written in French that it might almost be doubted that the same person was the author of these two pieces of work. This puzzled me considerably and still does.[50]

Clearly, it is not so much that Green's personality changes when he changes languages as that the language he has chosen changes the persona embodied in the work: "In reading the proofs of my book, I was struck by all that I had left unsaid and that I should most certainly have said in that book, had I written it in French. For instance, all that had to do with the development of religious feeling. I was even tempted to suppress the little I had said on that subject in the second half of the book. Why? I cannot say. Probably because I had written the book in English. It was as if the language itself had opposed certain disclosures in a book of that type" (*MFBIE*, 232).

By 1941, Green was pretty sure that "we may take it for granted that practically all our thinking is done in terms of a definite language. A language is not only a means of designating objects or describing emotions; it is in itself a process of thought" (*AEE*, 160), and later he would say that between two languages there is a concrete wall that one must somehow render transparent to translate even the simplest sentence. Thus, for Green, his languages are not communicating vessels, but two parallel systems that never mesh.

Green feels that those "differences" in his artistic "personality" which are created by his two languages are "puzzling" or "a little strange," but not particularly painful. This is because he believes that, in his case, there is one language "deeper than the other" (even if it is not literally his *Muttersprache*), and this priority provides an essential grounding and a basic "persona." Thus: "I am more and more inclined to believe that it is almost an impossibility to be absolutely bilingual. True, several languages can be mastered by the same person, sometimes to an amazing degree. I have heard people turn from French to English and from English to German with consummate ease and such perfection as to accent, intonations and choice of words that I wondered if there wasn't a trick about it. But this is not exactly what I mean. What I mean is that a man may speak half a dozen languages fluently and yet feel at home in only one; that is the language in which he will think when he is alone" (*AEE*, 172). Elsewhere, in French this time, Green added: "It is questionable whether one is really bilingual when one writes. I would tend to say that one is not. There cannot be a perfect balance between two languages, two ways of feeling, which is not tipped to one side or another by one's interior being"[51] [C'est une question que de savoir si l'on est vraiment bilingue lorsqu'on écrit. Je serais enclin à répondre par la négative. Entre deux langues, entre deux façons de sentir, il ne peut y avoir d'équilibre parfait que l'être intérieur ne penche d'un côté].

Green's solution is the weaker but safer one. More difficult and troubling is the task of those more or less balanced bilinguals who try to function linguistically as whole bilingual beings. Those for whom two languages are essentially parallel and equal often find that there is no way they can coincide with their total linguistic selves. Witness Claude Esteban, a well-known poet and translator from Spanish to French:

I have written elsewhere how, having been divided between French and Spanish since early childhood, I found it difficult for many years to overcome a strange laceration,[52] a gap not merely between two languages but also between the mental universes carried by them; I could never make them coincide within myself. I'm sure that I'm not the only person raised in bilingualism to have been torn in this way, even though I may have experienced it with exceptional intensity. . . . If [a translator] takes advantage of the bilingual knowledge that constantly splits his way of thinking and feeling, it is reality as a whole which teeters between two distinct ways of apprehending the world—and the two languages which he uses will also be affected by this ambivalence because he cannot manage to reduce them to pure systems of symmetrical and equivalent signs.[53]

[J'ai dit ailleurs comment, partagé dès la petite enfance entre l'espagnol et le français, il m'avait été longtemps difficile d'échapper à un étrange déchirement, non pas seulement entre deux langues, mais entre deux univers mentaux que l'une et l'autre véhiculaient sans que je parvinsse jamais à les faire coincider en moi-même. Un tel écartèlement, si je l'ai ressenti avec une intensité toute particulière, je ne pense pas être le seul de tous les individus élevés dans le bilin-guisme à l'avoir connu et subi. . . . s'il (le traducteur) tire parti d'un savoir bilingue qui dédouble inlassablement son mode de penser et de ressentir, c'est tout le réel, pour lui, qui bascule entre deux appréhe-nsions distinctes du monde—et les deux langues qu'il pratique seront, elles aussi, affectées par cette ambivalence, puisqu'il ne parvient pas à les réduire à de purs systèmes de signes, symétriques et équivalents.]

Tzvetan Todorov, born and reared in Bulgaria, where his second-ary schooling was in the Russian language, is also fluent in English. Now an influential critic, writing in French and completely at ease in the Paris literary world where he had made his mark as a pro-moter and translator of the Russian Formalist critics, Todorov was suddenly confronted by the same problem as Esteban. Todorov ex-perienced the psychic dangers and oppression of unsubordinated polyphony when he returned to Sofia, for the first time in eighteen years, to give a paper at a conference on the subject of "Bulgaria."

When he first arrived in France, Todorov wrote in Bulgarian and then translated into French. Except for occasional lexical and gram-matical problems, which he felt to be strictly mechanical, this sys-tem worked well for him, as he felt that there was a clear hierarchy between the two languages.[54] Later, Todorov began to write di-rectly in French, and by the time he sat down in Paris to write his paper for the Sofia conference, it was natural for him to write it in French. From his current situation—in Paris, in French—Todorov argued that the native-born person is always blinded to his own identity, that the history of a people is essentially the sum of the external influences to which it has been subjected, that, in any case, it is better to live in the present than to try to resurrect the past; in short, that there is no point in imprisoning oneself in traditional national values (*B, d, & s,* 20–21). He then began to translate this address into Bulgarian. Working in Bulgarian, he reacted to his ar-gument as would the Sofia intellectuals, one of whom he would have been had he not left Bulgaria. In Bulgarian, he felt obliged to replace his initial argument with its contrary. Todorov could no longer coincide with himself: he was neither in the situation of a Bulgarian intellectual nor in that of a Parisian writer; he was linguistically and spiritually of both places, and therefore not completely in either: "My double allegiance had a simple result: It seemed to me to brand each of my two discourses as inauthentic, since each could only correspond to half my being, whereas I am really double" [Ma double appartenance ne produit qu'un résultat: à mes yeux même, elle frappe d'inauthenticité chacun de mes deux discours, puisque chacun ne peut correspondre qu'à la moitié de mon être; or, je suis bien double] (p. 22).

This realization was confirmed during Todorov's actual visit to Bulgaria. And although, of course, shifts in attitude owing to circumstances such as those cited by Grosjean were an important factor in the malaise Todorov felt in Sofia, the fundamental source of his anxiety was the equal status of his two discourses. External circumstances dictated that he speak Bulgarian to Bulgarians and French to the French. Even though there is a pleasure and a kind of pride in being able to manifest different facets of one's personality and in being able to understand and identify with others, Todorov finds it impossible to make a *one* out of these two halves because, for him, his discourses are *not* so divided. From Todorov's point of view, his languages do not "split" according to function. Each is potentially *total*: "My two languages, my two discourses were, in a sense, too much alike: each could suffice for the totality of my experience, and neither was clearly subordinate to the other. One reigned here, the other there, but each reigned unconditionally. They were too much alike, and could substitute for one another, but could never combine to form a whole" [Mes deux langues, mes deux discours se ressemblaient trop d'un certain point de vue: chacun pouvait suffire à la totalité de mon expérience et aucun n'était clairement soumis à l'autre. L'un régnait ici, l'autre là; mais chacun régnait inconditionnellement. Ils se ressemblaient trop et ne pouvaient donc que se substituer l'un à l'autre, mais non se combiner entre eux] (B, d, & s, 24).

On his return to Bulgaria, Todorov had come up against a hurdle that all bilingual writers must face, sometimes more than once. His solution, like Green's, insists on the necessity of a clear subordination of one language to the other. His psychic equilibrium depends on it: "I feel the breath of madness in the equality of the voices. Their asymmetry and hierarchy is, on the contrary, reassuring" [L'égalité des voix me fait sentir le souffle de la folie. Leur asymétrie, leur hiérarchie est au contraire rassurante] (*B, d, & s,* 25). Most bilingual writers would agree with Todorov's caveat: "Just as I reject the idea that one necessarily loses one's soul if one belongs to two cultures, I also doubt that having two voices, two languages at one's disposal, is in itself a privilege that guarantees access to modernity. I wonder whether bilingualism based on neutrality and the perfect reversibility of two languages isn't an illusion, or at the least an exception, whether for it to be liberating, the practice of two languages doesn't require . . . a real disparity between them, a strict assignment of tasks, in short, a hierarchy" [En même temps que je refuse l'idée qu'appartenir à deux cultures c'est perdre son âme, je doute aussi que disposer de deux voix, de deux langues, constitue en soi un privilège qui vous garantit l'accès à la modernité. Je me demande si le bilinguisme fondé sur la neutralité et la parfaite réversibilité des deux langues n'est pas un leurre, ou tout au moins une exception; si son exercice libérateur n'implique pas, . . . un bon angle d'écart entre les deux, une répartition stricte des tâches; en un mot, une hiérarchie] (p. 26). In fact, most bilingual writers do suppress the active literary use of their first language almost entirely while they are in the process of investing their second language with psychic legitimacy (as Todorov had done before his return to Bulgaria). The period of suppression of the first language may last for years. Then, provided there is subordination, the bilingual writer can—indeed, should—function bilingually again, because, as Grosjean says, the bilingual is not the sum of two monoglots. He is a different kind of linguistic being altogether, and it is essential for him to have his languages maintain some kind of a dialogue.

Green's and Todorov's comments illustrate one of the few generalizations that one can safely hazard about bilingual writers. So long as a bilingual behaves toward himself as though he were a monolingual in each of his two languages, he may *surprise* himself when he switches, but he will be psychically safe. If he places one of his two languages in a position clearly subordinate to the other, even though he may use both professionally and be fully competent in both, he may feel guilt (if the subordinated language is his first language) and may experience considerable moral discomfort, but he will probably be psychically able to handle it. What is tricky is trying to function as a whole linguistic being, trying to write one's difference, rather than camouflaging or denying it. Very few bilingual writers attempt perfect equality in their two languages,[55] and one might suggest that those who do so, such as Samuel Beckett and Raymond Federman, know the risks and are deliberately tempting the "breath of madness," seeking to push both themselves and language to the limits.[56]

Trajectories

It is no accident that Todorov's discovery of his psychic need to subordinate clearly one of his two languages was touched off by an attempt at self-translation. Self-translation is the true test of whether a bilingual writer can ever totally coincide with himself. It is a crucial moment, a rite of passage endured by almost all writers who ultimately work in a language other than the one in which they have first defined themselves as writers. Self-translation is the pivotal point in a trajectory shared by most bilingual writers.

No matter when or how writers have learned their second language, they usually begin to write in it during a period of experimentation, continuing for several years or more, when the new literary language is tried out alongside the old one. During this time, writers continue to work in their first language and do translations of the works of other writers, sometimes in both directions, but mostly from the first language into the second. Then they attempt to self-translate, also from the first language into the second language—and they hate it. Although later in their careers bilingual writers frequently return to self-translation and may even become addicted to it, even these writers find self-translation exquisitely painful in the beginning. Nabokov, for example, wrote to Zinaïda Schakovskoy that putting *Otchaianie* [Despair] into English was "a terrible thing, translating oneself, sorting through one's own innards, then trying them on for size like a pair of gloves"[57] [Uzhasnaia veshch'—perevodit' samogo sebia, perebiraia sobstvennie vnutrennosti i primerivaia ikh, kak perchatki]. Other bilinguals make similar comments. So unpleasant is the exercise of self-translation that it precipitates writers into finally committing themselves to their second language. No matter how daunting it used to seem, compared to self-translation, writing directly in the second language now appears far easier, even a relief.

Usually the first attempts at writing directly in the second language are works thematically and stylistically similar to those recently written in the first language. This keeps the break to a minimum and helps the writer rediscover his personal voice in the new language. Although there may be a few linguistic difficulties at the beginning, starting to write in a second language seems at first amazingly unproblematical in other ways ("as many lovers as you please"). The real trouble starts afterward, when the writer has proven to himself and to others that he has a *real individual voice* in the second language, a voice that is as much his own as the voice in the first language had been. It is when the bilingual writer has two avowedly *legitimate* output systems at his disposal that writing in the second language ceases to be a mere "fling" and the horror of bigamy sets in.

At this point, and often with considerable internal and/or external theatrics, bilingual writers usually renounce writing in their first language, forcibly committing themselves exclusively to the new one, thereby violating their profound natures as bilinguals. All the writers who go through this most difficult period have good reasons for putting away their "first spouse" and choosing to throw in their lot, apparently once and for all, with the second language. Among the reasons offered for the decision to become a monolingual writer in an adoptive tongue are the following: a lack of audience in the first language; the inappropriateness of the first language for what one now feels one has to say; the cultural context; money, opportunity to publish, etc., etc. The technical justification offered most often by bilinguals for ceasing to write in their first language is the need to avoid linguistic interference. One can certainly understand, particularly if the second language is not as strong as the first, that newly fledged bilingual writers would want to isolate the second language from the first one. But even when this is the case, writers also admit that part of the reason for the decision to abandon active professional use of their first language is less the desire to avoid contamination of the second language by the first than the desire to avoid contamination of the renounced, yet infinitely more beloved, first language by the second language.

We have seen that the problems of transition are at least as much psychological as they are narrowly linguistic. Behind many of the exceedingly practical reasons offered by bilinguals for abandoning writing in their first language seems to be an attempt to avoid psychic split by committing the inner voice to only one of the output systems, albeit the most recently acquired. The bilingual writer senses that the first language must be cut off and dammed up because, although the self can speak in either language, and although the brain processes incoming information for both languages, the self apparently cannot *speak to itself* simultaneously in both. And thus, paradoxically, bilingual writers are more aware that they are not totally coinciding with themselves when they *do* write in both their languages than when they use only one.

In the long run, however, attempting to suppress all literary activity in the first language seems to be a mistake for most bilingual writers. Or perhaps it is a phase that seems or may in fact *be* necessary at the crucial moment of the investment of psychic legitimacy in the second language. But if so, it is a phase that must be left behind if bilingual writers are to realize their full promise. To be true to themselves, to their cerebral organization, and to their linguistic experience, bilingual writers must somehow remain *actively* bilingual. To profit from the greater number of processing strategies available to them, they must continuously exercise their option to choose among their languages and even to let them interact; for the possibility of such choice is the foundation of their particularity, part of their individual signatures.

The greatest modern writers writing in more than one live national language eventually come to see this, and the ends of their careers manifest an extraordinary reconciliation. The monogamy/bigamy metaphor ceases to be applicable, and for those bilingual writers who have gone the whole course, completing the full trajectory, a kind of constantly shifting balance or flexible synthesis is achieved. The details and proportions of this resolution vary from writer to writer, but usually involve major, long-term projects wherein the writer brings together both languages and both cultures. Frequently, the bilingual writer undertakes a major translation project at this stage of his career, usually from the first language into the second language. This involves the constant and intimate interaction of both languages (e.g., Triolet's translation of Chekhov's plays and her bilingual anthology *La poésie russe* [Russian poetry]; Nabokov's quirky and monumental translation of and commentaries on Pushkin's *Evgenii Onegin* [Eugene Onegin]). The new balance almost invariably also involves the previously execrated genre of self-translation, constituting a rejection of the writer's earlier certainty that something could or should be written in only one language or the other.

In their later years, fully "individuated" bilingual writers thus make concerted efforts to coincide completely with themselves. If they succeed in making their peace with their two languages, it is because they realize that although they cannot perfectly superimpose one language on the other and create a whole in that way, there is a third language at their command which overarches the others; and the existence of that third language enables them to reconcile the other two. This "third" language may, in polyglots, be in fact a fourth or a fifth, but whatever its numeral, it is separate from and additional to any of the natural languages the bilingual may speak or write. The third language does not really "cap" the others: it is not "higher"; it emerges from the depths, inextricably intertwined with the "natural" languages, and is as basic to the writer's mature linguistic identity as any of the others. Once again Steiner has observed this as only a true polyglot could:

> I harbour the feeling that the reticulations of inter-lingual contact and transfer in my own mind, as in that of any polyglot, belong to at least two principal hierarchies. The one seems to draw on the objective analogies ("cross-echoes") and mnemonically salient contrasts between phonetic units in several languages. The other would appear to be based on a prodigiously tangled and private network of associations between morphemes or semantic units on the one hand and the circumstances of my own life on the other. This second topology operates irrespective of formal linguistic barriers. In other words, at least one of the modes of spatialization of phonetic, grammatical and semantic material in my consciousness interleaves the languages I know according to criteria of proximity or antithesis, of cognateness or exclusion, which are wholly personal and interlingual. Thus one of the "languages" inside me, probably the richest, is an eclectic cross-weave

whose patterns are unique to myself though the fabric is quite palpably drawn from the public means and rule-governed realities of English, French, German, and Italian. [*AB*, 292]

Every really bilingual or polyglot writer has such an "eclectic cross-weave," and for each the pattern is unique, depending on the interaction of those individual associations and experiences of acquisition and usage that researchers into bilingualism find so endlessly frustrating. The "third tongue" is the sign of the bilingual writer's difference. Once bilingual writers accept its existence, it is evident that they cannot coincide fully with either of their other languages, or even with some kind of forcible superimposition and compression of them into a kind of laminate. Both languages and cultures are wholly theirs, but they do not belong wholly to either. For the "poly-linguistic matrix" is the determining fact not only of Nabokov's art,[58] but also of Beckett's, and of the art of all bilingual writers who, some more belatedly than others, have come to terms with their special artistic nature.

Once bilingual writers have made their peace with the fact that they have a "third" language, then they can allow themselves to behave linguistically *like bilinguals.* All bilinguals know that when they are speaking to another bilingual or polyglot, their language is radically different than when they are speaking to a monolingual in either of their two languages. The frequent code-switching and "borrowing" from the shared languages that is evident when bilinguals speak to each other may be highly efficient and enriching. The later works of writers who have made peace with their bilingualism may therefore be permeated by a personal idiolect in which elements from their various languages appear in a polyglot synthesis. When this occurs, the argument that bilingual writers have chosen to write in a second language in order to reach a larger audience ceases to be valid (if it ever was). They would seem to be addressing, first and foremost, a small audience of fellow polyglots.

Bilingual or polyglot writers perform an essential service to the vaster readership of monolinguals when they allow the pressure of their polyglotism to infuse, but not overwhelm, the "national" languages in which they write. By so doing, they serve the "purpose of expressing the central reciprocal relationship between languages," as they do when translating.[59] By allowing one or the other language to be "powerfully affected" by a foreign tongue—by expanding and deepening their "natural" languages, stretching them with elements from their personal idiolects which their mastery of the natural languages assures them will be ultimately compatible with them—they thereby revivify those languages. All bilingual writers who can do so, owe it to their languages, as well as to themselves, to allow creative interference. The languages and the readers can be trusted to reject whatever is indigestible or unsavory.

In their ability to switch languages, writers like Nabokov are comparable to the Joyce of *Finnegans Wake* and to the creators of certain kinds of *zaum* (transrational language) and *dada*. Yet there are significant differences. Having written extensively first in one language and then in another before allowing the "third" language to play through one or both, places strict limits on what bilinguals such as Nabokov or Beckett will allow themselves to do with their languages. To play is to stay within rules, even when one stretches them outrageously by one's originality and mental flexibility. In some ways, bilingual writers care more about the systematic spirit of each of their languages (because they have the other, also intimately known, as a counterweight and comparison) than do monolingual "experimenters" or polyglots who have never seriously tried to *pass* as writers in more than one language. Thus, bilingual writers are unlikely to indulge regularly in large, arbitrary macaronic structures, and whatever borrowings do occur tend to be bound by the systematically determined rules of bilingual code-switching that are natural to bilinguals when they communicate with one another. Their freedom of choice makes bilingual writers paradoxically more *responsible* to their languages. Having once stepped outside the system of a language, they can never return to the thoughtless and unprincipled literary use of it. They are conscious of the folding and interfolding of their languages in the space within their heads. They have "tempted alien tongues," and once having done so, each must proceed—in his own way, as best he can—to live and work in the ambivalent condition of knowledge.

Beyond the very general elements they share, which I have just considered, the trajectories of bilingual writers are significantly idiosyncratic. Let us therefore turn to a closer examination of individual artistic careers and to the solutions arrived at by some of the most significant practitioners of bilingual writing in the twentieth century: the generation of Russian writers who left their homeland after the Revolution of 1917 and who are usually known as the Russians of the "first" emigration.

CHAPTER THREE

Elsa Triolet

Don't forget the birds. The nightingale will sing neither *cou-cou* nor *cra-cra;* the crow doesn't trill. Never. Wherever birds may hatch, their language, like their plumage, is determined by their species.

[Ne pas oublier les oiseaux. Le rossignol ne chantera ni cou-cou ni cra-cra, le corbeau n'emettra pas de trilles. Jamais. Qu'ils sortent de l'œuf ici ou là, le language des oiseaux est, comme le plumage, attaché à l'espèce.]

Basically, one writes against oneself: to prove to oneself that one can do something different than what one has already done.

[Au fond, on écrit contre soi-même: pour se prouver qu'on peut faire autre chose que ce qu'on a déjà fait.]

—Elsa Triolet

Elsa Triolet (née Elza Iur'ievna Kagan) is known to readers of French literature as a prolific, frequently impressive novelist and as a kind of *monstre sacré*. A decisive woman, with clear pro-Soviet principles and loyalties, she was a major power in French literary politics for forty years. She is also one of the major *characters* in modern French poetry, the object of the public, published adoration of the poet Louis Aragon. He enshrined her in such works as "Elsa," "Cantique à Elsa" [Canticle for Elsa], "Le fou d'Elsa" [A fool for Elsa], and "Les yeux d'Elsa" [Elsa's eyes] at least as solidly as Vladimir Maiakovskii did her older sister, Liliia Iur'ievna Brik, in his "Pro eto" [About this] and "Fleita-pozvonochnik" [The backbone flute]. Elsa Triolet is also a heroine of Russian literature. Long before being so fulsomely adored by Aragon, she had appeared as the cosmopolitan, comfort-loving, and elusive Alia of Viktor Shklovskii's *Zoo, ili pis'ma ne o liubvi* [Zoo, or, Letters not about love]. Although she later wrote seventeen novels and a number of other books in French, Triolet's own first novels, written in Russian in the late 1920s and published in the Soviet Union, can stand comparison with any Russian prose of the period.[1] Throughout her career, she continued to translate in both directions and to promote Russian literature in France and French literature in Russia. Her own Russian books were translated into French less than twenty years ago, however, and like most bilingual writers, Triolet's total achievement has not been fairly estimated. She deserves to be considered whole, in her bilingual difference.

Elsa Triolet (1896–1970) was the second daughter of Iurii Aleksandrovich Kagan, a lawyer of Jewish extraction who specialized in contracts for actors and musicians. Her mother, Elena Iur'ievna, was an excellent amateur pianist.[2] The Kagans were well-off, assimilated, and cultivated; the girls learned French and German at an early age.[3] The parents spoke fluent German, and Elena Iur'ievna even took her daughters to Bayreuth to hear Wagner.[4] Nevertheless, for both girls, Russian was clearly the first and primary language (Elsa was six when she began to learn French, and she already knew how to read and write Russian). Neither the young Elsa nor her sister Liliia would ever have chosen to write in French as had Mariia Bolkonskii, Tatiana Larina, or, indeed, Pushkin himself. Nabokov has said with some justice that he was an English child,[5] but the Kagan sisters were unequivocally Russian.

Despite Elsa's passion for poetry (it was the sixteen-year-old Elsa who discovered Maiakovskii, championed his poetry, and brought him into the family), she had no ambition to become a writer herself. Except for some adolescent diaries, she had written nothing before she emigrated to rejoin and marry André Triolet, a dashing Frenchman whom she had met while he was posted in Russia during World War I. Nor did she take advantage of the isolation and idleness of her sojourn with her husband on the island of Tahiti to write anything but letters. It was in fact because of some of her letters that she more or less accidentally, and rather unwillingly, became a professional writer. Viktor Shklovskii included letters by Triolet in the text of his *Zoo, ili pis'ma ne o liubvi*; and Maksim

Gor'kii, unaware of their authorship, told him that the "letters from the woman" were the best thing in the book.[6] Some of these letters speak in the voice of the idle, passive heroines of Triolet's early novels.[7] Others presage the emergence of the active, talented writer, content only with a combination of solitude and activity, who would create these heroines and those of her French novels.[8] As Shklovskii put it, her letters show Elsa-Alia to be somehow both a Russian and an "acting foreigner" [zauriad-inostranka], but not entirely either one.[9]

Both Gor'kii and Shklovskii encouraged Triolet to write, and she began to do so seriously after she settled in Paris in one of the series of almost identical violet- and yellow-striped rooms in the Hotel Istria which she occupied until the beginning of her life with Louis Aragon. Alone in Paris,[10] Elsa wrote *Na Taiti* [Tahiti], a book that is both a traditional travel novel, portraying the curiosities of life on an exotic island, and a confession about the aimlessness and isolation of exile. Tahiti, in 1919 still an almost inaccessible speck lost in the ocean, became the symbol of the physical and linguistic distance now separating Elsa Triolet from her former Russian existence.[11] Yet her relation to her subject was somewhat more complex than it may at first appear. By the time she actually wrote *Na Taiti,* the island and her marriage were as much a part of the past as her life in Russia, perhaps even more so. For although she was writing about Tahiti and homesickness, about "a soul in pain, gnawed by homesickness for Russia, wallowing alone in an abyss of nostalgia" [une âme en peine, rongée par le mal du pays, seule à patauger dans mon abîme nostalgique] (OC, 1, 15), she was still writing in Russian for readers "back home." (For Triolet, "home" [u nas] would always mean the Soviet Union).[12] She was writing, in Russian, about an island at the end of the world, for readers in "a country that was just emerging from the cold, from hunger", [pour un pays qui sortait à peine du froid et de la faim] (1, 22), and writing from Paris, a place almost as inaccessible to her readers as Tahiti.

Although *Na Taiti* is a book about aimlessness, solitude, and exile, it is actually a first step back from passivity and separation. In her novel, Triolet looked at Tahiti through the prism of her Russian past. As she remarked years later: "Just think, I had gone to that island just as I was when I had left Moscow, more than a year before. I still belonged entirely to my past, brief as it had been, and I saw everything in relation to what I had left behind. Just think, I was writing in Russian, for Russians, and I was using everyday Russian to describe this exotic island—It was already a conscious artistic device—I was narrating the unknown in terms of the known." [Songez que je suis allée dans l'île, telle que j'avais été à Moscou, bien que je l'eusse quitté depuis plus d'un an. J'appartenais encore pleinement à mon passé pas trè long et tout se présentait à moi par rapport à ce que j'avais quitté. Songez que j'écrivais en russe, pour des Russes, et que je me servais pour décrire l'île exotique—et c'était là déjà un procédé conscient d'écriture—du quotidien russe. Je racontais l'inconnu par rapport au connu] (*OC*, I, 21). Triolet also insisted on the fundamental "Russianness" of her first novel, despite its exotic subject: "If I had written *Tahiti* in French, I would have done it quite differently.... French doesn't suit the complexion of *Tahiti*: the novel's simplicity appears to be naiveté, and the specificity of the Russian language with its associated ideas and feelings does not transfer into French" [Si j'avais écrit *A Tahiti* directement en français, je l'aurais fait tout autrement.... Le français ne va pas au teint de cet *A Tahiti*: la simplicité s'y fait naïveté, le langage spécifiquement russe ne trouve pas en français ses associations d'idées, de sentiments] (I, 22).

Triolet's comments on the language of *Na Taiti* seem to be truisms. Yet they are worthy of attention because of the context in which they were made: in a preface to her very belated self-translation of this, her first novel, done some forty-five years after its initial appearance. Her remarks are a disclaimer for not having already done something that deep down she still feels it should be impossible to do: rewriting her book in a language other than the one she had originally chosen. Triolet explains her long-term reluctance to translate her works by claiming that the deliberate "simplicity" of her style in either language makes the task almost impossible. This is nonsense. She is relatively easy to translate, and Léon Robel has rendered her second novel, *Zemlianichka* [Wild strawberry], and her third novel, *Zashchitnyi tsvet* [Camouflage], quite well into French. Triolet herself has successfully negotiated far more difficult tasks of translation, in particular her renderings of Celine's *Voyage au bout de la nuit* [Journey to the end of night] into Russian and of various modern Russian poets, including Khlebnikov, into French.

Triolet's reluctance to translate herself is therefore less a reflection of the objective linguistic difficulty of the task than of her need as a bilingual writer to assure herself that she had originally made the right choice of language for her works. She is also afraid of the high emotional cost of self-translation, which, as we have observed, threatens the bilingual writer with a far more serious split than does writing directly in two different languages. For Triolet, self-translation raises the terrifying spectre of noncoincidence with herself: "One would think that it should be easy for bilinguals to translate themselves. Not a bit! You look at yourself as though in a mirror, you try to find yourself, and you don't recognize the reflection as your own" [Pour les bilingues, *se* traduire devrait être facile? Non pas! On se regarde comme dans une glace, on s'y cherche, ne reconnaît pas son reflet] (*M en m*, 76). Nevertheless, in order to realize her project of publishing her works together with Aragon's in a multivolume garland of *Œuvres romanesques croisées* (an emotional priority of her last years), Triolet finally forced herself to put *Na Taiti* into French and, perhaps more difficult still, to translate part of her Paris diaries into French for the collection's preface.

Triolet frequently cannibalized her diaries for her novels, most extensively in her second novel *Zemlianichka*, an *autobiographie romancée*.[13] Its first part, about a Russian childhood and adolescence, incorporates actual entries from Triolet's early diaries and ends with a chapter entitled "Amputation" in which the heroine, known to all as Zemlianichka, declares her intention to marry and emigrate.[14] In the second part of the novel, we find Zemlianichka spending days on end on a divan waiting for the return of her fiancé or, at least, for a good letter from him. She takes to wandering the streets in despair, lives in a small hotel (the conversations she overhears there while ill are in French and English in the Russian text), and falls into an affair with a wealthy Monsieur Pierre, but all this occurs in a way too absent-spirited to count.[15]

In one of Zemlianichka's early entries in her grown-up Parisian diary, we see reflected that fear of life of which Shklovskii had only half-jokingly accused Elsa-Alia in *Zoo*: "When one's suffering for those who suffer comes from the realization of one's own powerlessness to defend oneself, from fear for oneself, from cowardice, it can never transform itself into active love for humanity. I have seen a lot, and as it happens, experienced a good deal of the 'the danger of living.' Why can't I get used to it then? Why do I react to everything so convulsively? Why do I brood so long over my impressions as though they were eggs?" [Kogda stradanie za strazhdushchikh proiskhodit ot soznaniia svoei sobstvennoi bezzashchitnosti, ot strakha za sebia, ot trusosti, ono nikogda ne prevratitsia v aktivnuiu liubov' k chelovechestvu. Ia mnogo videla, sluchaino mnogo perezhila iz "opasnosti zhizni," otchego zhe ia ne mogu privyknut', otchego ia tak sudorozhno ko vsemu otnoshus' i tak dolgo, kak iaitsa, vynashivaiu vpechatleniia?] (*Zemlianichka*, 110).

This fear of life and self-centered isolation are slightly dissipated at the end of the novel when the heroine returns to Moscow (as Triolet herself did, shepherded by Maiakovskii, for eight months in 1925–1926. Triolet was no longer entirely at home there either, however, and returned abroad).[16]

While in Moscow, Triolet began her third novel. *Zashchitnyi tsvet* [Camouflage] develops still further the themes of spiritual and linguistic homelessness (and of the fear of life which homelessness may foster) that had permeated *Na Taiti* and *Zemlianichka*. In 1938, writing in her private journal, in Russian, just before *Camouflage* appeared, Triolet observed that the real subject of her novel was "fear, or cowardice in the face of life. 'A corpse's life,' Babel says. I say, 'an accidental corpse's life.' . . . A convulsive fear of life that never lets go"[17] [Le véritable sujet de ce livre est la peur (ou la lâcheté) devant la vie. "Une vie de cadavre," dit Babel. Moi je dis "une vie de cadavre par accident." . . . Une peur convulsive devant la vie, qui ne la lâche pas] (*OC*, I, 25).

Camouflage is particularly interesting for our purposes because it speaks about spiritual split (which Triolet accented by dividing herself between two separate women characters, each of which embodies certain aspects of their author) and about an incipient linguistic split. The two turn out to be intimately related. One heroine, Lucille, a small, white-bodied woman,[18] pampered by a wealthy husband, abandoned by a lover who has left for the tropics, is a continuation of Elsa-Alia and the heroine of *Na Taiti*. Her friend Varvara, whom Lucille first met on one of her aimless wanderings through Paris, is a woman of Russian origin, adrift in Paris. Despite her many acquaintances, Varvara feels exposed and isolated, as though she were in a constant draft: "She thought to herself that she was really alone, that she had neither relatives nor family nor house nor opinions nor money nor a profession. She had nothing that could serve as a link between her and any group of people. In any milieu, she remained isolated, not knowing how to dissolve and blend with it. She was a foreigner in all countries, placed in the margins of life like a typographical error. In fact, she was an error" [Ona dumala o tom, chto ona voistinu odinoka. U nee ne bylo ni rodnikh, ni sem'i, ni doma, ni ubezhdenii, ni deneg, ni professii, nichego takogo, chto posluzhilo by sviaz'iu mezhdu nei i drugimi liud'mi, kakoi-nibud' gruppoi liudei. Vo vsiakoi srede ona ostavalas' odinochkoi, ne umeia rastvorit'sia i slit'sia, i vo vsekh stranakh byla inostrankoi. Eë, kak oshibku, vynesli na polia. Ona i byla oshibkoi] (*Zashchitnyi tsvet*, 69). Triolet saw that the whole novel suffered from the same lack of rootedness as its heroine. It may have been an "error" for several reasons, but she later recognized that the book's greatest flaw was that she had chosen the wrong language.[19] *Camouflage* had been written in Russian, but was not comfortable in it:

> The drama of *Camouflage* is played out in France among characters who speak, think and feel French. It would appear to be a book translated from the French, and yet the language of the novel is profoundly Russian. As a result, the novel is strangely, hopelessly out of phase with itself, and the novel as a whole is an illustration of what is said in it about Barbara, its Russian heroine who lives in France: the only thing Barbara had left was her mother tongue, and she was forced to mutilate even that, because her thought could not bend itself to fit the structure of the Russian language.

> [Le drame de *Camouflage* se joue en France, entre personnages parlant, pensant, sentant français. On croirait un livre traduit du français, et pourtant la langue du roman est profondément russe. Il s'ensuit un étrange, un irréductible décalage, et le roman tout entier est l'illustration de ce que l'on y dit de Barbara, son héroïne russe habitant la France: Tout ce qui restait à Barbara était sa langue maternelle, et encore était-elle obligée de la mutiler parce que souvent sa forme de pensée n'arrivait pas à se plier à la structure de la langue russe.] [*OC*, I, 24–25]

Thus, *Camouflage* seemed to Triolet to be fatally out of linguistic sync. Faced with what she felt as a contradiction between her life and her mother tongue, unwilling to write in French, she ceased for a time to write altogether:

> So I stopped writing, and it didn't seem really to matter, since I had only written idly, for lack of anything better to do. It wasn't worth thinking about—finished, over and done with. And it was better so, since my instrument—my language—had turned out to be useless for communicating with my readers. My mother tongue, my irreplaceable language . . . was no good to me anymore. . . . I had nothing more to say in this language which was part of my innermost self.

> [J'ai donc cessé d'écrire, et je semblais ne pas y tenir, puisque je n'avais jamais écrit que comme ça, parce que je n'avais rien de mieux à faire. Je n'y pensais plus, assez, fini. Et c'était mieux ainsi, puisque l'outil que je possédais s'avérait inutilisable pour communiquer avec mes lecteurs: la langue! Ma langue maternelle, mon irremplaçable langue . . . Elle ne me servait plus à rien. . . . Je n'avais plus rien à dire en cette langue que je connaissais jusqu'au fin fond de moi-même.]
> [OC, I, 26–27]

Of course, it did matter, and it was not over and done with. From Triolet's own descriptions of her career, it would appear that when she did begin to write again, she had made the break and was writing in the "other" language: French. But the actual process of changing language was far more complex and seems to have lasted at least a decade. Triolet did not in fact abandon writing in Russian because of the failure of *Camouflage*. When she started to write again in the 1930s, she wrote several articles in Russian as well as a whole fact-novel about the Paris fashion industry, also in Russian.[20] Despite Gor'kii's intervention on its behalf, the Soviet censorship prevented this novel, *Busy* [Necklaces], from being published in its entirety in the USSR.[21] Given the communist views that Triolet held by this time and that she shared with Aragon, there was no question of her writing for the Russian-speaking readership of the Paris emigration, some of whom still refuse to consider Triolet a legitimate member of the "first" emigration because of her politics (notwithstanding the fact that her leaving Russia to marry André Triolet had nothing to do with politics and that she appears as anything *but* a hard-nosed revolutionary in her own early books and in Shklovskii's *Zoo*).

Disturbed by the fate of *Necklaces*, lacking confidence in herself, Triolet had hoped that Aragon would tell her to go on writing.[22] But he would have had to encourage her on trust, knowing almost no Russian, and he did not do so. When Triolet started to write again, for a third time, she did write in French, *against him*, to affirm her integrity, so that he would have to consider her an artist in her own right, not merely the passive object of his adoration: "And when I did begin to write again, it was against you—in fury and despair, because you didn't trust me. I was going to try to write in French so that you could tell me 'Write' or 'Don't write' in full knowledge of the facts" [Et quand j'ai recommencé à écrire, c'était contre toi, avec rage et désespoir, parce que tu ne me faisais pas confiance. J'allais essayer d'écrire en français pour que tu me dises: écris!—ou n'écris pas! . . . en connaissance de cause] (OC, 1, 31).

Beginning to write in French was therefore an assertion of self more than an abdication of it. One hears the *same* voice—or, rather, the same *voices*—in both languages. Similar topics and genres produce the same tone in either. Her Russian news reports show the same heavy-handedness and rhythmic rigidity as some of her later "communist-committed" works in French, but she can be just as delicate and supple in French, when her themes are similar to those of her early Russian novels.[23]

Yet this flexibility and sensitivity did not at first come easily to Triolet. Later, she recalled the painfulness of writing *Bonsoir, Thérèse* [Goodnight, Thérèse], her first French novel:[24] "I had to throw myself into French. It was physically painful, as though someone had encased me in a plaster corset. I was limited on all sides; there were obstacles everywhere. I lacked verbal raw material, and what I had was as rigid and as hard to handle as tangled barbed wire" [Il me fallait plonger dans le français. J'en souffrais physiquement, comme si on m'avait mis un corset de plâtre. J'étais limitée de toute part, il n'y avait autour de moi que des bornes, je manquais de matériaux verbaux, et ceux que je possédais étaient rigides et commodes à manier comme du fil de fer barbelé, enchevêtré] (OC, 1, 32). Nor did the change of language really occur simply as the result of a single moment of decision to "show" Aragon.

Triolet's notebooks and diaries of the years up to and including 1939 document a complex, ten-year process through which she passed before emerging as a real French writer in *Bonsoir, Thérèse*. Particularly interesting in this regard is the evidence provided by two notebooks which show that Triolet had been trying her hand in French well before she stopped writing in Russian.[25]

In the first notebook, a little black one, Triolet wrote from both ends. One side begins with an exercise entitled "J'aime être heureuse" [I like being happy], written in a rather flat and rhythmless French, and including errors that have been crossed out and corrected. The script is large, rigid, and rather childish. After some descriptive notes on happiness, erotic objects, and women as the future of the world, there follows a text of several pages in length that is a self-translation of a chapter from *Zemlianichka*. Triolet had put into French a description of her adolescent heroine's walk through the streets of Moscow during a spring thaw (not, as one might have expected, a segment of the chapters that take place in Paris). Here again, the French is for the most part correct but ever so slightly stilted. There are also a few grammatical errors, particularly in agreement of verbs: e.g., "Elle portent [*sic*] des gants blancs immaculés" [She wear [*sic*] immaculate white gloves]. When one compares Triolet's draft version with the translation of the same passage some forty years later by Léon Robel, it is evident that he is far more faithful than Triolet to the flexibility of her Russian. To give but one example, Triolet translates the chapter title "Nailuchshaia vesna" as "Le plus beau printemps." Robel calls it "Le plus beau des printemps." Either version is correct French, but Robel's fuller, more metrically satisfying phrase is closer to the tone of the original.

This chapter of self-translation in the notebook is followed by drafts of parts of what would become *Bonsoir, Thérèse* (the gala at the theater and parts of the chapter "Je cherche un nom de parfum" [I try to find a name for a perfume]). When one turns the notebook around and begins to read from the other end, the text is a diary, begun on Triolet's thirty-second birthday. It is mostly in Russian, but there are frequent insertions of French words (e.g., part of an entry on her relations with Isaac Babel: "*Chuvstvuiu sebia* ridicule" [I FEEL ridiculous]) and bilingual comments on French usage (e.g., "l'allure pur sang, *nedarom* on vicomte . . . *a ranovor na* argot [*sic*] *tozhe* pur sang—*smeshno ochen'*" [looks like a real thoroughbred, NOT FOR NOTHING is he a viscount, BUT "RANOVOR" IN slang ALSO MEANS thoroughbred—VERY AMUSING]).[26] "Argot" could be written either in Russian or in French, but Triolet has done it in French, rather than in the Russian, ARGO.

The black notebook shows us that Triolet's French was still stiff when she began to consider translating herself into that language and that she was continuing to write in Russian, at least for herself, when she was already jotting down certain episodes of *Bonsoir, Thérèse* directly in French. It testifies to the period of linguistic interaction that is usual when bilinguals are just beginning to write in their second language. Triolet continued to write in both French and Russian in her private journal even after the completion of *Bonsoir, Thérèse*, sometimes, as we have seen, allowing herself to mix French and Russian even within a single sentence—a type of code-switching long considered by Russians to be a cardinal sin against the language—but she never allowed herself to code-switch in print.[27]

The yellow notebook provides even more interesting evidence of the complexities of Triolet's relations with her two languages and, more specifically, it tells a good deal about *Bonsoir, Thérèse*, during the writing of which Triolet took the plunge into French *quitte à se noyer*. The handwritten title on the notebook's cover is symptomatic of the halfway position in which Triolet found herself:

BONSOIR, THÉRÈSE
po russki   [in Cyrillic, meaning "in Russian"]
i   [in Cyrillic, meaning "and"]
La femme au diamant.   [the lady with a diamond]

The notebook contains a series of personal reminiscences, written in Russian, some of which were later translated into French by Triolet to become parts of *Bonsoir, Thérèse*.[28] A passage that begins "I am lying in the grass" [Ia lezhu na trave] is easily recognizable as a draft of the first scene of *Bonsoir, Thérèse*. Some of these texts reflect Triolet's more recent Paris experience. A passage about the Closerie des Lilas, including a description of how she met Aragon, reappears in shortened form in *Bonsoir, Thérèse*. There is also a description of a ball at the Salle Bullier and of the incidents that followed, elements of which appear in *Bonsoir, Thérèse*. The presence of these texts in Russian in the notebook confirms Triolet's assertion that *Bonsoir, Thérèse* was in part first written in Russian: "To tell the truth, I had actually written the beginning of my first French book in Russian and then translated it" [A vrai dire, le début de ce premier livre en français, je l'ai quand même écrit en russe, puis traduit]. (*OC*, 1, 32).

Other texts in the same notebook seem to indicate that, even as late as 1936, Triolet had not yet completely given up hope of being able to write in Russian for the audience "back home."[29] Yet there were equally strong internal compulsions for her to switch to French. This is shown by the existence of an extremely interesting text in the yellow notebook, one that does *not* subsequently reappear in *Bonsoir, Thérèse*. It is a nostalgic, birthday love poem, written in French, first in a rough draft, then in a clean copy. So at the time Triolet was writing parts of *Bonsoir, Thérèse* in Russian, there were feelings and emotions, similar to those which her earlier novels had expressed in Russian, that she could now express in French—indeed, that came to her directly in French.

As we have already seen, self-translation accentuates the consciousness of hiatus in bilingual writers such as Triolet. For Triolet, self-translation actually jeopardized the intimate conversation with herself that she prized above all in her writing. Because *Bonsoir, Thérèse* was an attempt to revive that conversation, writing directly in French was less inhibiting than writing first in Russian and then translating: "I lit *Bonsoir, Thérèse* from *Taiti* the way a chainsmoker lights a fresh cigarette from the previous one. Thirteen years later, it's the same voice, with the same timbre, with the same accent, the voice of a woman who once again takes up the author's conversation with herself" [Ainsi que le fumeur allume une cigarette à la précédente, j'avais allumé *Bonsoir, Thérèse* à *A Tahiti* au bout de quelque treize ans. C'est la même voix de femme, au même timbre, avec le même accent qui reprend la conversation de l'auteur avec soi-même] (*OC*, 1, 42).

Thus *Bonsoir, Thérèse*, which marks the moment when Triolet stops translating herself from Russian and accepts the idea that she will write directly in French, is not a book of rupture. It is the work that reestablishes the continuity of Triolet's intimate voice. Far better for the intimate conversation with oneself to go on in French, when one's emotional life goes on primarily in French with persons speaking French. Only in this way can Triolet avoid the deadly split embodied in the "failure" of *Camouflage*. Because the distance between thought and words is there in either language, from the very fact that there *are* two languages, the self can speak equally well in either.

Triolet's investment of her second language with psychic legitimacy in *Bonsoir, Thérèse* does not mean, however, that the themes of split, exile, and separation therefore disappear from her work. They recede, and become almost unnoticeable in some of her more socially conscious later novels, but they are still central to most of those novels which will endure. The travails of exiles in a particularly inhospitable period of French history pervade *Le rendez-vous des étrangers* [Foreigners' rendezvous].[30] Even after many years of adoration and power, Triolet's later books frequently still involve heroines who are isolated, eccentric, spiritual solitaries and wanderers, even when they are not exiles in the strict sense.[31] One of these women even becomes a "street-person," a *clocharde*. Madeleine Lalande, the heroine of *Ecoutez-voir* [See/hear] declares: "I am what I am, a vagabond. In this situation, which, as I have already said, is privileged, I see the world as though I were dead while I am still alive"[32] [Moi, je reste ce que je suis, une rôdeuse. Dans cette situation, comme j'ai déjà dit, privilegiée, je vois le monde comme si j'étais morte tout en étant vivante]. The heroine of Triolet's poignant last novel, *Le rossignol se tait à l'aube* [The nightingale falls silent at dawn], also manages to die alone, on her own terms, at sunrise, in the garden adjoining a house full of old friends.[33]

> Alia, forgive me my cheerless love; tell me, in what language will you speak your last words when you die?
>
> [Alia, prosti mene moiu neradostnuiu liubov'; skazhi, na kakom iazyke skazhesh' ty poslednee slovo, umiraia?]
>
> —Viktor Shklovskii

Toward the end of her life, Elsa Triolet wrote frequently about her bilingualism and her relations with her two languages. She proclaimed her continuing devotion to Russian: "My mother tongue, my irreplaceable language. . . . Being homesick for a language is as unbearable as being homesick for a country. You would think that no one could take a language away from you, that you carry it with you wherever you go, that it is alive within you—unforgettable, incurable, divine" [Ma langue maternelle, mon irremplaçable langue. . . . Le mal de la langue est insupportable comme le mal du pays. On croirait qu'une langue, personne ne peut vous la prendre, que vous l'emportez avec vous où que vous alliez, qu'elle vit en vous, inoubliable, incurable, divine] (*OC*, 1, 26). She realized, however, that a language cannot be preserved like an inanimate object in a breakfront: "In fact, a language is something you share with a people, a country; you cannot keep it safe deep within you, it must get some exercise. You must use it, or else it gets rusty, atrophies and dies" [En réalité, une langue, cela se partage avec un peuple, un pays, vous ne pouvez la conserver au fond de vous-même, il faut qu'elle s'exerce, il faut s'en servir, sans quoi elle se rouille, s'atrophie et meurt] (1, 26).

She came to feel that bilingualism need not tarnish the first language: "Pushkin wrote in French without its soiling his Russian. . . . There seem to be no rules about this. Richness and purity of language do not depend on whether or not the writer is monolingual or polyglot, and may be present in either case" [Pouchkine écrivait en français, sans que cela salisse son russe. . . . Pas de règles, semble-t-il, la richesse et la pureté de la langue appartiennent aussi bien aux monolingues qu'aux polyglottes, ou, plutôt, ne dépendent pas du mono ou polylinguisme] (*M en m*, 80–81). So Triolet did exercise her Russian. She maintained close contacts with the Soviet Union and at certain periods went there frequently. She translated, both into and out of Russian, and she watched her Russian as though it were a delicate child, keeping it healthy against all odds: "Perhaps it is my devotion to the Russian language that has enabled me to keep it intact, as pure as when it was born in me, without its being disturbed by any foreign accent" [Peut-être est-ce ma dévotion pour la langue russe qui me l'a conservée exceptionellement intacte comme à sa naissance en moi, et sans qu'aucun accent étranger vienne la troubler] (*OC*, 1, 26). Where she did have an accent, as she frequently noted, was in French, and she wore it proudly, refusing to "pass," rejecting all well-meaning offers to help her correct it: "It's in French, that I had, and still have, an accent. People have offered to help me get rid of it, but I always refused: an accent is like a hump, and only death can take it away"[34] [L'accent, c'est en français que je l'avais, que je l'ai. On m'a bien proposé de me le corriger, mais je m'y suis refusée: l'accent c'est comme une bosse, il n'y a que la tombe pour vous la supprimer] (I, 27).

Triolet kept her accent, although she did not find it in any way "charming." To the contrary: "My Russian accent embarrasses me, like ugly teeth which keep one from smiling . . . an accent seems to me to be ugly. I don't want to inflict ugliness on others" [Mon accent russe me gêne comme de vilaines dents qui vous empêchent de sourire . . . un accent, c'est laid à mon sens, je ne veux pas imposer à d'autres ce qui est laid] (M en m, 55). If she found her accent so ugly, why then did Triolet "prefer" to keep it? In part, of course, because it was *hers,* a part of her total persona. But, more important, her accent was a hostage, a sacrifice to Russian, a constant proof that she had not really betrayed her first linguistic loyalty. Her accent in spoken French balanced out the fact that, at least to the French reader, her written French was *without* accent. Triolet herself maintained: "I write with my authentic accent, it's in the character of my writing, in my style, in my madness: madness also has a nationality"[35] [J'écris avec mon authentique accent, il est dans le caractère de mon écriture, dans mon style, dans ma folie elle-même: la folie aussi a une nationalité] (p. 56). But her written accent, however "authentic," is not the same as her spoken one.

Her written French may be *hers,* but lexically and syntactically it has no coloration that can be separated out and that would mark it as "foreign," let alone "Russian." Triolet actually admitted as much in her somewhat testy remarks about the work of a Soviet professor who had undertaken a study of the "Russianisms" in her novels, meaning not her borrowing of Russian words or Slavic roots, but rather her capacity to create purely French equivalents of Russian expressions and words. Triolet observed that most of the examples cited by the professor as her coinages were actually "honest French words" [d'honnêtes mots français], even if, since they belonged to the contemporary language, they had not yet found their way into dictionaries (M en m, 86). Triolet did admit to consciously transposing certain Russian formulaic expressions into French, considering this to be her contribution to her adoptive lan-

guage, an enrichment she could offer because of her total bilingualism (pp. 87–88), but only very rarely, and then cautiously, did she
indulge in the kind of interlinguistic transfers that pepper all of
Nabokov's works, whether written in "Russian" or "American."
Beyond that, Russian and Russian literature sometimes affected the
"sources of her creation" without her being immediately aware of
it. Yet, in general, Triolet kept her two languages scrupulously
apart and her Russian pure—well exercised, beloved, but clearly
subordinate.

This is not to say that Triolet's mature writing in French is ex-
empt from the effects of her bilingualism per se, but most such effects are not directly visible to the reader. Although she had
masterfully subdued the rhythms of the French phrase, and although syntax posed no problems, Triolet always and inevitably
had to face the "distance" between thought and the words of either
language and, therefore, had to struggle to put thought into words.
In *La mise en mots* [Putting into words], the carefully chosen title
of her artistic self-portrait, Triolet discussed her difficulty at length:

> Oh how I wish it [writing] were simultaneous with thought. How
> wonderful it would be to leap on the backs of words as though they
> were a wild horse, to forbid myself to think about how best to formu-
> late what I want to express. To write in direct contact with thought.
> By enchantment. To forget the act of writing . . .
>
> I'm constantly struggling with words. I mustn't see them with their
> roots, the weight of their meanings, their shape. If I do, I can't use
> them anymore. Perhaps I'm really in hand-to-hand combat with *lan-
> guage itself*, a result of my bilingualism? . . .
>
> I could probably improvise a *speech* in Russian more easily than in
> French. It comes in a more orderly fashion in my mother tongue and
> all jumbled in French. Does that mean that the journey from thought
> to words is shorter for me in Russian than in French? But I don't
> notice the distance between them when I'm *speaking* French, and fre-
> quently a French expression comes to me more rapidly than the Rus-
> sian equivalent. What if everything I said about those happy moments,
> which are so rarely granted to me, when I can leap directly onto
> words without having to go through the deadly process of thinking
> about them, what if all of that is a result of my bilingualism? . . .
>
> At any rate, the less I think about it, the shorter the distance be-
> tween my thoughts and their "putting into words"; then the *what* and
> the *how* are one. It's the reverse of automatic writing, which attempts

to eliminate consciousness and liberate the unconscious. The process about which I am talking requires intense concentration on what you want to express. You are finally able to guess the lucky number and win the jackpot: if I had enough strength of will and power of concentration, I would always hit the jackpot in the game of writing.

Language and I are always quarreling. Words, the units of language, resist me, take to the hills, refuse to arrange themselves according to the demands of my thought, harden themselves, will not be bent, break, become hostile to any construction. They become parts that I no longer know how to assemble.... And yet, I love words, with a timid, unrequited love, that hides itself and doesn't speak out.

[Combien je la voudrais simultanée avec la pensée, combien je souhaiterais sauter sur les mots comme sur un cheval sauvage, m'interdire la réflexion de comment mieux formuler ce que j'ai à exprimer! Ecrire au contact de la pensée. Ecrire par enchantement. Oublier l'acte d'écrire . . .

J'ai maille à partir avec les mots. Il ne faut pas que j'y voie des mots avec leurs racines, le poids du sens, le dessin, je ne saurais plus m'en servir. Ne serait-ce plutôt un corps à corps avec la *langue,* conséquence de mon bilinguisme? . . .

J'improviserais sans doute plus facilement un *discours* en russe qu'en français, il s'ordonne plus naturellement dans ma langue maternelle et me vient en français dans le désordre. N'est-ce pas que le passage de la pensée aux mots est pour moi plus court en russe qu'en français? Je ne perçois pourtant pas la distance qui les sépare quand je parle en français, et même, souvent, une expression française me vient plus rapidement que l'expression russe correspondante. Si tout ce que je disais des moments heureux qui me sont rarement donnés où je puis sauter sur les mots directement sans passer par la réflexion néfaste, si tout cela provenait de mon bilinguisme? . . .

Et donc, moins j'y songe et plus courte est la distance entre la pensée et la mise en mots. Le *quoi* et le *comment* ne font plus qu'un seul tout. Au contraire de l'écriture automatique qui essaye d'éliminer la conscience, de libérer l'inconscient, c'est une concentration si intense sur la chose à exprimer, qu'elle vous fait deviner le numéro gagnant à la roulette: si j'avais assez de volonté, de force de concentration, j'arriverais à tous les coups gagnante dans l'affaire de l'écriture. C'est, entre le langage et moi, une perpétuelle dispute. Les mots, unités de la langue, me résistent, prennent le maquis, refusent de s'ordonner à la convenance de ma pensée, se durcissent, ne se laissent pas plier, se brisent, deviennent hostiles à toute construction, pièces détachées que je ne sais plus monter. . . . Et pourtant, je les aime, les mots, d'un amour timide et malheureux qui se cache, ne s'avoue pas.] [pp. 53–57]

The problem seemed to be that Triolet loved words less for them-selves than for the meanings they carried: "You will note that none of my writing ever organizes itself, or orders itself in verse. *I don't dance: I walk to get from one place to another.* I speak to say something. Words are numbers; what interests me is their sum to-tal: the novel. . . . Taken one by one, words are a necessary evil, I leave them behind so as to arrive the sooner at the total" [Remar-quez que rien de ce que j'écris ne s'organise, ne s'ordonne jamais en vers. *Je ne danse pas, je marche pour aller d'un point à l'autre.* Je parle pour dire. Les mots me sont nombres, afin qu'apparaisse la somme générale, le roman. . . . Les mots un à un me sont un mal inévitable, je passe outre, je suis pressée d'arriver au total] (*M en m,* 57–58; emphasis added).

It is because of this utilitarian, not to say socialist-realist, view of language that Triolet suffered so much from her bilingualism. She had all of the problems of bilingualism but, in her mature work, allowed herself few of its joys. Not for her the sensual pleasures of the young poet Fëdor Cherdyntsev, testing words on his tongue, holding them up to the light, in the first chapters of Nabokov's *Dar* [The gift], nor Khlebnikov's intimate creative relations with words. Triolet could translate Khlebnikov and in so doing could success-fully "imitate" Khlebnikov's *motcréation* (as she rendered one of Khlebnikov's own inventions),[36] but she would not venture into *motcréation* on her own, reserving such enlargement of language to "acrobats of the word, poets and erudite linguists who have the gift and knowledge that *motcréation* demands" [Cet élargissement de la langue est permis aux acrobates du mot, aux poètes, et aux savants linguistes qui ont le don et le savoir nécessaires à la motcréation] (*M en m,* 63). Triolet considered that she lacked this gift, as she lacked the gift for *writing* poetry, although she translated it with some ease:

A translation should be an imitation of a text in another language; one must undertake it with the care of a counterfeiter imitating a bank note. Translating is a strange activity, and I am even more aware of its strangeness when I have to translate a poem: I, who am not on speaking terms with words when they have their full, golden weight in a given language, can handle them much better when I have to make them *resemble*, when they're not there in their own right, when the game involves bringing foreign words to the sweet reason of French. If I have to do this in verse, I feel less awkward, less shy in *copying* them, than I would have in expressing myself directly in my language.

[La traduction devrait être l'imitation d'un texte écrit dans une autre langue; il faut y apporter le soin du faux-monnayeur à imiter un billet de banque. Traduire est un étrange travail et j'en ressens plus fortement l'étrangeté lorsqu'il s'agit de traduire un poème: moi qui suis brouillée avec les mots quand ils ont leur poids d'or propre à une langue, je les manie bien mieux quand il faut les faire *ressembler,* qu'ils ne sont plus là pour eux-mêmes, quand le jeu consiste à ramener des mots étrangers à la raison française. S'il me faut faire cela en vers, j'ai moins de gêne, moins de pudeur en les *copiant,* que je n'en aurais eu en m'exprimant directement, dans ma langue.] [*M en m,* 90]

Triolet's success as a translator of complex modernist poetry, on the one hand, and her own linguistic conservatism, on the other, are striking examples of the fact that translation is a special skill requiring particular and separate processing strategies.[37] As we saw in Chapter 1, not all fluent bilinguals are good translators. Triolet's practice shows that the reverse is also true: writers capable of exceptional inventiveness in "imitating" the work of others may reject or be incapable of similar flexibility in their own writing.

In Triolet's case, this is at least in part the result of a self-imposed and carefully cultivated rigidity. In the interest of ideological and linguistic purity, she seems to have deliberately squelched and disciplined the "tolerance for ambiguity," supposedly characteristic of bilinguals.[38] Her early Bohemianism and love of pleasure had to be sacrificed, at least in her own artistic practice.[39] Both the accent that she kept and the linguistic creativity that she would not allow herself are, at least in part, sacrifices on the altar of her bilingualism.

For although, having found her man and her party, Elsa Triolet vanquished her earlier "fear of life" and became "brave," as she said she would in her 1939 journal (*OC,* 1, 25), she was still afraid of words and would not give them their freedom. She would allow herself to use her languages only as tools, never allowing them to

play through her in the exuberant games to which Nabokov
Beckett were addicted. This puritanical attitude toward langu
made her bilingualism seem profoundly dubious. If language
not an area in which Triolet would allow herself to take her pleasure, if it was merely a utilitarian way of getting her thought "from
here to there," then why have two sets of instruments to perform
the same function? For her, having two languages was felt to be not
only physically abnormal but also a sinful luxury, paid for by the
intimate awareness that to use one was to betray the other. This is
why, in *La mise en mots,* Triolet returns several times to the metaphor of bigamy. "I am a bigamist. It's a crime in the eyes of the
law. As many lovers as you please; two legal husbands—impossible.
People look askance at me: to whom do I belong?" And: "Being
bilingual is a little like being a bigamist: but to which one am
I being unfaithful?" [. . . je suis bigame. Un crime devant la loi.
Des amants, tant qu'on veut; deux maris enregistrés, non. On me
regarde de travers: à qui suis-je? . . . Etre bilingue, c'est un peu
comme d'être bigame; mais quel est celui que je trompe?] (pp. 54,
84). Perhaps if her legitimate spouse had been Russian, as were
Nabokov's and Schakovskoy's, she would have felt her linguistic
bigamy less strongly.[40] As it was, the situation seemed hopeless.
Only if there were some miraculous way to speak two languages at
once could she be whole and faithful again. But since Triolet would
not permit herself to code-switch in print, the macaronic solution
was unacceptable.

Triolet never gave up her effort to resolve this insoluble problem
and, in her last works, succeeded in realizing her dream of being able to speak two languages simultaneously. She did this by
integrating elements other than words into her texts, creating an
interplay among several different means of communication.[41] Thus,
in *Le rossignol se tait à l'aube,* she uses a different, paler ink to
render the discourse of dream, and in *Ecoutez-voir,* a book that she
calls a *roman imagé,* the text is interlarded with *citations picturales.*

In *La mise en mots,* Triolet explains what she was doing in
Ecoutez-voir:

> Having exhausted verbal arguments, I saw images beckoning to
> me. . . . Not verbal images, but real pictorial images: paintings, draw-
> ings, photographs. . . . I had only to choose what I needed to add to

my verbal tree. . . . The image-novel became a magnet for me. . . . I wrote, and the image was born in me at the same moment as the words. . . . I began to write as much with images as with words: they were my pictorial quotations. The image is a prefabricated element, like the word. A complex element that I can select and place exactly where it can enlarge the meaning, the expressiveness and the atmosphere of the text. . . . Unlike an illustration, which is added after the text is written, *my* image appears *simultaneously* with the writing. . . .

Since the images which the author has chosen from among those already in existence form an organic part of the novel and are on an equal footing with words, only the author can place them properly in the text—just as he does with words.

[C'est à bout d'arguments verbaux que j'ai vu l'image me faire signe. . . . Non pas l'image verbale, mais bel et bien l'image picturale, le tableau, le dessin, la photo. . . . Je n'avais qu'à choisir ce qu'il me fallait pour l'ajouter à mon arbre verbal. . . . Le roman imagé devint cet aimant qui m'attire. . . . Je me mis à écrire autant avec des images qu'avec des mots: c'étaient mes *citations* picturales. . . . L'image m'est un élément tout fait, préfabriqué comme le mot, un élément complexe que je peux choisir et placer exactement là où il est susceptible d'élargir le sens et l'expression et l'atmosphère du texte. . . . L'illustration vient une fois le texte écrit, *mon* image apparaît *en même temps* que l'écriture. . . .

Tandis que les images choisies, trouvées par l'auteur parmi celles qui existent déjà, formant un tout organique avec le roman, sont là au même titre que les mots, l'auteur seul peut les mettre à leur place dans le texte, comme il le fait des mots.] [*M en m*, 107, 108, 110, 112]

Triolet claims that the images and the words are simultaneous and of equal status. Aragon, in his preface to the posthumously published French translation of *Zemlianichka* goes even further, claiming a kind of priority for the image in these last works. He describes *Ecoutez-voir* as a book "where the mechanism of thought begins with images, found or chosen, paintings, drawings, or photographs that generate the text rather than merely accompanying it"[42] [ce livre où le mécanisme de la pensée part d'images données ou choisies, peintures, dessins ou photographies, qui, moins qu'ils n'accompagnent le texte, le déclenchent].

Triolet's *La mise en mots,* in which she discusses *le roman imagé* is itself a *livre imagé,* containing a linguistic self-portrait made up of printed text and of passages in facsimile of Triolet's own handwriting, as well as of pictures that are moral self-portraits, emblematic of Triolet's spiritual position. Triolet framed the beginning and end of the text of *La mise en mots* within a small, brightly colored frieze of birds, borrowed from the Saint-Sever manuscript of the Beatus de Liebanus commentary on *Revelation* which is conserved in the Bibliothèque nationale. These birds accompany the text's opening observations on the language of birds, which Triolet says are saved from the burden of choice, because they can learn only the song of the species into which they were born (p. 7).[43] Triolet, despite (or in part because of) the birdsong name she acquired from her first husband, André, could—in fact *had to*—choose her song: "As for me, I am bilingual. I can translate my thought equally well into two languages. As a result, I have a double destiny. Or a half-destiny—a translated destiny"[44] [Ainsi, moi, je suis bilingue. Je peux traduire ma pensée également en deux langues. Comme conséquence, j'ai un bi-destin. Ou un demi-destin. Un destin traduit] (p. 8).

At the center of *La mise en mots* is a double page taken up almost entirely by the photograph of a Janus-faced, baroque statue of a smiling woman who is looking at one of her faces in a hand mirror (which returns a distorted image) while her second face looks back over her shoulder.[45] Just so, Triolet could mirror only one of her linguistic faces at a time, even though the two are almost identical. This beautiful but monstrous statue is the image of Triolet's bilingualism. She confirmed this identification by choosing to juxtapose with the picture of the statue one of her remarks about bilingualism as bigamy. The comment is written in fascimile of Triolet's own handwriting. Facing the first page of a chapter on translation which Triolet has titled "Vos pas dans ceux du créateur" [Your steps in the footprints of the Creator], there is a detail from the "Encounter of Souls in Paradise" segment of Giovanni di Paolo's *Last Judgment*. From among the couples of the blessed, Triolet has chosen to reproduce one consisting of two women, closely resembling each other in feature and dress, who are joyfully holding hands. As a caption, Triolet has added in her own handwriting the comment I quoted earlier: "One would think that it should be easy for bilinguals to translate themselves. Not a bit! You look at yourself as though in a mirror, you try to find yourself, and you don't recognize the reflection as your own" [Pour les bilingues *se* traduire devrait être facile? Non pas! On se regarde comme dans une glace, on s'y cherche, ne reconnaît pas son reflet]. Here, then, is Triolet's answer to Shklovskii's question, "Forgive me my cheerless love, but in what language will you speak your last words when you die?" Her last books were an attempt to speak two languages at once—if not Russian and French, then at least French and the language of images. But even this solution is only a *pis aller.* Last words prove nothing and cannot be used to determine a *true,* unique language, for it is only in Paradise that most of those condemned to the intimate separation of bilingualism will be completely joined with themselves again.

CHAPTER FOUR

Vladimir Nabokov

Now I shall spy on beauty as none has
Spied on it yet. Now I shall cry out as
None has cried out. Now I shall try what none
Has tried. Now I shall do what none has done.
—John Shade, "Pale Fire," canto 4, ll. 835–838

For decades, Vladimir Nabokov has been the despair of literary taxonomists who, unaware that they have in their hands an exceptionally beautiful specimen of a rare species which is unfamiliar to them, have kept trying to fit him into the pigeonholes of a classificatory system too narrowly conceived to describe him. The deceased had a horror of pigeonholes.[1] Was he a Russian writer? An American one? A Swiss one, on the basis of final residence? Initially, of course, he seemed to be a Russian writer, but even then many of his fellow exiles rejected him as "un-Russian."[2] Although in the second part of his career he wrote primarily in English, and although *Lolita* must surely be considered one of the great American novels, Nabokov also seemed to many readers to be unassimilable into the mainstream of American literature.[3] Some critics have even stressed the "Russianness" of his English-language novels.[4]

When pressed by interviewers, Nabokov classified himself variously. In the early 1960s, for example, in answer to the BBC's question, "Do you still feel Russian in spite of so many years in America?" he replied: "I do feel Russian and think that my Russian works . . . are a kind of tribute to Russia. And I might define them as the waves and ripples of the shock caused by the disappearance of the Russia of my childhood. And recently I have paid tribute to her in an English work on Pushkin" (*SO*, 13). Elsewhere he declared, "I think of myself today as an American writer who has once been a Russian one" (*SO*, 63), and, in his 1964 *Playboy* interview, he observed that with the passing of years he had grown less and less interested in Russia and more and more indifferent to the thought that his books would remain banned there (*SO*, 37),[5] adding: "I am an American writer, born in Russia and educated in England where I studied French literature, before spending 15 years in Germany. I came to America in 1940 and decided to become an American citizen and to make America my home" (*SO*, 26).

Despite his eventual installation in the permanent impermanence of the Montreux Palace Hotel, to which he was drawn in part because of the region's tradition as a *lieu de séjour* for *Russian* writers,[6] Nabokov continued to claim not only American citizenship, but also American attitudes: "America is the only country where I feel mentally and emotionally at home" (*SO*, 131). "It is in America that I found my best readers, minds that are closest to mine. I feel intellectually at home in America. It is a second home in the true sense of the word" (p. 10). Occasionally he even waxed (only slightly ironically) lyrical about his essential Americanness: "I am as American as April in Arizona" (p. 98). This (more or less) sincere pledge of allegiance provides a perfect example of why it is hopelessly silly to try to attribute Nabokov to a single country, a single culture, or even a dominant language. No "strictly" American writer would have come up with "I am as American as April in Arizona,"[7] which sounds peculiar to the American ear precisely because it conceals and transforms so many clichés of American culture: "as American as apple pie" (with its series of A's and P's); "as corny as Kansas in August" (with its *K* sounds, a state name, and the month); and it echoes the song "April in Paris," which may in fact be particularly American in its yearning for the lost chestnut blossoms of European springs. In its conjunction of tender, verdant, European Aprils and the flowering Arizonian desert spring, in the fact that the flora, fauna, and air of the western states are Nabokov's links with Asiatic and Arctic Russia (p. 98),[8] and in its playful phonetic complexity, Nabokov's little comment is a characteristic token of the multilevel, multicultural punning and interreferences that are an essential part of his work and to which he was obviously attracted from the very beginning (witness his early translation of *Alice's Adventures in Wonderland* into Russian as *Ania v strane chudes* [Berlin, 1923]).

Polyglot punning and allusion are among Nabokov's personal trademarks, or rather they are an important element in the "special pattern" that makes Nabokov distinctive and that, in his own judgment, is the only really acceptable basis for identifying him:

> I have always maintained, even as a schoolboy in Russia, that the nationality of a worthwhile writer is of secondary importance. The more distinctive an insect's aspect, the less apt the taxonomist is to glance first of all at the locality label under the pinned specimen in order to decide which of several vaguely described races it should be assigned to. The writer's art is his real passport. His identity should be immediately recognized by a special pattern or unique coloration. His habitat may confirm the correctness of the determination but should not lead to it. Locality labels are known to have been faked by unscrupulous insect dealers. [*SO*, 63]

But to say that Nabokov must be identified by his unique coloration rather than by his habitat is not to say that he is totally unclassifiable, that he was, as he says some would have him, "an ageless international freak."[9] Nabokov seems a freak only to resolutely monolingual and monocultural readers, whose categories are too narrow to encompass the complexities of linguistic reality.

As Nabokov himself adjusted from the antiquated German system of butterfly classification that he had first learned in his boyhood to a more sophisticated English system of nomenclature, so Nabokov criticism has increasingly come to understand that Nabokov is a splendid specimen, arguably the most spectacular ever netted, of the genus *Polyglot* and the species *scriptor*. George Steiner is perfectly justified in asserting that the "poly-linguistic matrix is the determining fact of Nabokov's life and art."[10] Neither Nabokov's abiding loyalty to the Russian language and its literature nor his virtuosity in English contradicts the fact that bilingualism has been crucial to his artistic sensibility from the beginning. Because there have by now been a number of splendidly detailed studies of the polylinguistic aspects of certain of Nabokov's novels, I will cite them where appropriate but will not try to repeat this maddeningly painstaking work here,[11] lest we be trapped (as some Nabokov scholars have been) by his Sirin song and remain enthralled forever.[12] I shall simply try to show how Nabokov's bilingualism is the warp of the elaborately contrived pattern of his

extraordinary artistic career. Or perhaps I should say, his "polyglotism," for Nabokov himself has observed: "I might have been a
great French writer."[13] Indeed he might have been, and he did well
to remind us of the implications of such dazzling polyglot
virtuosity.[14]

Vladimir Vladimirovich Nabokov (1899–1977) was born into an
exceptionally cultivated and enlightened Russian aristocratic family,
a number of whose members performed significant public service.
The values of his parents and family and their attitude of *noblesse
oblige* provided Nabokov with a profound sense of spiritual
security,[15] a knowledge of who and what he was that was totally
independent of external status and of property (the loss of which
undermined or destroyed many other Russians who found themselves impoverished and in exile after the Revolution). This unshak-
able sense of *self* in the context of enduring emotional and spiritual
relations sustained Nabokov even through the changes of artistic
language to which he subjected himself, changes that caused him
more torment than any of the other sufferings imposed upon him
by emigration.

Nabokov's father, Vladimir Dmitrievich, was a "patrician
democrat,"[16] an eminent jurist, and a member of the first Duma
who spoke out against the government's anti-semitic policies and
spent three months in prison in 1908 for having been a signatory
of the Viborg Manifesto. He was the editor of various newpapers,
the last one being the émigré publication *Rul'* [The rudder]. A
leader of the moderate faction of the Kadet party in emigration,
Vladimir Dmitrievich was killed in 1922 as he shielded his friend
and political opponent Pavel Miliukov from assassins' bullets. His
death was greeted with genuine regret by an amazingly wide spectrum of the Russian world.[17] The elder Nabokov, who, like his son,
was a passionate lepidopterist, spoke several languages very well
and delighted on occasion in indulging in simultaneous interpret-
ing (*SM*, 175). He wrote a study of Charles Dickens for volume 4
of the Russian-language *History of World Literature* (Saint Petersburg, 1912) and read Dickens aloud to his children.[18] It is to his
father's influence that the younger Nabokov attributes "appreci-
ating very early in life the thrill of a great poem" (*SO*, 46).

Nabokov's mother, Elena Ivanovna, née Rukavishnikov, was herself an amateur poet. She shared with her eldest surviving son the
gift of *audition colorée* (hearing in color), as well as "double sight,"

premonitions, and the sensation of *"déjà vu"* (*SM*, 39). She read to him in English before bedtime when he was small (p. 81), and later it was to her that young Nabokov carried his first completed poem (pp. 226–227).

While Russian aristocratic families have traditionally been bilingual in Russian and French, with degrees of competence and patterns of usage and code-switching that vary according to status and cultivation (see Tolstoi's *War and Peace* for the most elaborate illustration in Russian literature), Anglophilism was somewhat less commonplace and more prestigious. Nabokov's parents were thoroughly trilingual. Russian, English, and French were used domestically, and Vladimir Dmitrievich took advantage of his 1908 incarceration to work on his Italian. German was also known by Nabokov's parents, but it was not used in normal familial discourse.

In *Speak, Memory*, Nabokov records a conversation that gives one a good sense of how the family used languages:

> I soon noticed that *any* evocation of the feminine form would be accompanied by the puzzling discomfort already familiar to me. I asked my parents about it (they had come to Berlin to see how we were getting along) and my father ruffled the German newspaper he had just opened and replied in English (with the parody of a possible quotation—a manner of speech he often adopted in order to get going): "That, my boy, is just another of nature's absurd combinations, like shame and blushes, or grief and red eyes." "*Tolstoy vient de mourir*," he suddenly added, in another, stunned voice, turning to my mother.
>
> "*Da chto ti!* [something like "good gracious"]!" she exclaimed in distress, clasping her hands in her lap. "*Pora domoy* [time to go home]," she concluded, as if Tolstoy's death had been the portent of apocalyptic disasters. [pp. 207–208][19]

In later years, Nabokov frequently complained of the limitations of his English: "My English, this second instrument I have always had is however a stiffish, artificial thing, which may be all right for describing a sunset or an insect, but which cannot conceal poverty of syntax and paucity of domestic diction when I need the shortest road between warehouse and shop. An old Rolls-Royce is not always preferable to a plain Jeep" (*SO*, 106). Yet English had been a "domestic" language for Nabokov; he was a Russian-English bilingual from early childhood and, by his own admission, had spoken English with the same ease as Russian since infancy (p. 189), adding French when he was five (p. 5). His first goodnight prayers were in English—"Gentle Jesus, meek and mild, something-something little child" (*SM*, 85–86)—and he remembered a bewildering series of English nurses and governesses (p. 86).[20] He and his brother Sergei could read and write English before they could do so in Russian (p. 79), his first magazines were *Little Folks* and *Chatterbox*,[21] and he recorded his boyhood butterfly notes in English (*SO*, 5). He was, as he himself admits, an English as well as a Russian child: "In common with many other English children (I was an English child), I have always been very fond of [Lewis] Carroll" (p. 81).[22]

At a certain point, English governesses were replaced by French-speaking ones and by male Russian tutors. Formal, at-home study of English was reduced to occasional afternoon conversation sessions with two Saint Petersburg Englishmen (*SM*, 87–94). Still, Nabokov continued to devour English, as well as Russian and French, books: "I was a perfectly normal trilingual child in a family with a large library" (*SO*, 43).[23] Between the ages of ten and fifteen, he read Wells, Poe, Browning, Keats, Kipling, Conrad, Chesterton, Oscar Wilde, Flaubert, Verlaine, Rimbaud, Chekhov, and Aleksander Blok. He also relished the adventures of the Scarlet Pimpernel, Phileas Fogg, and Sherlock Holmes (pp. 42–43), and he claimed to have read or reread all of Tolstoi in Russian, all of Shakespeare in English, and all of Flaubert in French by the age of fourteen or fifteen (p. 46). Little wonder that when he became a pupil at the Tenishchev School at age eleven, he was accused of showing off by "peppering his Russian papers with English and French terms which came naturally" to him (*SM*, 185).

When Nabokov began to compose poems as an adolescent, however, these were in Russian. And although Nabokov's first collection of early poems (1916), published at author's expense in Saint Petersburg, had one epigraph in French (from Musset) and another in English (from Wordsworth), and although he published a few lepidopterological articles in English and wrote some English poems in 1919 when he went up to Cambridge, he chose to study not English but French and Slavic literature there.[24] In fact, the main intellectual and artistic endeavor of his Cambridge years was to make himself into a Russian poet.[25]

Having been forced to leave Russia after the Revolution, Nabokov's primary concern was to reconstruct the "artificial but beautifully exact Russian world" of which the Revolution had deprived him (*SM*, 270) and to protect his cherished Russian language from interference and decay: "My fear of losing or corrupting, through alien influence, the only thing I had salvaged from Russia—her language—became positively morbid, and considerably more harassing than the fear I was to experience two decades later of my never being able to bring my English prose anywhere close to the level of my Russian" (p. 265). In an effort to enrich his Russian, deprived of the resonance of an actively Russian-speaking environment, Nabokov for a time read about ten pages a day of Vladimir Dahl's four-volume *Tolkovyi slovar' zhivogo veliko-russkogo iazyka* [Interpretative dictionary of the living Russian language], jotting down such words and expressions as especially pleased him (p. 265).[26] Then he would make "polished and rather sterile Russian poems not so much out of the live cells of some compelling emotion as around a vivid term or a verbal image that I wanted to use for its own sake" (p. 266).[27] Later it became obvious to Nabokov, though no longer traumatic, that the Russian structures of his Cambridge-period poems were in fact heavily subject to the direct influence of "various contemporaneous ('Georgian') English verse patterns that were running about my room and all over me like tame mice" (p. 266).

Of course, Nabokov continued during his Cambridge period to read literature in languages other than Russian. He also began the impressive series of translations that Roy Judson Rosengrant persuasively argues are an essential part of the body of Nabokov's work and a principal source for the replenishment of the multilingual wellsprings of his creativity.[28] In the 1920s, these translations were into Russian, rather than from it, thus enlarging Nabokov's active literary capacities in his chosen language. The most significant of these translations was Nabokov's "Russianing" of Lewis Carroll's *Alice's Adventures in Wonderland,* accomplished three years before the publication of his first novel. This diabolically difficult, virtuoso performance gave strenuous exercise to his gift for linguistic inventiveness and was a foretaste of the multilingual playfulness of such novels as *Ada.*[29] It is also a good early example of Nabokov's willingness to transform, to transpose, and to sacrifice sense for sound—a practice he rejected for his *Eugene Onegin,* but retained for his self-translations.[30] Nabokov translated poetry by Rupert Brooke (on whom he also published a nineteen-page article in Russian in 1922)[31] and, in addition, translated works by Seamas O'Sullivann, Verlaine, Supervielle, Tennyson, Yeats, Byron, Keats, Baudelaire, Shakespeare, Rimbaud, Musset, and a novel by Romain Rolland, *Colas Breugnon* [Nikolka Persik].[32]

At first, it may seem something of a paradox that Nabokov should have devoted his Cambridge years primarily to writing in Russian, but throughout Nabokov's career the dominant language of his literary expression was frequently *not* the ambient language of the place where he was physically located. Thus, in Russia, he learned to write in English; in England, he increasingly wrote in Russian. Creatively, the Berlin years were almost untouched by German and were devoted almost exclusively to Russian, except for a preparatory excursion into French with "Mademoiselle O." While in France, he did dabble in French, but it was there, not in the United States, that Nabokov wrote his first novel in English. Nabokov "Russianed" *Speak, Memory* into *Drugie berega* in the American West and Midwest, but *Pale Fire* came to him on a steamer going *from* the United States to France, thus reversing Kinbote's pilgrimage. John Shade's quintessentially Anglo-American poem, with its echoes of Pope and Frost ("the hardest stuff I ever had to compose"), was mostly written in Nice, and Kinbote's commentary on it was largely written in the gardens of the Montreux Palace Hotel (*SO*, 55–56). It was there, in the French-speaking part of a trilingual country (none of whose languages is either Russian or English), that Nabokov Russianed *Lolita* and did most of the exhaustive Englishing of Pushkin's *Evgenii Onegin*.[33]

After his Russian years at Cambridge, Nabokov settled in Berlin (1922–1937). This fertile period of Nabokov's career is relatively unproblematical for our purposes. During these years, Nabokov supported himself primarily by giving lessons in English, Russian, and tennis; and, using the penname Sirin, he defined himself as a Russian writer.[34] He still thought of himself primarily as a poet but also wrote a number of stories, as well as the novels *Mashen'ka* [Mary], *Korol', dama, valet* [King, queen, knave], *Zashchita Luzhina* [The defense], *Podvig* [The exploit], *Camera obscura* [Laughter in the dark],[35] *Otchaianie* [despair], and *Priglashenie na kazn'* [Invitation to a beheading]. While Margaret Byrd Boegeman makes a persuasive case that *Priglashenie na kazn'* can be read as a kind of "dream vision" of Nabokov's initial impulse to make a change of language, as the hortatory fable of a writer arguing himself into a new medium of expression,[36] and while it is important to note that there are some polyglot allusions (particularly to English literature) even in these Berlin works, *Dar* [The gift], the last, warmest, and greatest of Nabokov's Russian novels, is intensely—almost exclusively—permeated with Russian language and Russian culture. *Dar*'s heroine is Russian literature,[37] and its hero, the young poet, biographer, and future novelist Fëdor Godunov-Cherdyntsev, is steeped in Pushkin, in Gogol', and in the memories of a Russian childhood.

Although *Dar* has an inventive, idiosyncratic structure, being at the same time a collection of poems, several biographies, and a novel, almost nothing in it prefigures Sirin's future transformation back into Vladimir Nabokov. For whatever determined Nabokov's initial decision to use a pseudonym, it is in some way appropriate that he settled into signing his real name to his works only after he had accepted his destiny as a polyglot writer. This occurred during the Paris years (1937–1940), when Nabokov slowly shed his image of himself as an exclusively *Russian*-language writer, an image he had so carefully nurtured since 1919. While continuing to work in Russian, he also began to write experimentally in French and seriously in English.[38]

In the late 1930s, many factors prompted Nabokov to try to write in languages other than Russian. Certainly among them was the refusal of émigré journals to print the fourth chapter of *Dar* (Godunov-Cherdyntsev's devastating biography of that darling of the Russian liberal intelligentsia, the radical writer and critic Nikolai Chernyshevskii), not to mention Nabokov's subsequent awareness that the audience for his works in Russian was being still further narrowed. The sense that, with the looming Nazi threat, the Nabokovs might have to leave Europe forever—"Oh, I did know I would eventually land in America" (*SO*, 88)—may also have played a part. But the precipitating *internal* reason for writing in languages other than Russian was surely the experience of self-translation.[39] For Nabokov, as for most potentially bilingual writers, the early experience of self-translation is so painful and distasteful that writing directly in one's current second language (in his case, English) or even in an ambient third language (in his case, French), is clearly preferable to the continued prospect of such self-inflicted torture. Nabokov translated two of his novels into English in the second half of the 1930s: *Otchaianie* and *Camera obscura.* In a letter to Zinaïda Schakovskoy, written while he was translating *Otchaianie,* Nabokov complained that putting his novel into English was "a terrible thing, sorting through one's own innards, and then trying them on for size like a pair of gloves" [uzhasnaia veshch'—perevodit' samogo sebia, perebiraia sobstvennie vnutrennosti i primerivaia ikh, kak perchatki].[40] Far better, at least some of the time, "for the first available idiom / to exchange all I have; my own tongue" [promeniat' na liuboe narech'e / vse, chto est' u menia—moi iazyk].[41]

Given Nabokov's refusal to use German, his frequent trips to Paris for readings of his work, and the Nabokovs' subsequent decision to move there from Berlin, the "first available idiom" was obviously French. Nabokov's spoken French was good enough, though accented,[42] and his written French was excellent. He wrote, directly in French, a graceful and interesting article on Pushkin for the celebration of the centenary of his death and, even before that, he had written "Mademoiselle O," an essentially autobiographical reminiscence of his French-speaking governess. In "Mademoiselle O," Nabokov immediately found in French the unmistakable Nabokovian "childhood" tone that permeates parts of the novels *Mashen'ka* and *Dar,* as it would the English versions of Nabokov's autobiography, *Conclusive Evidence* and *Speak, Memory*—to say nothing of the penultimate Russian version, *Drugie berega*—in all of which "Mademoiselle O" was included.

Nabokov's decision to choose precisely a Francophone and Francophile aspect of his childhood for his first foray into artistic prose in French was a logical one. In so doing, however, he also refocused on the essentially polyglot nature of his Russian childhood, something that was not emphasized in the reminiscences he had used in his Berlin novels. Thus, Nabokov slowly moved toward a redefinition of himself which would recognize the centrality of the polylinguistic matrix of his creativity. He took a further step by translating several Pushkin lyrics from Russian *into* French,[43] thus reversing the direction of his previous translations. These verse translations of Pushkin are brilliantly successful in maintaining the Pushkinian lightness of foot, and they are more graceful and faithful than any I have seen done by native speakers of French translating from Russian into their mother tongue (a feat that should be impossible, if we are to believe such translators as D. M. Thomas).[44] In recognition of Nabokov's first-try success in criticism, in artistic prose, and in the translation of Russian poetry, it seems only fair to agree with his comment to Andrew Field, however outrageous it may seem, that Nabokov might (also?) have become a great French writer, had circumstances not led him to leave France for America in 1940.[45]

As we have already observed, it is usually the case that the first time a writer "works without net" in another language,[46] the book will be thematically similar to those already written in the first language, both in order to facilitate finding one's personal tone again in the new language and to minimize the inevitable sense of rupture. All of Nabokov's French works from the 1930s have Russian subjects and follow this pattern. Taken collectively, they resemble different aspects of *Dar*.

Echoes of other Nabokov Russian novels are likewise audible in his first major effort to become a writer in English. Having convinced himself, on the strength of his translation of *Otchaianie*, that he could use English "as a wistful standby for Russian" (*SO*, 88–89), Nabokov wrote *The Real Life of Sebastian Knight*, ostensibly the biography of a Russian-born, Cambridge-educated, English-language writer. For the "biographer," Knight's younger, Paris-based half-brother, English is in fact a third language. Thus, the problems of writing in English are a surface part of what is being talked about in this first of Nabokov's English novels, which is an investigation of psychic and artistic identity.

According to his brother, Sebastian Knight's struggle with words had been unusually painful for two reasons: "One was the common one with writers of his type: the bridging of the abyss lying between expression and thought; the maddening feeling that the right words, the only words are awaiting you on the opposite bank in the misty distance, and the shudderings of the still unclothed thought clamouring for them on this side of the abyss."[47] As we have seen, bilingual writers are particularly conscious of the "distance" between thought and words, but this experience is also shared by some monoglots. The second reason for Sebastian's difficulties, however, is peculiar to bilingual writers:

I know, I know as definitely as I know we had the same father, I know Sebastian's Russian was better and more natural to him than his English. I quite believe that by not speaking Russian for five years he may have forced himself into thinking he had forgotten it. But a language is a live physical thing which cannot be so easily dismissed. It should moreover be remembered that five years before his first book— that is, at the time he left Russia,—his English was as thin as mine. I have improved mine artificially years later (by dint of hard study abroad); he tried to let his thrive naturally in its own surroundings. It did thrive wonderfully, but still I maintain that had he started to write in Russian, those particular linguistic throes would have been spared him. Let me add that I have in my possession a letter written by him not long before his death. And that short letter is couched in a Russian purer and richer than his English ever was, no matter what beauty of expression he attained in his books. [*RLSK*, 84–85]

Obviously, Nabokov is neither Sebastian Knight nor his half-brotherly biographer.[48] Yet even though Nabokov himself had first begun to write in Russian, he had already experienced, or was later to experience, many of the problems that the narrator of *Sebastian Knight* has just evoked. Nabokov was particularly concerned about the "fragility" of his English while he was writing *Sebastian Knight,* so much so that he went over the manuscript, sentence by sentence, with Lucie Léon Noël, reading it out loud, testing for awkwardness.[49] Subsequently, he asked Agnes Perkins, the head of the Wellesley English Department, to read the galley proofs. The narrator's comments about the inadequacy of his own English provide additional cover. As Nabokov observed to Edmund Wilson (who had seen the proofs of *Sebastian Knight* and had noticed some "slips" that had eluded all these Arguses), "There are many clumsy expressions and foreignish mannerisms that I noticed myself when reading the book again after five years had passed; but if I started correcting them I would rewrite the whole thing. My suggestion (which I know is not quite fair) is that the assumed author of the *Life* writes English with difficulty."[50]

Nabokov's main concern in his first English-language novel, then, was to *pass*. Subsequently, he continued to use narrators for whom English (particularly American English) is not the first language— now not to cover "slips," but to allow his English to flower into Humbertisms and Kinbotisms, to say nothing of monstrous, sneeze-provoking Pninisms and insistently hybrid Vanisms. (As Jane Grayson so aptly observes, "while Nabokov's command of English undoubtedly improves, it does not for all that become more conventional.")[51]

After writing *Sebastian Knight,* Nabokov had arrived at a watershed.[52] Experimenting with writing in two other languages, while continuing to write in Russian, did not at first pose too great a problem ("as many lovers as you please"). The crucial moment for Nabokov, as for other bilingual and polyglot writers, came when he had proven to himself that he had two (or more) avowedly legitimate output systems at his disposal. As I have already noted, at this point, and frequently with considerable internal and external theatrics, the bilingual writer usually renounces writing in his first language, forcibly committing himself exclusively to the new one, thereby violating his profound nature as a bilingual. Nabokov was no exception in this regard. For years after his apostasy, despite whatever "beauty of expression" he had achieved in his English novels, Nabokov continued to complain that he had been obliged to abandon "my natural language, my natural idiom, my rich, infinitely rich and docile Russian tongue, for a second-rate brand of English" (*SO*, 15). Of course, Nabokov was not forced to abandon Russian. Many Russian writers in exile did not, including some who could have.[53] He chose to. And Sebastian's brother's comment that "a language is a live physical thing which cannot be so easily dismissed" is directly relevant to Nabokov's own problems in the late 1930s. For it was not enough for Nabokov to *wish* to abandon Russian and Russia, justifying his apostasy with the reasoning that Russia had betrayed him first. Russia and Russian seemed unwilling to allow themselves to be abandoned.

The pain of Nabokov's attempt to abandon Russian is visible in "K Rossii" [To Russia], a poem written in Paris late in 1939. In it, the poet pleads with the feminine figure of Russia to let him be, not to search for him with her beloved, blind eyes, but to allow him to live, even at the cost of all that he has held most dear:

> Will you leave me alone? I implore you!
>
> . . . .
>
> I'm prepared to lie hidden forever
> and to live without name. I'm prepared,

lest we only in dreams come together,
all conceivable dreams to forswear;

to be drained of my blood, to be crippled,
to have done with the books I most love,
for the first available idiom
to exchange all I have: my own tongue.

.   .   .   .

do not grope for my life in this hole

because years have gone by and centuries,
and for sufferings, sorrow, and shame,
too late—there is no one to pardon
and no one to carry the blame.
    [The English is Nabokov's—E. K. B.]

[Otviazhis'—ia tebia umoliaiu!

.   .   .   .

Navsegda ia gotov zatait'sia
i bez imeni zhit'. Ia gotov,
chtob s toboi i vo snakh ne skhodit'sia,
otkazat'sia ot vsiacheskikh snov;

obeskrovit' sebia, iskalechit',
ne kasat'sia liubimeishikh knig,
promeniat' na liuboe narech'e
vsë, chto est' u menia,—moi iazyk

.   .   .   .

ne ishchi v etoi ugol'noi iame,
ne nashchupyvai zhizni moei!

Ibo gody proshli i stolet'ia
i za gore, za muku, za styd
—pozdno, pozdno!—nikto ne otvetit,
i dusha nikomu ne prostit.]

It seemed to Nabokov that his break with Russia and its language would leave him with almost nothing that he valued, except the ability to go on, albeit amputated of the language, the literature, and even the dream of Russia. Only much later, after he had gone further in the process of his individuation as a bilingual writer, would Nabokov discover that what had seemed in 1939 and the early 1940s to be a betrayal and a wrenching *proshchanie,* or *adieu,* was in fact only a *do svidania,* an *au revoir.*

> But now thou too must go; just here we part,
> softest of tongues, my true one, all my own . . .
> And I am left to grope for heart and art
> And start anew with clumsy tools of stone.
>   —Vladimir Nabokov, "Softest of Tongues"

Once he and his family were safely in the United States, Nabokov committed himself to writing prose only in English. Giving up Russian prose cold-turkey was a most disagreeable experience. It left stranded an uncompleted Russian novel that Nabokov feared would "soon start to ooze from some part of my body if I go on keeping it inside"(April 29, 1944, *Letters,* 44). His abandonment of Russian for English prose was, he declared, "a very difficult kind of switch. My private tragedy . . ." (*SO,* 15). "My complete switch from Russian prose to English prose was exceedingly painful—like learning anew to handle things after losing seven or eight fingers in an explosion" (p. 54). Despite Nabokov's initial fears that his allegiance to Russian grammar might interfere "with an apostatical courtship," his regret for his painfully amputated Russian, his complaints about the problem of learning to handle things again, his "stiff" English, and his lack of "intimacy" with English words,[54] the true difficulty, as he finally admitted, was less linguistic than emotional: "I had spoken English with the same ease as Russian, since my earliest infancy. I had already written one English novel in Europe besides translating in the thirties two of my Russian books. *Linguistically, though perhaps not emotionally, the transition was endurable*" (pp. 189–190, emphasis added).

The worst torment seems to have been resisting the temptation to write in Russian. Less sure of himself than Odysseus, Nabokov tried to stop his ears to Russian's Sirin call. Because he had "thoroughly and early mastered English and French" [sovershenno vladeia s mladenchestva i angliiskim i frantsuzskim] (*Db,* 7), unlike Sebastian Knight, it would have been easy for Nabokov to write in English had he not already defined himself as a writer and a stylist in another language. Thus, for Nabokov, leaving Russian, in which he had written for fifteen years, was not bidding farewell to the Russian of Avvakum, Pushkin, Tolstoi, and the rest—that is, to the Russian literary language in general—but rather to his own individual expression, to his lifeblood as an artist [slovom, ne ot obshchego iazyka, a ot individual'nogo, krovnogo narechiia] (p. 7). Nabokov insisted that no one before him had imposed upon himself this sort of anguishing transformation: "There is no need to speak at length of the enormous difficulty of the impending reincarnation and of the state into which I was plunged at first by the horror of parting with this live, familiar creature. Suffice it to say that no writer of any real stature had ever endured it before me" [Chudovishchnye trudnosti predstoiavshego perevoploshcheniia, i uzhas rasstavan'ia s zhivym, ruchnym sushchestvom vvergli menia snachala v sostoianie, o kotorom net nadobnosti rasprostraniat'sia; skazhu tol'ko, chto ni odin stoiashchii na opredelennom urovne pisatel' ego ne ispytyval do menia] (pp. 7–8).

At the end of 1942, Nabokov wrote to his wife: "On my walk, I was pleasantly pierced by a lightning bolt of inspiration. I had a passionate desire to write, and write in Russian, and I must not. I don't think that anyone who has not experienced the feeling can really understand its tortuousness, its tragic aspect."[55] He later wrote to Edmund Wilson that "the urge to write is something terrific but *as I cannot* do it in Russian I do not do it at all" (September 27, 1945, *Letters,* 156; emphasis added). In 1942, he admitted to George Hessen: "The Sirin in me is beginning to arise since the time you were here. . . . It seems to me that not a single writer in the world has executed my *Kunststück.* (It is as though I created the person who composed *The Real Life of Sebastian Knight* and the poems in *The New Yorker* and all the rest, *but it's not I who am creating*—my relation to it is in the category of the pleasure one experiences in sport)"[56] (emphasis added).

Nabokov was clearly convinced that the only way to overcome this incomplete, merely "sporting" investment of self in English was to reject ruthlessly the blandishments of the Russian half of his linguistic nature. This was the way that he had "read in [himself] how the self to transcend" [i v sebe prochital chem sebia prevozmoch'], as he put it in 1942 at the conclusion of his Russian poem "Slava" [Fame].[57] Ultimately, the violence to himself seems to have worked, and a fundamental psychic and linguistic investment in English was achieved. By 1966–1967, Nabokov could look back and say that "the excitement of verbal adventure in the Russian medium has faded away gradually after I turned to English in 1940" (*SO,* 106).

To describe Nabokov's "switch" in this way is, however, an oversimplification. Despite his claim in 1966 that he could no longer write in Russian because the "adventure" was gone, he never really abandoned using Russian in one way or another, and he did not stop writing in Russian altogether for more than a year or so. What he did was to compartmentalize, reserving the right to write poetry in Russian while writing prose only in English. So he slaved away at his English prose and rewarded himself with (sometimes simultaneous) "trysts" with his Russian poetic muse. In his correspondence with Edmund Wilson, Nabokov makes frequent reference to these trysts:

> The only thing that really bothers me is that apart from a few sneaking visits I have had no regular intercourse with my Russian muse. [April 29, 1941, *Letters,* 44]

> For more than a year I have had no relation with my Russian muse. [July 18, 1941, p. 46]

> The book is progressing slowly, mainly because I get more and more dissatisfied with my English. When I have finished it, I shall take a three months' vacation with my ruddy robust Russian muse. [August 9, 1942, p. 69]

> I have lain with my Russian muse after a long period of adultery and am sending you the big poem she bore. . . . Please, do read it. I have also almost finished a story in English. [June 3, 1944, p. 121]

By the end of the 1940s, Nabokov was therefore in an extremely peculiar position vis-à-vis his languages. On the one hand, he was writing prose and some poetry in English, and the "verbal excitement" in prose was now securely in the domain of his newly legitimized second language. On the other hand, even as he wrote prose in English, he intermittently and guiltily sneaked back for poetry to his beloved first language, for which his affection was still so intense as to make the "verbal adventure" (which he craved and which was essential to his creativity) seem a kind of adultery. Luckily for Nabokov, although he still grumbled about sometimes feeling constrained, his confidence in his mastery of the kind of English that he cared about had by then developed to the point where he could declare unabashedly to Wilson: "Conrad knew how to handle *ready-made* English better than I; but I know better the other kind. He never sinks to the depths of my solecisms, but neither does he scale my verbal peaks" (November 18, 1950, *Letters,* 253).[58] Nabokov was thus reassured, as Vadim Vadimich of *Look at the Harlequins!* would also be, that he *had* indeed been able to switch, "not to the dead leaden English of the high seas with dummies in sailor suits, but an English I alone would be responsible for, in all its new ripples and changing light" (*LATH,* 124). A wondrous additional bonus was Nabokov's discovery that the poems birthed by his Russian muse were not rachitic or deformed by his frequentation of English. In fact, his Russian fallow period had "caused [his] Russian poetry to improve rather oddly in urgency and concentration" (*SO,* 54). He even declared later that the Russian poems he had written in New York were his best (p. 89). With these assurances, Nabokov unstopped his ears and openly embraced Russian again.

Retrospectively, one wonders whether the unhappy years of rejecting Russian were really necessary. The answer for Nabokov, as for Triolet and many other bilingual writers, would seem to be *subjectively yes* (at least during the crucial phase of the investment of psychic legitimacy in the second language), but *objectively* (insofar as objectivity exists in linguistic matters) *no.* As we have noted, while Nabokov frequently repeated that he *must not* write in Russian, he did, guiltily, allow himself to break training and compose an occasional Russian poem (a practice that he continued throughout his American and Montreux periods). This violation of his own draconian prohibition does not seem to have done Nabokov's "transfer" to English prose any harm. Nor should it have. For what is necessary in the long term to write in a second language, after already defining oneself as an artist in a first language, is not the absolute suppression or replacement of the first language, but rather a rearrangement of the linguistic layers, a shift in subordination. In Nabokov's case, the subordination involved both language and genre. With the shift to English, Nabokov's well-founded definition of himself as primarily a prose writer, rather than a poet, solidified. This allowed him to use poetry as a kind of double holiday.[59]

Perhaps it took Nabokov so long to realize that what was happening was more a refolding than a reincarnation because he had been led astray by his proclivity for entomological imagery. But linguistic metamorphosis need not, by analogy to the transformation from egg to caterpillar to pupa to butterfly, be serial, proceed in one direction, and involve the permanent disappearance of the first state of being. To be true to himself, to his cerebral organization and his experience, a bilingual writer must remain actively bilingual. Insofar as Nabokov's bilingualism was implicit even in his earliest state as a "normal" trilingual child, the butterfly model is even less applicable. A better scientific metaphor would have been that of the "normal" human brain, whose two hemispheres, though to some extent specialized, constantly work together and communicate through the corpus callosum, which runs below and connects them.

Even though entomology may have provided a spurious metaphor, in other ways it was a real help to Nabokov during the 1940s. It gave him a precious area of personal psychic and intellectual continuity. His passion for it reached all the way back to his Russian childhood and to his father and continued up through the period of his struggle to complete the psychic investment of his literary self in English. In fact, precisely during the latter period, entomology reemerged as a serious professional concern for Nabokov ("For nearly 15 years after moving, in 1940, to America, I devoted a tremendous amount of time [more in fact than I did to writing and teaching] to the study of lepidoptera") (*SO*, 314). Lepidopterology provided both an alternative and a ballast; entomology was, in a sense, another language, secure beyond the conflict of Russian and English, and providing a point of view external to Nabokov's linguistic system (in the narrow sense) from which he could come to the realizations that "the writer's art is his real passport" (p. 63) and that the art of literature is essentially one.[60]

Thus, by the late 1940s, after almost a decade of self-imposed barriers and exclusions, Nabokov began progressively to allow his polyglot nature to reappear *in his prose itself.* At first, in *Bend Sinister,* he used polyglotism tendentiously as a defamiliarizing and unnatural factor in the depiction of a vilely stupid, totalitarian ministate that used French, German, Russian, and macaronic combinations thereof which constituted its own language: "a mongrel blend of Slavic and Germanic with a strong strain of ancient Kuranian running through it (and especially prominent in ejaculations of woe)" (*BS*, x). Nabokov himself pointed out his use in *Bend Sinister* of paronomasia ("a kind of verbal plague"), his puns crossed with anagrams, spoonerisms, the hybrid tongues, and polyglot quotations (pp. ix–xii).

As Antonina Filonov Gove has noted, the resulting code-switching in *Bend Sinister* does not correspond to a simple linguistic labeling of nationality but imparts a specific stylistic tone to the narrative, a tone that is frequently parodic, especially when perfectly ordinary English words are supplied with parenthetical, invented glosses.[61] Code-switching in the mode of literary translation is treated more seriously (and possibly with some despair) in the passages of *Bend Sinister* that discuss the poet Ember's translation of *Hamlet* and the hero Krug's mental speculation on the ontological value of the exercise of trying to imitate in another language the words of Shakespeare's genius.[62] In general, however, the effect of Nabokov's use of frequent code-switching among three or more languages (one of them invented) in *Bend Sinister* is to provide the reader with a constant flow of defamiliarization. While code-switching in *Ada* will be integrative and "natural," here it is primarily a means of distancing the reader from a deeply unpleasant and inhuman invented land.

Although there is less overt code-switching in *Lolita* than in *Bend Sinister* (there *are* a few gems like Humbert's series: "Personne. Je resonne. Repersonne. From what depth this re-nonsense"),[63] *Lolita* is, linguistically, still a very "busy" book. In the preface to his exhaustive *Annotated Lolita*, Alfred Appel, Jr., describes it as "surely the most allusive and linguistically playful novel in English since *Ulysses* (1922) and *Finnegans Wake* (1939)."[64] *Lolita* has been profusely commented on by "a number of wise, sensitive, and staunch people" to whom the reader is referred for a detailed analysis of its language.[65] I will merely note in passing that in *Lolita*, which the author himself has called the result of his love affair with the English language,[66] Nabokov surreptitiously returned to materials from Russian literature that he reworked and parodied, protected and distanced by doing so in English. Katherine O'Connor has persuasively demonstrated the ways in which the final meeting between Humbert and Dolly Shiller is a variant on Svidrigailov's last confrontation with Dunia in *Prestuplenie i nakazanie* [Crime and punishment].[67] In fact, one might even argue that as Makar Devushkin is a saved Akakii Akakievich, so Humbert is a saved Svidrigailov!

By the second half of the 1950s, then, Nabokov's literary activity was firmly bilingual. He had translated the *Slovo o polku Igoreve* [The song of Igor's campaign] from Russian into English, had supervised and commented on his son Dmitri's translation of Lermontov's *Geroi nashego vremeni* [A hero of our time], was beginning his monumental work on Pushkin, and had almost completed the lengthy process of working his memoirs through English, French, and Russian and then back into English. Somewhere along the way, the insidious fear of involuntary contamination of one language (whichever) by the other had been allayed. The triumphantly controlled, bittersweet *Pnin* seems to mark the crucial moment of distancing and recovery of good humor and balance in linguistic matters. With *Pnin*, Nabokov confirmed the final consolidation of his awareness of himself as an intrinsically polyglot writer.

Plexed Artistry

> Whereas so many other language exiles clung desperately to the artifice of their native tongue or fell silent, Nabokov moved into successive languages like a traveling potentate.... The multi-lingual, cross-linguistic situation is both the matter and form of Nabokov's work.
>
> —George Steiner

Once one has accepted the argument that the polylinguistic matrix is the determining factor in Nabokov's art,[68] then other elements of his work can also be seen to participate in the patterns of polyglotism. As I mentioned briefly in my general introduction to bilingual writing, Nabokov is a spectacular instance of the characteristics that neurolinguistics has shown to be associated with "additive bilingualism"—enhanced capacity to seek out and create

structure, superiority in "divergent thinking" and "cognitive flexibility," as well as increased metalinguistic awareness, continuing
advantage in the capacity to generate synonyms and new uses.[69]
Bilinguals have also been shown to manifest other qualities that
are not themselves narrowly linguistic in nature, such as "greater
awareness of the relativity of things" and high "tolerance for
ambiguity."[70] Like the purely linguistic advantages listed above,
"greater awareness of the relativity of things" and, more particularly, "tolerance for ambiguity" are obviously central to Nabokov's
novels. For although Nabokov was notoriously *intolerant* of cruelty,
soft music in elevators, *poshlost'*,[71] and Sigmund Freud, his novels
do frequently present certain kinds of unresolved moral ambiguities,
as well as what might be called "reality ambiguities"—Whom was
Gradus/Jack Grey trying to kill? Who was he? And Kinbote?
Which is the "real life" of Sebastian Knight? (*See under real*), etc.
etc. Furthermore, as D. Barton Johnson has noted, Nabokov's mature novels all seem to follow one of two models of ambiguity: the
schizophrenic model or the twin-world model, finally culminating
in the ambidextrous universe theme of *Look at the Harlequins!*[72]

Nabokov also seems to be the perfect incarnation of Lambert's
working hypothesis that "bilingualism provides a person with a
comparative, three-dimensional insight into language, a type of
stereo-linguistic optic on communication that the monolingual
rarely experiences."[73] Lambert's synesthetic coinage "stereo-
linguistic optic" is appropriate in a variety of ways to Nabokov's
practices. The term "stereo-linguistic optic" is itself a variant of
tmesis (the insertion of another linguistic element between two that
normally occur together), which we shall shortly see to be one of
Nabokov's own preferred stylistic devices. The stereopticon is, of
course, an instrument that creates a single, three-dimensional image
by combining images from two separate points of view (eyes?
languages?).[74] It also frequently uses mirrors to deflect rays coming
from corresponding points in the two pictures, giving the impression of solidity or relief, as does the ordinary vision of the object
itself.

Nabokov's practice of the related combinational delights of stereolinguistic and visual stereoscopy are among the most salient characteristics of his "plexed artistry," enabling him to "transform the
figure of rupture back into a figure of connection."[75] They provide

a context for the persistence of mirror worlds in his novels, for his creation of idiosyncratic wholes by the juxtaposition and superposition of opposite or contrary elements (e.g., transparent/opaque), and for his passion for palindromes and "word golf."[76] One of the uses of a stereopticon is to "cause the image of one object or scene to pass gradually into that of another with a dissolving effect" (*OED*).

Perhaps the most important manifestation of Nabokov's "stereolinguistic optic on communication" is not purely linguistic: namely, his habitual use of synesthesia as a literary device, which, as D. Barton Johnson notes in his remarkable article "Synesthesia, Polychromatism, and Nabokov," may in turn correspond to psychological synesthesia.[77] One might even speculate that psychological synesthesia itself may be heightened by bilingualism. If one accepts the "dual coding" position that language is mediated by two independent, interconnected symbol systems—an image system and a verbal system—then Nabokov's exceptional capacity for "cosmic synchronization," for "feeling everything that happens in one point of time" (*SM*, 218) may well be related to the fact that, as a bilingual, his language system itself is dual, and so there are *three* interconnected systems at work of which the aesthetically primary one may well be the image system that interacts with the separate language systems.

Let us not forget that Nabokov repeatedly claimed to "think in images," even in his last interview: "Yes, I write in three languages, but I think in images. The matter of preference does not really arise. Images are mute, yet presently the silent cinema begins to talk and I recognize its language."[78] The hypothesis that Nabokov's bilingualism encouraged (or was encouraged by) his "thinking in images" is further supported by his gift for drawing and painting ("I think I was born a painter—really!" [*SO*, 17]), activities that obviously draw heavily on the image system and on holistic right-hemisphere strategies.[79] Nor should one forget the energy that Nabokov devoted to the invention of chess problems, which he considered a sufficiently important part of his *œuvre* to be published along with a bilingual selection of his poems in *Poems and Problems*: "Chess problems demand from the composer the same virtues that characterize all worthwhile art: originality, invention, conciseness, harmony, complexity, and splendid insincerity" (*P & P*, 15). It is interesting to note in passing that Nabokov was not alone among modern bilingual writers to work at least tangentially in several artistic disciplines. One might even speculate that there may be some correlation between being bilingual and being artistically polymath (e.g., Wassily Kandinsky, Jean Arp, David Burliuk, Il'ia Zdanevich).

If one looks at Nabokov's bilingual-synesthetic literary practice from a slightly different angle, his description of one type of sense perception through words and images normally appropriate to others is the linguistic equivalent of a kind of perceptual polyglotism, allowing for—indeed encouraging—sensual code-switching. One should also observe that Nabokov's insistence on the simultaneity of his most synesthetic passages (e.g., the bravura description of an encounter with the village schoolmaster in *Speak, Memory*, during which Nabokov was "all the while . . . richly, serenely aware of my own manifold awareness" [pp. 218–219]) is related to his at first rather startling assertion that, in the summer of 1914 "when the numb fury of verse-making" first came over him (p. 215), he discovered that "a person hoping to become a [bilingual?—E. K. B.] poet must have the capacity of thinking of several things at the same time" (p. 218).

While some of these suggestions must remain speculative, there can be no doubt that the final decades of Nabokov's literary career demonstrate both the relative peace and the variety of benefits that can accrue from a bilingual writer's "stereo-linguistic optic on communication," when both languages are active and when the blandishments of a stereolinguistically "meshed world" have been recognized and firmly accepted. Every bilingual or polyglot writer who achieves full individuation *as* a bilingual writer finds his own idiosyncratic, constantly shifting, active balance or flexible synthesis of his languages. This balance may involve the creation of an idiolect in which elements from the various languages combine in a polyglot synthesis.[80] Jane Grayson, Alexander Nakhimovsky, J. T. Lokrantz, William W. Rowe, Roy Judson Rosengrant, and others have written carefully and exhaustively about the peculiarities and interactions of Nabokov's languages properly speaking and their mutual contribution to what is sometimes called "Nabokovese." While I cannot retrace their arguments in detail here, some of their observations are particularly relevant to our discussion.

Everyone agrees that Nabokov's English is *sui generis* and unmistakable. We may grant Nabokov certain linguistic lapses and rigidities in his first English novels (he seems to insist on them), but it is fair to say that his English, even in these "apprentice" novels, was not a "second-rate brand." It was richer and more flexible than the language wielded by almost all of his monoglot contemporaries writing in English. Nabokov's great advantage was his bilingual's awareness of option and his sensitivity to the potential for defamiliarization provided by even the slightest variants in levels of usage and vocabulary. Ronald Hingley has stated that Nabokov's English is "justly described as masterly, perhaps for the very reason that he puts twists on it such as would never occur to a native user,"[81] but it would have been more accurate to have said "as would never occur to a *monolingual* native user." For Nabokov's bilingualism has made him *both* a "native user" and a "foreigner." Grayson has quite rightly observed: "The brilliance of Nabokov's later English style owes not a little to his viewpoint as a foreigner. He sees the English language through different eyes. He sees patterns of sound and potential meanings in words which the [monoglot] native speaker, his perception dulled through familiarity, would simply pass over. He deviates more readily from set modes of expression and conventional registers of style, inventing new and arresting word combinations, employing high flown, recherché vocabulary alongside the most mundane colloquialisms."[82] But it is *bilingualism,* rather than "foreignness" per se that is crucial, because Nabokov's bilingualism constantly and everywhere reinforces his consciousness of language(s) as such. This effect of bilingualism was already visible in the Russian period but, of course, increased after Nabokov became actively bilingual as a writer.

By the time Nabokov wrote *Lolita* and *Pnin* (to say nothing of the subsequent novels), the "oddnesses" of Nabokov's vocabulary and phraseology were almost never inadvertent. Upon close scrutiny of what at first appeared to be "little mistakes," Rowe found that nearly every such "mistake" turned out to be "a grammatically correct but faintly fresh, or 'foreign' effect probably left on purpose."[83] In Nabokov's later English works, it is not possible to draw a clear distinction between what is "foreign" or nonstandard and what is "original and calculated to enrich the scope of the English language."[84] In fact, the former is probably *also* the latter. If, as Rowe says, Nabokov is "uniquely and justly deemed a master stylist in both languages,"[85] then this is true in part *because* he has adapted the English language to certain Russian modes of expression. Or, rather, Nabokov has stretched the boundaries of American English by grafts (mostly Russian but frequently also French) which have increased the vigor and fertility of the host plant in ways that may turn out to be broader and more general than the interferences with Yiddish which Murray Baumgarter says provide the enduring linguistic interest of American writers such as Philip Roth, Saul Bellow, and the like.[86]

One of the simplest of Nabokov's techniques, the literal transplantation of wordings from one language into a work written in another, is invisible to any but a bilingual reader.[87] Thus a cliché may be reborn into a live metaphor in a new language, and the bilingual reader reacts both to the origin and to new associations from the counterpart.[88] Nabokov was fond of coining new words, and he also enjoyed creating and naturalizing neologisms (which frequently use stems deriving from languages other than English) and new combinations resulting in part-of-speech changes. As Rowe has indicated, prefixes and suffixes play a particularly vital role in the normal formation of Russian words, and Nabokov's English often displays similar manipulations resulting in a variety of odd effects. Nabokov also played with roots, and he frequently associated words containing similarities between letters and/or sounds, thus creating unexpected interplays of sense (Rowe offers "apprehensive hen," "our common hour," etc.).[89] Proffer notes that, while sound instrumentation is a foremost element of Nabokov's prose, it usually turns out that the "phonetic deftness is complemented by novelty of expression and precision of meaning."[90] Thus the sound instrumentation of Nabokov's prose in either language is usually related to other matters. As Nakhimovsky says: "Nabokov makes use of the entire linguistic and cultural context of the word. Moreover—and this distinguishes him from many other linguistically oriented authors—he never uses a stylistic device in isolation. A neologism appears in a metaphor, a metaphor is supported by an alliteration, an alliteration leads into a bold grammatical construction."[91] In particular, Nabokov's use in English of a grammatical construction that Peter Lubin has dubbed "phrasal tmesis" (whereby a set or fixed expression is "ruptured by an alien verbal insertion") would seem to be strongly influenced by the looser word order characteristic of an inflected language such as Russian.[92]

While it is easier to see the effects of Nabokov's bilingual practice in the American English works of his maturity, the same devices of alliteration, extensive lexical manipulation, and use of "a broad range of diction as well as unusual collocations" are visible in Nabokov's Russianing of his autobiography.[93] Rosengrant sums up these bidirectional effects: "In short, the Russian, like the English of which it is a recreation, is rich in device and marked by conscious and sometimes elaborate technique, but whatever its stylistic resources and however it may use them, their ultimate purpose, indeed their true *raison d'être*, is to produce a fundamental disjunction or discontinuity between form and meaning, a sort of verbal cleft through which the brilliant light of Nabokov's individuality can properly emerge."[94] If you define style as does Rosengrant—not as a variable, changing radically from work to work, but as "the manner in which an author's personality, his individual psychological, intellectual, and cultural identity informs the text at the verbal level, thereby constituting, for good or for ill, depending on the degree of assimilation, an important dimension of textual meaning"[95]—then Nabokov's style is a constant, a stable element, independent of the dynamics of any particular work. In Nabokov's case, style, growing out of a fundamentally bilingual set of processing strategies and involving certain kinds of transformations, is often paradoxically, eminently (self?)translatable, not in the sense that any given work can be adequately rendered in every detail (even, as Nabokov would have it, by means of a trot and an apparatus), but rather in the fact that it can be *transposed*.[96]

For example, Rosengrant remarks that Nabokov's "English style is characterized by a strong tendency to contrast registers—whether within the phrase (as in the collocation) or within a larger unit (as in the diction)—and to use that contrast both for rhetorical effect and as a means of authorial self-expression, of manifesting the governing sensibility of the maker within the verbal texture of the discourse."[97] Nabokov's habitual diction (in particular, his use of rare and unusual words) as well as his collocations (his technique of combining words from different, even divergent linguistic strata) are, in Bakhtinian terms, already a kind of code-switching, characteristic of Nabokov's prose in either language, properly speaking. Therefore, when translating himself from Russian to English or from English to Russian, as in the transformation of *Conclusive Evidence* into *Drugie berega* and back into *Speak, Memory*, Nabokov would frequently change the meaning of the lexical items in the translation, but the *effect* of these changes was "*to retain the underlying principles of stylistic organization* that governed the selection and combination of the English expressions in the first place" (emphasis added).[98] Thus, in a self-translated version of a Nabokov prose text, the neologisms and word play will be different, not an immediate mirror image, but they will be there in whatever guise the target language allows, and some kind of pendent Anti-Terra will be realized. Under these circumstances, the works that will be hardest to transpose into another language will obviously be those which already contain many polyglot elements and much code-switching (in the strong sense) in the original version. The hardest to translate of all Nabokov works would therefore be *Pnin,* where a given texture of language is foregrounded,[99] and, of course, *Ada.*

In *Ada,* Nabokov's profligacy in engendering neologisms, "new uses," allusions, and parodies reached its apogee. Surface interference and interreference permeate the entire fabric of this novel. In *Ada,* Nabokov allowed himself to behave linguistically very much as polyglots behave when they communicate with each other, rather than with monoglot speakers of any of their languages. In these special circumstances, bilinguals frequently allow their languages to interact or mix. As Grosjean and Soares have noted, this change of speech mode also has profound effects on the language-processing mechanisms involved in production and perception.[100] While no neurolinguistic studies have been made on the processing strategies used by bilingual writers, I would be inclined to wager that in both languages, but especially in English, and most particularly in *Ada,* Nabokov used a combined processing strategy[101] rather than any of those typical for either monolingual Russians or monlingual Anglophones.

Whatever the mysteries of the creation of *Ada,* it is evident that only a polyglot has any chance of fully apprehending its linguistic complexity. Without knowing Russian, as Rowe has remarked, one cannot completely understand even the first paragraph of *Ada,* and the polyglot may also miss a lot if he is not careful.[102] Proffer explains: "Many of the Russian words and phrases in *Ada* are not

translated. Sometimes these are bilingual puns which even a bilin-
gualist will miss if he does not examine both members carefully.
Russians may not notice that English sentences are actually translations (or adaptations) from Russian works. English song titles may
be metamorphosed Russian romances—which the English speaker
cannot know and the Russian speaker may well overlook."[103] Thus,
in *Ada* and (to an almost equal, if less obvious, degree) in *Look at
the Harlequins!* Nabokov was primarily addressing the select audience of polyglots who, like him and with him, had overcome the
barriers of linguistic compartmentalization. In these two works,
more than anywhere else, Nabokov was giving rein to "his own
sweet will" and writing "for myself in multiplicate" (*SO*, 114).[104]

The linguistic complexification of *Ada* has repelled even some
readers who are closest to being, linguistically at least, Nabokov
clones. The thoroughly polyglot George Steiner found *Ada* self-
indulgent, in spots irredeemably overwritten, and in its "mixture of
English, French, Russian and private esperanto" labored.[105] Robert
Alter thought that the novelist permitted himself too much, missing
the perfect selectivity and control of *Lolita* and *Pale Fire* through
his "eagerness to pursue every linguistic quibble, every gratuitous
turn of a sexual or literary double meaning."[106] *Ada*'s exuberant
linguistic promiscuity, its profusion of allusions and parodies, its
complex, distorted mirror worlds, its mixing of clean and unclean,
its loss of habitual distinctions—strike even some polyglots as not
only excessive, but even incestuous.

Once again, the familial trope of legitimate and illegitimate cou-
plings resurfaces! Although Nabokov made it abundantly clear that
he didn't "give a damn for incest one way or another" (*SO*, 123),
he recuperated the *trope* (from the Romantic novel or elsewhere)
and critics have pounced on it as a metaphor for his bilingualism:
e.g., "Incest is a trope through which Nabokov dramatizes his abiding devotion to Russian, the dazzling infidelities which exile has
forced on him"[107] and "On the most abstract level it would not
seem inappropriate to see incest as a metaphor for the interaction
of V. V.'s Russian and English works."[108] Steiner goes so far as to
claim that "mirrors, incest, and a constant meshing of languages
are the cognate centers of Nabokov's art."[109]

In *Ada*, Nabokov was testing the limits of the linguistically possible and the readerly bearable. (Proffer might have said of *Ada*,
even more than of *Look at the Harlequins!*, that the author of its

ultimate annotation "will no doubt go directly from the reference room to a padded cell."[110] Could the neurolinguists possibly have envisaged something like *Ada* when they spoke of the bilingual's greater tolerance for linguistic and situational ambiguity? As a proverb of Blake's antiworld declares, "The road of excess leads to the palace of wisdom," and those who "have not the taste for it" may consider *Ada* to be Nabokov's *Finnegans Wake* (a novel of which Nabokov thoroughly disapproved, even though he considered *Ulysses* to be one of the two or three greatest books of the century).[111]

Self-translation

> And from the inside, too, I'd duplicate
> Myself, my lamp, an apple on a plate
> —John Shade, "Pale Fire," canto 1, ll. 5–6

If *Ada* is arguably the most problematic of Nabokov's fully polyglot works, the self-regenerating and self-translated autobiographical text "Mademoiselle O"/*Conclusive Evidence*/*Drugie berega*/ *Speak, Memory* is indisputably one of the most successful, and brings us to a consideration of the role of translation and self-translation per se in Nabokov's artistic practice.

The fully polyglot period of a bilingual writer's career usually involves major translation projects, generally from the first language into the second language, though sometimes also from the second language into the first. Neurolinguistics has told us that not all bilinguals have an aptitude for translation, since translation is a skill separate from "simple" proficiency in two languages and uses a distinct set of neural passageways.[112] Nevertheless, it seems reasonable to posit that *most* actively bilingual writers do have both the talent and the taste for translation. This is frequently obscured by the fact that writers who are bilingual but monoglot *as writers* often complain that translation paralyzes them and gets in the way of their own creativity.[113] If, however, one examines the career of actively bilingual writers, one finds that they are generally very prolific (one even begins to suspect that polyglotism might actually be conducive to graphomania). For them, the practice of translation is a source of renewed vigor for their own bilingual writing, not an obstacle to it—especially when they translate in both directions.

Over the years, and from the beginning, Nabokov devoted a considerable amount of time and creative energy to translation or self-translation. As I have mentioned, Rosengrant argues very plausibly that Nabokov's translations are of such "prodigious extent and diversity" that they must be regarded as a principal part of his life's work.[114] Even if one considers only Nabokov's translations of the works of other writers, his production was voluminous, and his work on Pushkin's *Evgenii Onegin* was the focus of his activity for a number of years during his fully polyglot period.

Nabokov's idiosyncratic (but not entirely unprecedented) prose translation of *Onegin*,[115] with its symbiotic, monumental, and exhaustive commentary on nuances of language, meter, and culture, would seem to be a departure from the principles Nabokov used in translating his novels (and, as we shall see, his memoirs or, for that matter, his Russian rendition of *Alice's Adventures in Wonderland*). But what may be possible in prose is not necessarily so in poetry, and D. Barton Johnson's demonstration of the impossibility of the systematic transfer of phonoaesthetic effects from one language to another provides strong support for the legitimacy of Nabokov's *Onegin* format.[116] Still, one cannot help believing that Nabokov, had he so decided, might have done the *best possible* poetic translation of *Onegin*. (This unfulfilled possibility should be tucked away with the tantalizing suggestion that Nabakov might have been a great French writer.)[117]

If translation was a major activity of Nabokov's mature, polyglot period, self-translation was even more important. As we have repeatedly seen, self-translation is an essential attribute of the activity of bilingual writers. It usually precipitates the commitment to writing directly in a second language, and, years later, bilingual writers frequently return to self-translation, even though they may previously have rejected it as hateful. In the twilight of their careers, most bilingual writers are no longer content to have functioned separately in two different languages. They are in search of unity, and in their efforts to fully realize their *bi-destin,* or "double destiny," they want their collected works to exist in both languages. Beckett, who came quite early to the decision to transpose all his works from either language into the other, has for many years practiced something that is in fact a kind of dual creation, translating his works almost immediately after their composition. Nabokov, however, self-translated to a quite different rhythm. By the time he returned to self-translation, there was a major backlog of works to be trans-posed from Russian into English. Several of these he placed in the hands of the excellent professional translators whose services he could now command, particularly Michael Scammell, who did an exceptionally fine job on *Dar*. Even then, however, Nabokov trans-lated the poetry in *Dar* himself, and he oversaw, corrected, and amended the work of his translators, retaining full artistic control over the final product. In those cases where Nabokov self-translated his own books and where the project of transforming his artistic corpus into a completely bilingual one was fully operative, he was engaged in an activity that Paul de St. Pierre has described as "not . . . a process of translation, but rather one of writing *across* languages."[118] In the terms of our discussion in Chapter 2, what was involved was not simply horizontal movement, but a par-abolic return to those sources of the texts which are either bilingual or beneath either language.

Because self-translation and the (frequently) attendant reworking makes a text retrospectively incomplete, both versions become ava-tars of a hypothetical total text in which the versions in both lan-guages would rejoin one another and be reconciled (as in the "pure" language evoked by Benjamin).[119] The practice of self-translation by a mature writer who has successfully defined himself in more than one language is therefore a reassurance of wholeness and may in fact actually bring about additional creative interac-tion between the two languages on a quite different level from that of the deliberate interferences, code-switching, interreferences, and parodies that characterize *Ada*. In Nabokov's case, many of these self-translations were also a manifestation of a continuing and de-veloping domestic solidarity, for Nabokov often worked on them with his wife or with his son Dmitri or with both.

Probably the most significant of Nabokov's self-translations was his linguistically chameleonic autobiography. It developed slowly over almost three decades, beginning with "Mademoiselle O," which was written in French, published in 1936, and first Englished by Hilda Ward. The other chapters that would constitute *Conclu-sive Evidence* were written in English between 1946 and 1950 and published separately in various magazines.[120] Rearranged and somewhat revised, they were then grouped together as *Conclusive Evidence* in 1951. Nabakov admitted that writing *Conclusive Evidence* was particularly agonizing because his memories were attuned to one (musical) key, a Russian one, but had to be expressed through another—which, through force of circumstance, was English [Kniga *Conclusive Evidence* pisalas' dolgo (1946–1950), s osobenno muchitel'nym trudom, ibo pamiat' byla nastroena na odin lad—muzykal'no nedogovorennyi, russki—a naviazyvalsia ei drugoi lad, angliiskii i obstoiatel'nyi]. He was, however, relatively satisfied with the result—until he embarked on the "insane project" [bezumnoe delo] of self-translating *Conclusive Evidence* into the Russian [na prezhnii, osnovnoi moi iazyk], which would have been the "natural" language for his memoir in the first place (*Db*, 8).

Nabokov's transfer inevitably involved some of his usual transformations (e.g., sacrificing specific images in order to maintain the underlying principles of lexical control and sound instrumentation). Writing in Russian again also provoked substantial changes, particularly additions and elaborations. The savor of Russian prose acted as a Proustian madeleine, after tasting which the writer had to *work* to liberate, illuminate, and deepen the impressions of lost time.[121] Nabokov tells us that, by dint of "intense concentration," vague memories could be clarified and expanded: "the neutral smudge might be forced to come into beautiful focus so that the sudden view could be identified, and the anonymous servant named." On the other hand, the use of Russian made unnecessary numerous "explanatory" English phrases the retention of which would have been "a caricature of Mnemosyne." Nabokov even felt that writing in Russian actually *prohibited* the inclusion in *Drugie berega* of chapter 2 of *Conclusive Evidence* "because of the psychological difficulty of replaying a theme elaborated in *Dar*" (*SM*, 12).[122] Thus, as Grayson remarks, in *Drugie berega*, language itself assumes a compositional role, and *Drugie berega* is stylistically and structurally in many ways an independent work.[123] "While retaining the general design, I changed and added a great deal" [uderzhav obshchii uzor, ia izmenil i dopolnil mnogoe], Nabokov said in his preface, noting that the relationship of *Conclusive Evidence* to *Drugie berega* was like that of block-capital letters to cursive—as a chapbook's oversimplification and rigidity are to the live movement of the writer's hand, or as a stylized silhouette is to an encounter with a stranger on a train who, in the course of a night's trip, tells you all the secrets of his life (*Db*, 8).

Given what we know of the need felt by fully individuated bilingual writers to try linking the two linguistic faces of their creativity in order to create not two half-lives but one double destiny, and given Nabokov's taste for accepting particularly difficult artistic challenges (*The Dare*, as Vadim Vadimich was to entitle one of his books), it should not be surprising that Nabokov went one step further and *re*transformed the Russian *Drugie berega* (augmented by some additional corrections, mostly of fact) into the final harmony of *Speak, Memory*.[124] This last transfer was perhaps the hardest of all: the "re-Englishing of a Russian re-version of what had been an English re-telling of Russian memories in the first place, proved to be a diabolical task, but some consolation was given me by the thought that such multiple metamorphosis, familiar to butterflies, had not been tried by any human before" (*SM*, 12–13).

Nabokov's accomplishment in transferring his memoirs in and out of his principal literary languages illuminates two other efforts that many critics have judged to be less successful: his pony-*cum*-commentary of Pushkin's *Onegin* in English,[125] about which we have already spoken, and his translation of *Lolita* into Russian. Since Nobokov considered that the Russianing of his American novels was "like completing the circle of my creative life. Or rather starting a new spiral" (*SO*, 52), it was the obvious choice to begin this process with *Lolita*, a book to which Nabokov was particularly attached.[126] "In a spirit of justice to my little American muse" (*SO*, 37), he undertook to translate this most American of his works into Russian himself, thus protecting her from the clumsy attentions of future, well-intentioned incompetents.[127]

Even for Nabokov, Russianing *Lolita* posed a number of difficulties. The Americanness of the material would have resisted not only Nabokov's Russian, but even the efforts of someone whose Russian had continued to develop and change with Russian life, that is, someone living in the Soviet Union. Nabokov had problems finding appropriate terms, particularly when dealing with cars, clothing, varieties of shoes (sneakers? Nabokov would have been pleased, no doubt, to learn that the kind currently in favor with California skateboarders bears the trademark "Vans"), items of furniture, and the like (*SO*, 52–53), as well as with larger problems of tone. He declared himself to be deeply disillusioned with the result. In part, he attributed his disappointment to the fact that his Russian had grown "rusty":

> Alas, that "wondrous Russian tongue," that, it seemed to me, was waiting for me somewhere, was flowering like a faithful springtime behind a tightly locked gate, whose key I had held in safekeeping so many years, proved to be non-existent, and there is nothing behind the gate but charred stumps and a hopeless autumnal distance, and the key in my hand is more like a skeleton key.

> [Uvy, tot "divnyi russkii iazyk," kotoryi, sdavalos' mne, vsë zhdet menia gde-to, tsvetet, kak vernaia vesna za naglukho zapertymi vorotami, ot kotorykh stol'ko let khranilsia u menia kliuch, okazalsia nesushchestvuiushchim, i za vorotami net nichego, krome obuglennykh pnei i osennei beznadezhnoi dali, a kliuch v ruke skoree pokhozh na otmychku.][128]

But while there may be some truth to Nabokov's sense that his Russian had gotten stiff from infrequent compositional use, or even that it had slightly atrophied, his complaint was clearly hyperbolic and must be seen as the counterweight to his endlessly repeated assertions that his English was never *that* good—a plaint that must be taken with a whole *pood* of salt. Not only *Drugie berega*, but even the very postface in which he bemoaned the rusting of his Russian, is proof that Nabokov's loss of control and prowess in lyrical and expository Russian prose was not critical or even considerable. As his English was more original and vibrant (and idiosyncratic) than that of most monoglot contemporary writers of English prose, so his Russian, barnacles and all, was in fact, more aware and complex than that of almost any contemporary writer of Russian prose. The real problem was probably less that his Russian had deteriorated than that his English, in particular the language of *Lolita*, had become so subtle "in all its new ripples and changing light,"[129] as to pose particular difficulty for so extraordinarily exigent a self-translator as Nabokov, especially since he held, with Goethe, that the best translations "insist on retaining [the original text's] distinctive conventions and forms, however awkward and inconvenient they may at first prove to be in their new guise."[130]

In the end, Nabokov, consoled himself with the thought that the "clumsiness" of his translation of *Lolita* was in large part owing to the characteristics of the "amazing languages" [izumitel'nykh iaz-ykov] in which he wrote. On the basis of his two years of work on the translation of *Lolita*, Nabokov concluded:

> Gestures, grimaces, landscapes, the torpor of trees, odors, rains, the melting and iridescent hues of nature, everything tenderly human (strange as it may seem), but also everything coarse and crude, juicy and bawdy, comes out no worse in Russian than in English, *perhaps better* [emphasis added]; but the subtle reticence so peculiar to English, the poetry of thought, the instantaneous resonance between the most abstract concepts, the swarming of monosyllabic epithets—all this, and also everything relating to technology, fashion, sports, the natural sciences, and the unnatural passions—in Russian become clumsy, prolix, and often repulsive in terms of style and rhythm.

> [Telodvizheniia, uzhimki, landshafty, tomlenie derev'ev zapakhi, dozhdi, taiushchie i perelivchatye ottenki prirody, vse nezhno-chelovecheskoe (kak ni stranno!), a takzhe vsë muzhitskoe, gruboe, sochno-pokhabnoe, vykhodit po-russki ne khuzhe, esli ne luchshe, chem po-angliiski; no stol' svoistvennye angliiskomu tonkie nedogov-orennosti, poeziia mysli, mgnovennaia pereklichka mezhdu otvlechen-neishimi poniatiiami, roenie odnoslozhnykh epitetov, vsë eto, a takzhe vsë otnosiashcheesia k tekhnike, modam, sportu, estestvennym naukam i protivoestestvennym strastiam—stanovitsia po-russki to-pornym, mnogoslovnym i chasto otvratitel'nym v smysle stilia i ritma.][131]

But while Nabokov's comments as to the varying characteristics of Russian and English are founded, they are not a sufficient explanation.

More important, not only for poetry but also for Nabokov's prose, is the impossibility of systematically transferring phonoaes-thetic effects from one language to another. For as D. B. Johnson has demonstrated, the difficulty does not result from one language being inherently richer in its potential for sound patterning or from the *direction* of the translation. In either direction, "the phonoaes-thetic density of the translation is vastly inferior to that of the original."[132] Nabokov evidently could not accept that sometimes he, even he, could not fully transmute and re-create his own prose from one of his languages into another. Johnson has wondered, in some despair: "if one of the greatest stylists of modern literature, a man bilingual from earliest childhood, cannot successfully translate his own poetry, then who can?"[133] The same question could also be put for *Lolita*. But if Nabokov had not been the translator, we would not have *expected* a perfect transformation of a text in one language into one in another which would then make a flawless whole with the original. And if he had not been the translator, or if he had been translating someone else, Nabokov himself might have been able to accept compromises that his bilingual's vision of the total coincidence of his work in both languages would not allow.

Thus it would seem that Nabokov's project of "closing the circle of his artistic career" (or of opening a new spiral) was foredoomed to be an incomplete success. In fact, the effort of bilingual writers late in their careers to self-translate in order to form a bilingual corpus is frequently a partial failure. Perhaps the final spiral (the one subsequent to the attempt at "closing the circle") entails the realization that being a bilingual writer, like being a bilingual *tout court*, involves not only the pleasures of code-switching and inter-reference in a bilingual context, but also, sometimes, the definite choice of a given language for certain circumstances or the acceptance of major losses in translation. The reality of the bilingual situation may require the renunciation of the dream of clarity, complete transferability, and perfect closure. The bilingual writer may have to accept the ambiguities of an incompletely ambidextrous linguistic universe. Like Vadim Vadimich, the bilingual writer who is the protagonist of Nabokov's last completed novel, *Look at the Harlequins!*, he may be obliged to renounce his obsession with his inability to mentally transpose right and left (a problem not infrequent among talented language learners)[134] so as to accept "with a bellow of joy" the entrance of Reality (*LATH*, 250).[135] In Nabokov's case, this was the continuing reality of a meshed, but not entirely symmetrical, linguistic world. Only through the recognition of the constantly shifting strata, the complicated enfoldings, and the slowly changing subordinations of his languages could Nabokov (in the words of one of John Shade's prototypes) finally "drink and be whole again beyond confusion."[136]

CHAPTER FIVE

Other Bilingual Writers of
the Paris Emigration

Although Vladimir Nabokov and Elsa Triolet are the writers of the "first" emigration who have made the most lasting impact on the literatures of the languages other than Russian in which they wrote, less well known Russian bilingual writers are also interesting from both the literary and the linguistic point of view. The more of these writers one considers, the better one understands why bilinguals, and even more certainly bilingual *writers,* have driven linguistic research to a state closely resembling despair.

Because the elements that determine the relationships of the languages commanded by any bi- or multilingual person are in many respects idiosyncratic, it is almost impossible to measure or compare them. Unless one is willing to "restate bilingual problems in a more general form" using experimental conditions that only "approximate the real bilingual case,"[1] one is faced with crucial variables that are mind-boggling in the complexity of their possible recombinations. The problem is evident even in considering our narrowly limited primary sample, those writers who left Russia in the period from 1917 to 1923, who became bilingual or polyglot as writers, and who, wherever they may have been finally tossed by war and chance, spent at least a decade in Paris, willy-nilly becoming members of the "first" Paris emigration.

If one were to try constructing a table, one would have to list ten to fifteen of these writers on the paradigmatic axis. This is simple enough, but the number of variables that one would have to include on the syntagmatic axis—involving time and manner of language acquisition and of linguistic practice—would be daunting, and no clear regularities could emerge. One would have to consider *at least* the following factors: family background, childhood and domestic language patterns; whether the writer left Russia before reaching adulthood; the nature of the writer's Russian and/or foreign education; whether the writer has produced a major body of work in both languages; whether there is a preponderance of one language over the other—and for which genres. In what order were the languages used? Sequentially, over long or short periods of time, or simultaneously? If both languages were practiced during the same time period, were both used for the same kinds of writing? Was Russian, for example, reserved for poetry or fiction, or for both, while criticism was written in French? Or was Russian reserved for poetry, while artistic prose and criticism were written in French? And are these combinations consistent, or did they vary from one year to another? Was the development away from writing exclusively in Russian steady and progressive? Or was there a reversal? If so, when? Was it temporary or permanent? Was there only one reversal, or were there several? For which genres? Did the writer translate his own works? In one direction (which?) or in both? When? At the beginning of his career, at the end, throughout? Was there a third language? Was the writer in fact *polyglot* as a writer? If so, how did this change the linguistic balance? Perhaps the writer also tried mixed media? Which? When? Given these variables, and the consequent hopelessness of attempting any statistically based analysis of my sample, the most useful way of approaching the bilingual writers of the "first" Paris emigration would seem to be anecdotal. I will therefore consider the specific trajectories of the most significant of these bilingual writers, each of whom is "an interesting case" in his or her own right.

Zinaïda Shakhovskaia (Zinaïda Schakovskoy)

The life and career pattern of Zinaïda Schakovskoy[2] are in some ways different from any we have seen so far. Born in Moscow on August 30, 1906, she was the fourth child and third daughter of Prince Aleksei Shakhovskoi and the former Anne von Kninen. On her father's side, she can (and does) trace her ancestry back through twenty-nine generations to Rurik and through fourteen generations to Prince Konstantin "Shakh" of Iaroslavl.[3] Her great-grandfather fought at Borodino and is supposed to have been the first Russian general to enter Paris after the defeat of Napoleon. Her grandfather married Nataliia Trubetskaia. Schakovskoy's mother was the granddaughter of Carlo Rossi, the architect whose buildings were the glory of Saint Petersburg (as they are still of Leningrad). Leonid von Kninen, her maternal grandfather, was a renowned Austrian pianist and composer, a darling of Saint Petersburg society, whom Schakovskoy remembers to have spoken Russian with a strong Austrian accent *(L & o, 87)*. According to Schakovskoy, her father was everything that Tolstoi would have wished to be but did not succeed in being (p. 28). (Shakhovskoi and his family were, in fact, protected several times after the Revolution by their former peasants, servants, and local shopkeepers from threats of death and imprisonment [p. 34]).[4] Her mother frequently took the children abroad, and Zinaïda's earliest memories are of trains, the Berlin Zoo, the ponds in the Tuileries Gardens, Lake Geneva, and Toulon in 1910 when she was four (p. 21).

Three languages were in everyday use in the family, and Schakovskoy's memories would indicate that she was a true example of primary bilingualism with its attendant early sortings-out and confusions: "The people around me spoke Russian, German, and French, but Russian, German, and French words jostled one another in my mouth, and never seemed to express what I wanted"[5] [Autour de moi on parlait le russe, l'allemand, le français, mais les mots russes, allemands et français se bousculaient dans ma bouche, n'exprimant jamais ce que je voulais] *(L & o, 20)*. Her childhood, other than the trips abroad, was spent either in Saint Petersburg or at the paternal estate of Matovo, near Tula, in a sprawling old house, without electric light or running water, but nonetheless comfortable and inviting.[6] At Matovo, along with a series of German, Baltic German, or German Swiss nurses, there was also old Tatiana, who filled the role of Pushkin's nurse and told the future author tales about Baba Iaga and other folk spirits as well as stories from the Christian Apocrypha. There followed a series of more or less virtuous and serious *mademoiselles* accompanied by the (boring) children's books of the *Bibliothèque rose* (p. 44).[7]

During the winters from 1910 to 1913, the family lived on Vasil-'evskii Island in Saint Petersburg, and Zinaïda was allowed to sit in on the lessons of her brother Dmitrii and sister Natasha. So it was at about the age of four that Schakovskoy awakened to her passionate vocation as a reader: "I think one can be born a reader as one can be a born painter or musician" [Je crois qu'on naît lecteur comme on naît peintre ou musicien] *(L & o, 90).* At the age of eight, she went to a French kindergarten during the mornings, and in the fall of 1914, she entered the preparatory classes of the Mogilevskii *Gymnasium.* In 1916, she passed the entrance exam to the exclusive Catherine Institute, an extremely strict boarding school to which her older sister had also gone. Here Schakovskoy wrote her first literary "work"—a story called "Three Kisses," which, she says, was a shameless plagiarism of Turgenev—and continued to read everything she could get her hands on (p. 145). The four months that Schakovskoy spent at the Catherine Institute constituted the only formal secondary schooling that she had in Russia, but even this was not really schooling *in Russian,* because at the Catherine Institute the girls used French one day and German the next, despite the war. They were, however, allowed to speak Russian during recess.[8]

In the summer of 1917, after the first revolution, the family returned to the Matovo estate, where, aside from practical domestic cares (shared among the family and the few remaining servants) and romps with her faithful dogs, Schakovskoy consecrated herself to reading:

> Although my studies had virtually stopped since I had left the Institute at the age of ten, the library at Matovo gave me the opportunity to educate myself at the age of eleven. That winter, I read Molière and Shakespeare, *War and Peace, Anna Karenina,* all of Aleksei Tolstoi and all of Nadson, Knut Hamsun and Verhaeren, Grigorovich, Pisemskii, Gogol', Turgenev, Maikov, Goncharov, Sir Walter Scott . . . Poets and prose writers, good and bad, I swallowed them as a shark swallows fresh meat. . . . I tried Dostoevskii, too, but gave up, annoyed at not being able to understand him. . . . This orgy of premature reading has hovered over my whole life.
>
> [Si mes études étaient virtuellement arrêtées depuis que j'avais quitté l'Institue, à l'age de dix ans, la bibliothèque de Matovo me donna à

onze ans l'occasion de m'instruire. Cet hiver-là je lus Molière et Shakespeare, *Guerre et Paix, Anna Karénine,* tout Aleksis Tolstoi et tout Nadson, Knut Hamsun et Verhaeren, Grigorovitch, Pissemsky, Gogol, Tourguéniev, Maïkov, Gontcharoff, Walter Scott . . . Poètes et prosateurs, bons et mauvais, je les engloutissais comme un requin engloutit la chair fraîche. . . . Je m'attaquai à Dostoievski mais je l'abandonnai, vexée de ne rien comprendre. . . . Cette débauche de lectures prématurées a plané sur toute ma vie.] [*L & o,* 194–195]

In the spring of 1918, Schakovskoy's mother was arrested and almost executed. For several months Zinaïda was left alone at Matovo, which was then occupied by the Bolsheviks, an isolated eleven-year-old hostage. During this time, she witnessed the painful death by poison of her beloved dogs.[9] She also received nightly visits from one of her guards, a sailor, who told and retold in a monotone, with numerous gruesome details, how he had dived down to see how the corpses of some massacred officers (who had been thrown overboard with weights attached to their feet) were doing at the bottom of the harbor.

Many adventures and hardships as well as some almost miraculous strokes of luck were to follow before she, her mother, brother, and sisters arrived safely at Constantinople in 1920.[10] Schakovskoy then spent two years in Turkey before she and her older sister managed, by hook and by crook, to wangle passage to Paris to rejoin their mother, who had left somewhat earlier. For part of those years, Schakovskoy had a scholarship to an American school, where, not knowing the language of instruction, she could take no courses other than beginner's English. Although she had been an early polyglot, the obligation to learn yet another language after the disruption and hardships of the previous three years provoked a psychophysiological reaction, and Schakovskoy developed a serious stutter (which, however, was much less pronounced when she returned to a Russian-speaking environment).[11] Once safely in Brussels where her mother settled in 1923, she became a boarder at the Catholic convent of Berlaymont. Although French was a language with which she had been acquainted since childhood, the new shift of language and milieu aggravated her stuttering problem, which now reappeared in French. Her written French at this time was more developed than her spoken command of the language, but it was full of errors of syntax and spelling and suffered from highly romantic passages of "purple prose" (*M de v*, 78, 80); it was not miraculously better a year later when, at the age of sixteen, she abandoned her studies at Berlaymont.

Having been buffeted from place to place and language to language, Schakovskoy was therefore essentially an autodidact in the French and Rusian languages as well as in French and Russian culture. Any further formal studies were of a practical nature. At sixteen, she attended a socialist-leaning school of social work in Belgium for one year, and then, after a brief English interlude, she enrolled at eighteen in a Protestant school of social work in Paris (*M de v*, 95, 100). Not surprisingly, in the exercise of her social work, where she was actively integrated in a French context, her stutter disappeared (p. 107). At the same time, now nineteen years old and on her own in Paris, she began to get involved in the life of the Russian colony, especially with the Russian literary world.[12] She herself wrote some short poems in Russian at this time.

Soon after meeting and marrying Sviatoslav de Malewsky-Malevich, Schakovskoy left with him for the Belgian Congo, where they spent a rather unhappy two years (1926–1928) in the vile climate of the Congo River port town of Matadi. It appears to have been a kind of purgatory. Her husband had a job he disliked, far from the painting and politics and philosophy that interested him. At twenty, without books, in a climate too torrid and unhealthy for exploration or ethnographic pursuits, Schakovskoy's African sojourn was analogous to—but far less pleasant than—Triolet's stay on Tahiti.

Upon their return to Belgium in 1929, the two threw themselves into the pursuits they had missed. Although she dutifully participated in the activities of the "Eurasian" movement in which her husband was deeply involved, Schakovskoy's own leanings were toward the West.[13] While she wrote and published two volumes of poetry in Russian, *Ukhod* [Departure] (1934) and *Doroga* [The road] (1935), and wrote numerous articles for the émigré press in both Paris and Belgium, Schakovskoy felt the need to stop "crying over the ruins of Carthage" and to break out of what she increasingly felt to be her stifling and isolated situation as an émigré: "I was fed up with being separate from the world in which I lived. I was thirsty to write and communicate with readers—with a considerable number of readers—and so I wanted to write in French. I wanted something tangible to hold on to instead of merely the phantom of a fatherland. I was in search of a new country, although I had no intention of ever forgetting the one where I had been born" [J'en avais assez d'être séparée du monde où je vivais, et cette soif que j'avais d'écrire et de communiquer avec les lecteurs—un nombre considérable de lecteurs—me faisait souhaiter d'écrire en français. Je voulais m'accrocher à quelquechose de réel et de tangible, et, face à un fantôme de patrie, j'étais en quête d'une patrie de rechange (bien que je n'eusse aucune intention d'oublier celle où je suis née)] (*M de v*, 200). Having become a Belgian citizen, while continuing to share the spiritual and cultural destiny of her fellow émigrés, Schakovskoy "enlarged her domain" by voraciously annexing French culture: "I read and read and read: the *Roman de la rose,* the fabliaux, the *Miracle de Saint Théophile,* Villon and Claudel, Maurice Scève and Valéry, Montaigne and Mme. de Sévigné, Saint-Simon and Malraux . . . and there came a moment (I would be tempted to say, just in time) when I found myself in the position of someone who gets married and finds she has lots of new relatives without, of course, giving up her own family" [Je lisais, je lisais, je lisais: *Roman de la rose,* fabliaux, *Le miracle de Saint Théophile,* Villon and Claudel, Maurice Scève and Valéry, Montaigne et Mme de Sévigné, Saint-Simon et Malraux . . . Et il arriva un moment, juste à point serais-je tentée de dire, où je me trouvai dans la position de quelqu'un qui, en se mariant, se découvre une nouvelle parenté sans pour cela renoncer à sa famille] (p. 263).

As a result of frequent association with Belgian poets, Schakovskoy began to write in French for Belgian magazines and newspapers during the early 1930s at the same time that she was writing poetry and articles in Russian for the magazines and newspapers of the Russian emigration.[14] She wrote critical articles (primarily about Russian literature) for *Le rouge et le noir* [The red and the black] and also published short stories. She participated in the preparation of the special Pushkin issue of *Le journal des poètes* [The poet's paper] in which Nabokov published his translation of two Pushkin lyrics into French. Schakovskoy herself did a good deal of translation in this and in other contexts and wrote a biography of Pushkin in French. There was also some poetry written directly in French,[15] and Schakovskoy continued to write in both French and Russian until after World War II.

During the war, she produced a few poems but was generally otherwise occupied. The year 1940 found her in the Service de santé of the French army. She fled south and was reunited with her husband in 1942 in London, where she worked for the Agence française d'information. A correspondent at the Nürnberg trials and in Greece during its civil war, she was also in Morocco in 1953. Despite her continuing activities as a journalist, in 1949 she also turned to fiction, publishing her first (prize-winning) novel in French under the pseudonym Jacques Croisé. More than a dozen other books in French followed, including several novels over the signature Jacques Croisé, her multivolume autobiography, a study of daily life in Moscow in the seventeenth century, and several other works on Russia, among them the account of her return to the Soviet Union on the occasion of a diplomatic mission that her husband performed for Belgium.[16] From 1949 to 1968, Schakovskoy published *only* in French, even though some of her books were about Russia or Russian characters, and even though, from 1960 to 1968, she was in charge of the broadcasts of the Russian section of the ORTF (Office of French Radio and Television). In 1968, she returned to publishing in Russian: "It was through force of circumstance and, to tell the truth, because of a sense of duty that I returned to the Russian language in 1968, when I became the editor of *Russkaia mysl'* [Russian thought], which was in grave danger of folding had I refused the job"[17] [C'est par la force des choses—et à vrai dire par devoir—que je suis revenue en 1968 seulement à la langue russe, en devenant rédacteur en chef de la *Pensée russe* laquelle était menacée de disparition en cas de mon refus.] Since 1968, Schakovskoy has written in a variety of genres, but almost entirely in Russian.[18] She is still active.

Schakovskoy, we have seen, did not initially define herself as a Russian writer, and her commitment to Russian was initially less intense and emotionally exclusive than was that of other, slightly older writers of the "first" emigration. Certainly this was due at least in part to her youth and to her having been deprived of a Russian secondary education and of any adolescent participation in the lively Russian cultural life that immediately preceded the Revolution—years that were formative for both Nabokov and Triolet.[19] That she was essentially an autodidact in both French and Russian, and that she acquired her impressive cultural baggage literally without benefit of context, may help to account for the apparent psychological ease with which Schakovskoy ultimately moved back and forth between writing in French and in Russian.[20] On the other hand, the lack of a solid basis also explains the earlier, painful transitional period of shifts of language (clearly traumatic for an adolescent who had already undergone a great deal) which resulted in Schakovskoy's debilitating stutter, first in English and then in French. This had made her early days in Paris in 1925 a torment: "Badly dressed, with a foreign accent, and looking younger than I was, I was robbed right and left. . . . In cafés, they would never give me my change. I tried to protest, but my stuttering made my protest ineffectual and only provoked jeers. 'She doesn't even know how to talk and she still wants to complain!' "[21] [Mal vêtue, ayant un accent étranger et l'air plus jeune que je ne l'étais réellement, je fus volée comme dans un bois. . . . Dans les bistrots on ne me rendait pas le change.[22] J'essayai de protester; mon bégaiement rendait mes protestations inefficaces et ne provoquait que des railleries. "Ça ne sait pas parler et ça veut faire des histoires!"] (*M de v*, 102).

By the 1960s not only had Schakovskoy long since lost her stutter, but she could say that her long cohabitation with the French had erased the superficial signs of accent and behavior that had once marked her as Russian. Even her newsdealer (the acid test) frequently complained to her about how the country was being "overrun with foreigners" [de sales étrangers] (*L & o*, 13). This does not mean that Schakovskoy had made any particular effort to "pass" as something she was not; nor, in fact, had her accent completely disappeared. She never tried to define herself as exclusively Russian or exclusively Francophone. Nor was she inclined to be a "joiner." Therefore, at various moments, she was considered an outsider by different groups. In the early 1930s, it was the Russian writers inclined to the "Paris Note" of hopelessness and despair who viewed her as an outsider: "Impermeable as I was to all influences, refusing the discipline of belonging, and, above all, naturally averse to 'decadence,' I realized that some of my fellow members [of the Union of Young Russian Writers and Poets of Paris] considered me an *outsider* [in English in the text—E.K.B.]. Here, too, I was not completely integrated, and I frequently played the role of the peasant who dared cry out that the emperor had no clothes"[23] [Imperméable à toute influence, refusant de m'embrigader, et surtout, par ma nature même hostile à tout esprit décadent, je comprenais que certains de mes confrères me considéraient comme un *outsider*. Là encore je ne m'intégrais pas et il m'arrivait souvent d'être ce paysan qui ose crier que le roi est nu] (*M de v*, 226). In the 1940s, Charles Plisnier dedicated his novel *Matriochka* to Schakovskoy, who found its Russian characters too afflicted with the stereotypical "Russian soul" that Westerners attribute to Slavs. But she accepted as fitting for herself the epigraph from Montaigne that Plisnier had chosen for his book: " 'Je fus pelaudé de toutes mains: au Gibelin j'éstois Guelfe, au Guelfe, Gibelin.' Je restais étrangère aux Occidentaux, je semblais Occidentale aux Russes" (*M de v*, 220) [I was belabored from every quarter; to the Ghibelline, I was a Guelph, to the Guelph a Ghibelline.][24] Thus she seemed a "Westerner" to the Russian "Eurasians," but remained a foreigner to "Westerners."

Schakovskoy's strong sense of duty, which frequently obliged her, when faced with two solutions, to choose the most difficult one, as well as her clear view of the extent and limits of her artistic talent, seem to have been very important in helping the mature writer avoid that psychic conflict which is the greatest threat to bilingual writing.[25] She insists that she feels neither interference nor psychic conflict between her French and her Russian. Although the fictional tone in the Jacques Croisé novels may be slightly different from that of her Russian prose, this is as much because it is written under a male pseudonym as it is because of the difference in languages.[26] Nor did returning to Russian after many years of writing primarily in French feel like a new departure or a break, for she had always maintained close ties to the émigré community, to Russian Orthodoxy, and to Russian culture (it may not be irrelevant to note here that her brother is Archbishop John of San Francisco).[27] And, while Schakovskoy may paradoxically have been helped by being an autodidact in both languages and by the fact that she had, from the start, written in both, certainly at least as important as either of these factors was the strong sense of psychic legitimacy that protected her despite linguistic shifts, just as a similar sense protected

Nabokov. She was, and always would be, Princess Schakovskoy, a descendant of Rurik. Furthermore, she had a strong religious faith. Despite her disrupted childhood and separated family, or perhaps because of it, she had developed an intransigent honesty, a firm will, and a sense of self capable of resisting *toute épreuve*, including change of language. While Triolet agonized over being a linguistic bigamist, Schakovskoy does not worry about the illegitimacy of writing in two languages, and she has cheerfully declared that neither language is her legal husband: both are lovers.[28]

Marina Tsvetaeva

> Nor shall I crave my native speech,
> its milky call that comes in handy.
> It makes no difference in which
> tongue passers by won't comprehend me.
> —Marina Tsvetaeva
> (trans. Joseph Brodsky)

> [Ne obol'shchus' i iazykom
> Rodnym, ego prizyvom mlechnym
> Mne bezrazlichno—na kakom
> Neponimaemoi byt' vstrechnym!]

While Schakovskoy and Nabokov, being married to Russians, felt less guilty about writing in French or English than did those members of the "first" emigration whose legitimate spouses were French or English, one should hasten to say that, as in other areas having to do with bilingualism, one can easily find exceptions to what might for a moment seem to be an emerging pattern. In this, as in so many other matters, Marina Tsvetaeva was an anomaly. Despite her many physical and spiritual extramarital relationships, she was also irrevocably committed to her husband, Sergei Efron, and in her case this unbreakable bond was a major factor in discouraging Tsvetaeva from committing herself to writing French prose.[29]

Marina Ivanovna Tsvetaeva (1892–1941), one of the greatest, most unsettling, and tragic of Russia's modern poets, was technically capable of writing in both French and German as well as in

Russian. Furthermore, she did not conceive of poetry in narrowly nationalistic terms. In 1926, she wrote in German to Rainer Maria Rilke:

Goethe says somewhere that one can never achieve anything of significance in a foreign language—and that has always rung false to me.... Writing poetry is in itself translating from the mother tongue into another. Whether French or German should make no difference. No language is the mother tongue. To write poems is already to write "after" something. That's why I am puzzled when people talk of French or Russian poets. A poet may write in French; he cannot be a French poet. That's ludicrous. I am not a Russian poet and am always astonished to be taken for one and looked upon in this light. One becomes a poet ... to be not Russian or French, but in order to be *everything*.[30]

[Goethe sagt irgendwo, dass man nichts Bedeutendes in einer fremden Sprache leisten kann—und das klang mir immer falsch.... Dichten ist schon übertragen, aus der Muttersprache—in eine andere, ob französisch oder deutsch, wird wohl gleich sein. Keine Sprache ist Muttersprache. Dichten ist nachdichten. Darum versteh ich nicht, wenn man von französischen oder russischen etc. Dichtern redet. Ein Dichter kann französisch schreiben, er kann nicht ein französischer Dichter sein. Das ist lächerlich. Ich bin kein russischer Dichter und staune immer, wenn man mich für einen solchen hält und als solchen betrachtet. Darum wird man Dichter ... um nicht Franzose, Russe etc. zu sein, um alles zu sein.]

Tsvetaeva is therefore a particularly interesting case: a poet who could have become a real bilingual—perhaps even a *trilingual*—writer, but who ultimately rejected bilingual practice although she did not believe that poetry was "national." As we shall see, Tsvetaeva's resistance to writing in French was ferocious and emotional, and her refusal to write poetry in German was more spiritual than linguistic.

Tsvetaeva came from a much more modest background than Schakovskoy and Nabokov. Her father was a provincial priest's son who eventually became professor of Roman literature and art history at Moscow University and founded the Aleksander III Museum of Fine Arts. Her mother, Ivan Tsvetaev's second wife, was the half-

Polish (aristocratic) daughter of a wealthy Baltic German business-man and publisher.[31] Mariia Aleksandrovna was an accomplished musician who read French and German literature to her children. Her father, Aleksander Mein, recited German poetry to them. Tsve-taeva herself began to write Russian verse at the age of six (a pen-chant mocked and discouraged by her mother, who was determined to make her daughter into a musician).[32] As a child and adolescent, Tsvetaeva also wrote some poems in German, as well as a few in French (her first graded prose composition in French, at age eleven, received the judgment "trop d'imagination, trop peu de logique" [too much imagination and too little logic]).[33] In childhood, then, Tsvetaeva had learned both German and French not only from her mother and grandfather and from the usual parade of Baltic Ger-man and French governesses, but also in the Swiss and German boarding schools abroad that she and her sister attended while their mother was undergoing treatment for tuberculosis. For a short while after her mother's death, Marina even took over the French and German correspondence for her father's museum.[34] Although she always felt a particularly close emotional link to the German language, it was to France that Tsvetaeva went alone the summer when she was sixteen—to study (with a Mademoiselle James), to see her idol Sarah Bernhardt (who was not there), and to pay hom-age to her other idol, Napoleon (who was). She even took lodgings on the rue Bonaparte.[35]

Tsvetaeva married Sergei Efron when she was nineteen and he was eighteen. Subsequently, after the war and the hardships of the Revolution and civil war, she and their surviving daughter, Ariadna,[36] left Russia to rejoin Efron (who had fought with the Whites) in Czechoslovakia, where he had obtained a student schol-arship. In Czechoslovakia, they lived in straitened circumstances and on an emotional roller coaster. It was in Czechoslovakia that their son Georgii (soon known to all as "Mur") was born.[37] The last years of Tsvetaeva's life abroad (1926–1939) were spent in France, mostly in dire poverty.[38] While living in Paris and its sub-urbs, writing poetry and then prose primarily in Russian, Tsve-taeva also did some writing in French. As one might have expected, her first major effort in French was precipitated by self-translation. In 1929, while Tsvetaeva was writing a study on Nataliia Gon-charova, the painter did a series of illustrations for Tsvetaeva's long poem "Molodets" [The swain] and wanted to publish them together with a French translation of the poem. Tsvetaeva, dissatisfied with the self-translation of "Molodets" which she undertook for this purpose, then wrote, directly in French, "Le gars," a poem loosely based on the original text.[39] Her public reading of this, her first (and last) mature poem in French was, however, a fiasco, and the French version was never published.[40] Tsvetaeva's next effort in French, *Les nuits florentines* [Florentine nights], "an epistolary meditation on the love of a strong woman for a weak man," was a reworking of some letters she had written many years earlier to Abram Vishniak.[41] *Les nuits florentines* was sent to several journals in 1933, but none accepted it.

In December 1932, Tsvetaeva wrote "Lettre à l'Amazone" [Letter to the Amazon], a response in French to Natalie Clifford Barney's 1920 pro-lesbian tract *Pensées d'une Amazone* [An Amazon's thoughts].[42] While Tsvetaeva herself had several serious emotional involvements with women and had always been attracted to the image of the Amazon,[43] her essay puts forward a view of lesbian love that is essentially hopeless and very different from Barney's.

In 1936, when Tsvetaeva was deeply involved in a series of autobiographical prose pieces, she decided to write some of them in French, in the hopes of placing them in French-language publications. "Sharlottenburg" [Charlottenburg], "Mundyr" [The uniform], and "Lavrovyi venok" [The laurel wreath] were all written in French.[44] Although economic motives explain Tsvetaeva's decision to try writing in French once more, they do not explain why these *particular* sketches were chosen for what Tsvetaeva clearly considered a dubious honor. The answer may be that, while Tsvetaeva wrote about her relations with her mother only in Russian, these texts are about the period after her mother's death and concern Tsvetaeva's relations with her father and sister. The impetus to write in French *precisely these sketches*, about her father and the preparations for the opening of his museum, may have been furnished by the plaster bust of an Amazon which plays a major role in "Charlottenburg," thus providing a thematic link with Tsvetaeva's previous work in French, the "Lettre à l'Amazone."[45]

Tsvetaeva's work in French was almost completely ignored by the Paris literary world, and both for this reason and for the more important spiritual and emotional ones that I shall consider shortly, it is unlikely that Tsvetaeva would have ever really committed herself to writing in French. The question became moot, in any event, when Sergei Efron, who had gradually become not merely pro-Soviet but even a Soviet agent, was implicated in the assassination of a KGB official who had defected from the Soviet Union.[46] Efron fled to the USSR (their daughter Ariadna had already returned in March 1937). Ultimately, and with many misgivings, Tsvetaeva yielded to her son's urgings and to her own sense of her unbreakable tie to Efron, and she herself returned to the Soviet Union in 1939.[47] There, as might have been expected, her husband was arrested and shot, and her daughter arrested and imprisoned. Unable to find work, Tsvetaeva hanged herself on August 31, 1941, in the small town of Elabuga, to which she and Mur had been evacuated.

Tsvetaeva's relation to life and art was above all passionate. She was a great defender of lost causes,[48] and her *engouements* for men, women, and a few select poets, notably Pasternak and Rilke, were of such force as frequently to frighten off their objects. Her relationships with her languages were also passionate. For while Tsvetaeva felt that there is no such thing as a "Russian" or a "French" poet, and that one becomes a poet to be *everything*, this does not mean that it was a matter of indifference to her in which language she wrote, especially because she believed that, for each poet, one language, independent of nationality, is spiritually *closer* than any other.[49] Tsvetaeva referred to this closeness as being *rodnei*, or "more native," and although she was to claim that "Angelic" was most native to her, she also said that, among earthly languages, German was certainly "more native" than French and even "more native" than Russian.[50]

If Russian was not the language "most native" to Tsvetaeva, why did she not abandon it for another? At least part of the answer may be that, although Russian was not Tsvetaeva's mother tongue in the spiritual sense of being most "native" to her, yet it was the language in which she wrote about her mother and, more important, the language *in which she was a mother;* and, of all Tsvetaeva's passions, none was stronger than the maternal one.[51] As Karlinsky has remarked, the maternal instinct, which in Tsvetaeva's case extended to her husband as well as to her children, "imprisoned this rebellious poet more securely and guided the tragic turns of her fate more imperiously than any government or revolution ever could."[52]

Together, Russian and motherhood had claims on her that out-weighed all others.

Tsvetaeva's obsessive maternal love was strongest of all for her son,[53] and the interdependence of her love for Mur with the Russian language is already visible in the letters Tsvetaeva wrote to Ol'ga Eliseevna Chernova-Kolbasina three months after his birth: "I don't want to hear Czech on his lips. Let him be completely Russian, to prove to all those snivelers that what counts is not *where* one is born but *to whom*"[54] [I ne khochu na ego ustakh cheshskogo, pust' budet russkim—v polne. Chtoby dokazat' vsem etim khnykal'shchikam, chto delo ne *gde* rodit'sia a *kem*]. Three weeks later, Tsvetaeva wrote to Ol'ga Eliseevna that when alone with Mur, she tells him:

> "You're an émigré Mur, the son of an émigré, that's what your passport will say. Yours will be a wolf's passport [i.e., a passport marked "unreliable"], but it's a fine thing to be a wolf, better than being a sheep. Your patron saint had a wolf, too. And, my dear, that wolf is now in Paradise, for there is a Paradise for wolves too." I tell him other things about Russia, about how Russia is within us, and not somewhere out there, or on a map, it's in us and in our songs and in our coloring, in the slant of our eyes and in our all-forgiving heart, that through me and the songs I have started him off with he will be more Russian than X or Y will ever be, even though they may have been born in "white-stoned Moscow."[55]

> [Ty—emigrant, Mur, syn emigranta, tak budet v pasporte. A passport u tebia budet volchii. No volk—khorosho, luchshe, chem ovtsa, u tvoego sviatogo tozhe byl volk—liubimyi, etot volk teper' v raiu. Potomu chto est' i volchii rai—... I eshchë o Rossii, o tom, chto Rossiia—v nas, a ne tam-to ili tam-to na karte, v nas i v pesniakh, i v nashei rusoi raskraske, v raskososti glaz i vo vseproshchenii sertsa, chto on—cherez menia i moe pesennoe nachalo—takoi russkii Mur, kakim nikogda ne byt' X ili Y, rozhdennomu v "Belokamenoi"].

In 1932, by now a longtime resident of France, Tsvetaeva wrote a brief, virulently anti-French, three-poem cycle, "Stikhi k sinu" [Verses to my son].[56] The third of these poems, with its exhortation *Ne byt' tebe frantsuzom* [Do not become French] demands (and declares) that Mur must not join the young émigré generation which was becoming more French than Russian. While Tsvetaeva knows that there is no place for her in Russia, and that Mur's return there would distance him from her in every respect, yet it is her maternal duty to keep Mur Russian, even if this means encouraging him to leave her in order to return to his country, to his century, to "Mother Russia"⁵⁷ [Ezzhai, moi syn, v svoiu stranu / . . . Ezzhai, moi syn, domoi, . . . / v svoi krai, v svoi vek, v svoi chas—ot nas / V Rossiiu].

Almost simultaneously with "Stikhi k sinu," Tsvetaeva was writing, in French, her rebuttal to Natalie Clifford Barney's *Pensées d'une Amazone.* Tsvetaeva's argument in "Lettre à l'Amazone" rests on the overriding instinctual claims of motherhood. Her basic point is that, no matter how close and passionate a lesbian relationship may be, it will eventually be destroyed by the powerful desire of one partner (usually the younger one) to have a child: "It is the only weak point, the only point vulnerable to attack, the only breach in the perfect wholeness of two women who love each other. It is possible to resist the temptation of men, but it is impossible to resist the need for a child" [C'est le seul point faillible, le seul point attaquable, la seule brèche dans cette entité parfaite que sont deux femmes qui s'aiment. L'impossible, ce n'est pas de résister à la tentation de l'homme, mais au besoin de l'enfant].⁵⁸ Because it is impossible to have a child by her beloved, the woman will make do with some man, and thereafter it is the child who will be the focus of the mother's love.⁵⁹

The fact that Tsvetaeva wrote poems (in Russian) urging her son to remain Russian at the same time that she wrote (in French) a regretful but firm repudiation of lesbian relationships in the name of *motherhood,* helps us to understand Tsvetaeva's attitude toward things French and writing in French. In this period of hesitation over whether to make a real psychic commitment to writing in French, it would seem that Tsvetaeva made her decision by symbolically defining herself not as a wife, or a lover, but in terms of the most instinctive and irrevocable of blood relationships: that of a mother to her child. And because, as Jane Taubman has rightly noted in her comments on "Stikhi k sinu,"⁶⁰ Tsvetaeva's exhortation to her son not to become French appears to be addressed as much to herself as to Mur—despite her stormy and widely ranging affective life—Tsvetaeva turns out to be the *only* bilingual Russian writer we have considered who formulated her (his) relationship to

her (his) languages not in metaphors of bigamy, legitimate husbands (wives) or lovers, marriage or adultery (or even fraternal—
sororial or step-paternal—filial incest), but rather in the old-
fashioned terms of *Muttersprache* and motherhood. Ultimately, it is
in the name of *her* motherhood that Tsvetaeva, despite her earliest
verses, cleaved to the "milky call of Russian" and abandoned not
only working in French, but France altogether.[61]

> . . . The Gods learned early to
> pretend to create halves. But inscribed in the orbit, we
> filled out to become whole, like the disk of the moon.
>
> [. . . Frühe erlernten die Götter
> hälften zu heucheln. Wir, in das Kresen bezogen,
> füllten zum Ganzen uns an, wie die Scheibe des Monds.]
> —Rainer Maria Rilke, "Elegie für Marina"
> [Elegy for Marina Tsvetaeva]

If Tsvetaeva's maternal commitment to Russian and her lack of
emotional bonds with the French language made her reluctant to
commit herself to French, her relations with German were far more
complex, and far more positive. As Karlinsky has noted, German
and German literature were an integral part of Tsvetaeva's cultural
heritage, a constant feature of her education from earliest
childhood.[62] German was more *native* to her than Russian because
she felt that only German could accurately express her characteristic
spiritual traits: *Übermass* ("a condition of excess or extravagance")
and *Schwärmerei* ("a state of being either ecstatic or gushing").[63] It
was, wrote Tsvetaeva, her "German component" that forced her to
"take everything so seriously" and to submit to the "all-too-real
puddle of soapy dishwater" in which she felt she had been drown-
ing during the years of her emigration.[64] Another "German" aspect
of her character, her *Furchtlosigkeit*, or "fearlessness," would, she
said, stand in the way of her ever melting quietly into Soviet life.[65]
The pro-German poems that she had written and read publicly during the First World War, and her article "On Germany" also attested to her long-standing attachment to Germany, as did her use
of German themes in several of her longer works.[66] Why, then, did
Tsvetaeva never write poetry or "artistic prose" in German? The
answer may lie in the most significant manifestation of Tsvetaeva's

involvement with German and German culture: her relationship with the poet Rainer Maria Rilke.

Rilke's linguistic and cultural configuration was in many ways a mirror image of Tsvetaeva's. For him, it was *Russia* that "made me what I am. I emerge internally from there! . . . the whole homeland of my instinct. All my inner resources are there"[67] [Alle Heimat meines Instinkts, all mein innerer Ursprung ist dort! . . . die Grundlage meines Erlebens und Empfangens]. Russia was the "homeland of Rilke's instinct" despite (or because of) the fact that his actual experience of Russia was quite early and rather limited. The identification was essentially emotional, and filtered through temporal and spatial distance. Rilke's passionate attachment to Russia as corresponding to something essential in him is therefore similar to Tsvetaeva's sense of the "nativeness" of German and German culture to her.

Rilke was also perfectly fluent in French. His last book of poems, *Vergers* [Orchards], was in French, as were various other works written after 1922[68] and as was the little dedicatory poem he wrote to Tsvetaeva in the copy of *Vergers* he sent her. Thus it would at first seem that Tsvetaeva's passionate worship of Rilke should have encouraged her to emulate him and to write in either French or German, or (perhaps) in both. But, as was frequently the case with Tsvetaeva, the empirically obvious choice was not the one she made.

Tsvetaeva's epistolary relationship with Rilke was part of a triangular pattern of letters also involving Boris Pasternak, upon whose insistence Rilke had initiated the correspondence with Tsvetaeva.[69] Although Rilke was deeply attached to Russian and to Russia and could read Russian, by 1926 he could no longer write Russian easily. He therefore sent his first letter to Tsvetaeva in German,[70] mentioning that French was as familiar to him as German, in case she herself wrote more easily in French and would prefer to answer him in that language. Tsvetaeva replied with a dithyrambic burst of German, characteristically choosing the solution of difficulty and spiritual authenticity, in homage to the language in which Rilke had written the works she knew and admired. In her second letter to Rilke, she inquired: "I wonder if you can understand me, given my bad German. I write French more fluently; that's why I don't want to write to you in French. From me to you, nothing should flow. Fly, yes! And failing that, better to trip and stumble." [Ob Du mich wohl in meinem schlechten Deutsch verstehst? Französisch schreib ich fliessender, darum will ich Dir nicht Französisch schreiben. Von mir zu Dir darf nichts fliessen. Fliegen—ja! Und wenn nicht—lieber stocken und stolpern.][71] In fact, her German is very interesting, full of plays on words of the folk-etymological type to which bilinguals are particularly given, and of the purely phonetic type, to which Tsvetaeva was attracted in any language.[72] Rilke replied:

> No, your German doesn't "stumble." It just takes heavier steps now and then, like the steps of someone who is going down a stone staircase with stairs of unequal height and cannot estimate as he comes down when his foot is going to come to rest, right now, or suddenly further down than he thought. What strength there is in you, poet, to achieve your intent even in this language, and be accurate and be yourself. *Your* gait ringing on the steps, your tone, *you!* Your lightness; your controlled, bestowed weight.

> [Dein Deutsch, nein, "stolpern" tut es nicht, es fällt ab und zu schwerer auf, wie die Schritte von einem, der eine Steintreppe von ungleich tiefen Stufen abwärts kommt und nicht ermessen kann, im Herabsteigen, wann sein Fuss ins Aufruhn gerät, jetzt schon oder plötzlich erst weiter unten als er dachte. Welche Stärke Du hast, Dichterin, auch in dieser Sprache Deine Absicht zu erreichen, genau zu sein und Du. *Dein* Gang, der an die Stufen anklingt, Dein Ton, *Du.* Dein Leichtsein, Dein beherrschtes, geschenktes Gewicht.][73]

If Rilke is right, and how could he not be in a judgment of German prose, Tsvetaeva's voice *passed* into German. So there was no purely linguistic obstacle to Tsvetaeva's writing not only letters but also other prose texts and even, perhaps, poetry in German.

Tsvetaeva frequently wrote poems or poem cycles *in memoriam,* and the death of Rilke, on December 30, 1926, while Tsvetaeva was deeply involved in her extremely passionate (if entirely epistolary and poetic) relationship with him would have seemed to provide the perfect occasion for her to write a poem for him in German. Instead, she wrote one last letter in German, the language of their correspondence, and then developed the letter into a Russian poem, "Novogodnee" [New Year's greeting], which she completed on February 7, 1927.

Tsvetaeva's reaction to Rilke's *Vergers* and her own "Novogodnee" addressed to him are the keys to her linguistic fate, insofar as it was to be determined by her own choice rather than by force of circumstance. For, to Tsvetaeva, Rilke's bilingual accomplishment in *Vergers* was a sign both of his incomparably high status among earthly poets and of something still higher—and at the same time suspect.[74] In the letter she wrote to Pasternak on January 1, 1927, two days after Rilke's death, Tsvetaeva told him:

> He [Rilke] was weary of his mother tongue: "Tired of you, my foes, of you my friends, and of the pliancy of Russian speech . . . (1916)" [Tsvetaeva is quoting her *own* very early lines here, thus comparing Rilke's attitude to German with her own previous comments about Russian—E.K.B.]. He was weary of his omnipotence, he wanted to learn all over again, so he seized upon the language least congenial to a poet—French *(poésie)*—and, once again he could do it, was doing it, was suddenly weary again. It turned out not to be a matter of German but of human. What he took to be a longing for French was a longing for the language of angels, the language of the other world. In *Vergers* he gave himself away by speaking in the language of angels. See, he is an angel. I constantly feel his presence always at my *right* shoulder (which is not my side).

> [On ustal ot iazyka svoego rozhdeniia. (Ustav ot vas, vragi, ot vas, druz'ia, i ot ustupchivosti rechi russkoi . . . 1916). On ustal ot vsevozmozhnosti, zakhotel uchenichestva, skhvatilsia za neblagodarneishii dlia poeta iz iazykov—frantsuzkij ("poésie")—opiat' smog, eshche raz smog, srazu ustal. Delo okazalos' ne v nemetskom, a v chelovecheskom. Zhazhda frantsuzskogo okazalas' zhazhdoi angel'skogo, tusvetnogo. Knizhkoi *Vergers* on progovorilsia na angel'skom iazyke. Vidish', on angel, neizmenno chuvstvuiu ego za *pravym* plechom (ne moia storona).][75]

Tsvetaeva seems to disapprove of Rilke's attempt to transcend his earthly linguistic mastery of German through choosing to write also in the "least congenial" language for a poet, French, thereby approximating "Angelic." She seems to feel that, on earth, the poet must accept the bonds of earth: Angelic is for the other world.[76] In "Novogodnee," as Joseph Brodsky has noted, Tsvetaeva sees death and the next world not as an extra-linguistic experience, but as one where the soul is "all-tongued" [ne bez—a vse iazychen].[77] Thus, in "Novogodnee" Tsvetaeva can justify herself to Rilke for writing her poem to him in Russian rather than in German by her belief that, because Rilke is immortal, Russian is now completely accessible to him. She, however, is still earthbound, considerably lower on the scale of incarnate poetry of which she considers Rilke to have been the pinnacle.[78] Nevertheless, Tsvetaeva does allow herself two German words in "Novogodnee": *du Lieber*. This German *du Lieber* is Tsvetaeva's modest equivalent of Rilke's final work in French—a momentary earthly approximation of "Angelic."[79] She allows it to herself once, to call on Rilke—"a winged touch" (their metaphor for their entire earthly correspondence)—but otherwise does not permit herself to use German in poetry as a way to "Angelic."[80]

Thus, Tsvetaeva refuses the one moment when she might have begun to write poetry in German. She refuses it both because Rilke can now read her without hindrance in Russian and because she is convinced that "Angelic" is for the next world—even for Rilke, the absolutely greatest of poets, who through his artistry was closest to it.[81] Furthermore, Rilke had written to her that, of all *earthly* languages, Russian came closest to being the *totalizing* one to which Tsvetaeva aspired, and which Rilke recognized as being the ultimate language: "[Seen] in that light in which all languages are a *single* language (and this one, yours, Russian, is so close to being *all* of them anyway!)" [. . . in *das* Licht halte, in dem alle Sprachen *eine* Sprache sind (und diese, Deine, die russische, ist ohnehin so nah, *alle* zu sein!)].[82] So, in obedience to Rilke, into whose hands she committed herself and her poetry in the last lines of "Novogodnee," in response to Rilke's sense of the high status of Russian (in which he can now read Tsvetaeva) relative to the highest of all languages, Angelic (which is now legitimately his), Tsvetaeva wrote poetry, even to him, in Russian. And although she subsequently did try to break into the Parisian literary world on several occasions, she did not consider that she had come anywhere near scaling the poetic heights achieved by Rilke in his work, and she therefore had not the right to attempt an earthly version of Angelic. She therefore cast her poetic lot irrevocably with Russian, the language in which she was herself a mother. Thus, both her most elemental instinct and her highest spiritual one joined forces to keep Tsvetaeva tied to Russian, to the heights of which, as she herself put it in another context, she "shrieked herself" [dokrikivalas'].[83]

Boris Poplavskii

> I remember the lacquered wings of the crew,
> The silence and falsehood. Fly, sunset, fly.
>
> . . . .
>
> But the captain concealed from the crew
> the extent of the distance traveled.
>
> [Ia pomniu lakovye kryl'ia ekipazha,
> Molchanie i lozh'. Leti, zakat, leti.
>
> . . . .
>
> No kapitan skryval ot ekipazha
> Velichinu proidennogo puti.]
> —Boris Poplavskii, "Orly" [Eagles]

It is illuminating to compare briefly Marina Tsvetaeva's essentially nonlinguistic rejection of French with the choice of another Russian poet of the first emigration who seemed predestined by all objective factors (age, linguistic training, and literary tastes) to become a French writer, but who instead insisted on writing only in Russian. Boris Poplavskii (1903–1935) might have been a major, if not great, French writer in the Surrealist vein. Anthony Olcott has declared that Poplavskii was at least half-French: having left Russia in 1919, when he was sixteen, Poplavskii died in Paris at the age of thirty-two. Thus, exactly half his life was spent in Russia and half abroad.[84] But this chronology is misleading. Linguistically, Poplavskii was much more than half French and nowhere near half Russian. He had had a German nurse and French governesses, had gone to live abroad with his mother when he was three, and had some schooling in Switzerland and Italy. According to his father, when Poplavskii and his brother returned to Russia they had forgotten Russian to such an extent that their parents enrolled them in the French *lycée* of Saint Philippe Néri, where Poplavskii remained until the Revolution.[85] After his arrival in Paris in 1921, what further education Poplavskii had was, of course, also in French. His literary tastes inclined him toward French poetry, so that Karlinsky, one of Poplavskii's strongest supporters, can quite reasonably declare: "I did not know then, as I know now, that Boris Poplavsky was in a sense a very fine French poet who belongs to Russian literature mainly because he wrote in Russian."[86]

But why *did* he write in Russian? Aside from the elements mentioned above, all of which would have seemed to incline him to write in French, there are still other factors that should have encouraged Poplavskii to write in French rather than in Russian. His control of Russian appeared to many to be sometimes shaky, and there was really nothing specifically Russian in the content of Poplavskii's poems and prose that might have demanded or justified their being written in Russian, rather than in French.[87] In fact, although they are written in Russian, his poems frequently have French titles.[88]

That Poplavskii wrote in Russian was the result of a quite deliberately paradoxical choice: how better to be a *poète maudit* (and be one up on Rimbaud) than to write in the *wrong language!* This choice also continued the linguistic anomalies of Poplavskii's earlier life. For as Vladimir Padunov has rightly noted, Poplavskii's life in Russia took place in French, whereas his intellectual and artistic life in France took place in Russian.[89] The resultant tension is attested to by those passages in Poplavskii's diaries where identical entries are made first in Russian, then in French.[90] Such parallelism is unusual in bilingual diaries, where one typically finds macaronic passages or switching from one language to another but not the same entries in both languages. Diaries are essentially a form of conversation with oneself. If the self can speak to itself in one language or the other, then why use both? Does this mean that the self cannot adequately speak to itself in either? Or that there *is* no integral self? (Poplavskii was not above trading on the latter possibility. Schakovskoy records a letter to a girl in which Poplavskii had written, "come to me, we must see each other; I have a split personality"[91] [Prikhodi, nado uvidet'sia, u menia razdvoen'e lichnosti]. Because Poplavskii declared that "the private letter, the diary, and the transcript of a psychoanalysis are the best methods of expression [of the spiritual life],"[92] perhaps one could simply see these parallel entries as exercises in self-translation, with an eye to eventual publication for one (or both) of his potential linguistic audiences. But, insofar as a diary is ostensibly private to start with, there is a paradox of intention here too, which Poplavskii's early death left unresolved, as it did his ultimate linguistic destiny.

One factor that had surely influenced Poplavskii to choose the apparently least appropriate language is what might be labeled the *lycée français* syndrome, whose symptoms are seen in adolescents who have been molded into caricatural little Frenchmen: they have French intellectual tastes but cannot fully identify themselves as French emotionally; at the same time, they have lost or have never developed any mental and linguistic fluency in their native cultures. However idiosyncratic Poplavskii's fate was in some respects, one should not forget that he was also in many ways a quite typical, almost commonplace, product of the colonial *lycée* system. Not only does this cultural schizophrenia help to explain the poverty of Poplavskii's spoken Russian (what Nina Berberova calls Poplavskii's *absence of language*),[93] it must also have exacerbated the need for social, as well as linguistic, legitimacy which Poplavskii sometimes displayed. His remark to Zinaïda Schakovskoy, whom he had just met, may be revealing: "You know, I find it very pleasant to go walking with a Schakovskoy. Our family were only merchants, so it is rather flattering. And I can even take your arm" [A znaete, mne priiatno idti s Shakhovskoi! My iz kuptsov, tak vot kak-to lestno. I pod ruchku vziat' vas mozhno].[94] (It is worth noting that while Poplavskii's father was indeed a merchant, he had also been vice-president of the Moscow Association of Manufacturers, and Poplavskii's mother's family was old aristocracy.)[95] Of course, Poplavskii's rather distasteful snobbery may have been no more genuine, though probably no less so, than many of the other postures he was constantly adopting. Schakovskoy later remarked that Poplavskii had no fixed world view, merely moods.[96] Poplavskii's life was a curious compound of drugs, various forms of spiritualism, outrageous behavior, poverty, and hard work on his poetry and prose. It is difficult to make any causal judgments,[97] but one might hazard the hypothesis that, in large part, there was no solid psychic ground beneath Poplavskii because he had no dominant language—or, rather, because he *did* have a (technically) dominant language and did not wish to recognize and capitulate to the fact that it was not Russian but French.

It is interesting that Poplavskii had attempted, whether consciously or not, to avoid the linguistic problem altogether by initially defining himself as a painter. In 1922, his father sent him to an art academy in Berlin,[98] yet apparently not only his teachers but also his fellow students felt that he had no talent. As Karlinsky notes, Poplavskii appears to have believed them and, probably in consequence of this, suffered a nervous breakdown. Poplavskii returned to Paris, where he committed himself to poetry while continuing to seek the company of painters in preference to members of the literary emigration.[99]

Poplavskii's poetry is strikingly visual; critics have commented on his eye and his imagery.[100] Karlinsky sees it as the verbal equivalent of the visual imagery he "knew and loved in the work of the exiled Russian, neo-Romantic painters Pavel Tchelitchew and Eugene Berman."[101] Gleb Struve remarked that Poplavskii's poems had been compared to Marc Chagall's paintings (these critics probably had in mind such images as the sky-blue horse of "Dolorosa"— E.K.B.).[102] Struve himself considered that Poplavskii's "Surrealistic" world was created illegitimately, but the adjective is nonetheless apt. One can see in poems such as "Roza smerti" [The rose of death] images straight out of Giorgio de Chirico and Paul Delvaux.[103]

No one is now in a position to say whether Poplavskii was indeed untalented as a painter and whether he therefore found a more valid outlet for his imagery in poetry, but perhaps Poplavskii should not have given up so easily. Had Poplavskii continued to paint, or *also* continued to paint while writing poetry, he might have found the necessary nonlinguistic ground that could have helped him to bear his linguistic homelessness and his desire to subordinate his stronger language to his weaker one. Or perhaps, as Poplavskii is obviously one of those bilingual writers who "think" primarily in images, continuing to paint might have allowed him to commit himself psychically to making a shift and writing in French with a concomitant reduction of psycholinguistic dissonance. As it was, Karlinsky observes, there was in Poplavskii a "never-resolved dichotomy between poetry and painting. . . . Much of his prose and poetry testifies to his never-ending yearning for mastery of the visual arts."[104]

Il'ia Zdanevich (Iliazd)

Combining writing and the visual arts has been a rather common and generally integrative practice among twentieth-century bilingual artists: e.g., Hans Arp and Wassily Kandinsky.[105] As we have seen, bilingual Russian writers such as Triolet have sometimes resorted to integrating the visual arts with their writing in periods when psychological, political, or practical constraints prohibited them from an easy alternation between their languages or (even more so) stood in the way of the creation of a new idiolect.

The career of Il'ia Mikhailovich Zdanevich [Iliazd] (1894–1975) integrated several languages and the visual arts in a way that enabled him to solve the problem of artistic expression without deliberately abandoning either language. His first published work, in 1913, was a commentary on Larionov and Goncharova (with whom he was closely linked), written in standard Russian under the pseudonym Eganbiury (a bilingual pun).[106] As a very young man, Zdanevich was involved in the beginnings of Futurism in Russia and himself wrote and published a series of *dras* (*zaum*, or "transrational," dramas with increasingly complex typographical layouts) already actively using visual as well as linguistic elements.[107] With its echoes of regional Russian speech and dialects, and occasionally of Georgian, Zdanevich's *zaum* is not entirely arbitrary as was Aleksei Kruchenykh's. But while it is securely based in "natural language," it is certainly not simply Russian. One would therefore either have to consider that Zdanevich's *dras* are in a new idiolect or to say that he is already a bilingual writer, the two languages he practices being Russian and *zaum*. One should also note that these two languages are already presented in a form that privileges visual over standard, and therefore quasi-invisible, typographic form.

In Paris in the 1920s, Zdanevich, now definitively become Iliazd (again, the pseudonym is a bilingual pun),[108] wrote lectures in French, which he spoke well, his father having been a teacher of French in Tiflis. But he also continued to write novels in Russian—subliminally marked by *zaum*, but now purified to the point of being easily comprehensible to any native reader of Russian. Several of these remain unpublished, notably *Parizhach'i* [The Parisians] (1923), a *tour de force* having to do with four couples who pass through all possible variants of sentimental recombination in two hours of one morning before they all meet in the Bois de Boulogne for lunch. *Posmertnye trudy* [Posthumous works] (1928), an ironic depiction of the worlds of high fashion, art, and politics in Paris during the 1920s, was finally published beginning in 1988 in numbers 168 to 169 of *Novyi Zhurnal* [New review]. Iliazd's greatest novel is *Voskhishchenie* [Rapture], which, despite a rave review from D. S. Mirsky, was more or less ignored when it was published in Paris in 1930.[109] *Voskhishchenie,* a mountain novel, draws on Zdanevich's Georgian roots; it combines sociological accuracy, mythic imagination, and a primitivism subsumed and transformed by modernist techniques. *Voskhishchenie* stands out almost as a lone peak among Soviet and émigré Russian prose of the late 1920s. There were also Russian poems, almost classical in form and language: a cycle of seventy-six sonnets, *Afat,* illustrated with six engravings by Picasso;[110] a fifteen-sonnet *couronne* (a very difficult form in which each of the first fourteen sonnets begins with the last line of the preceding one, the fifteenth sonnet being made up of the last lines of the other fourteen), which took ten years to perfect and which he published as *Prigovor bezmolvnyi* [Sentences without words] (1961) with a cover design by Georges Braque and a frontispiece by Alberto Giacometti. There was also "Brigadnyi" [The member of the brigade], a narrative poem about the Spanish Civil War in twenty complexly rhymed, ten-line stanzas.[111]

By the end of the 1920s, Zdanevich, who did not belong to any of the factions of the fragmented "first" Paris emigration, felt isolated and without a Russian audience. The lack of attention to *Voskhishchenie* was a particularly severe blow. Still, he did not simply abandon Russian for French. At first, largely for economic reasons, he turned instead toward the visual arts, designing textiles for Chanel and other *couturières.* He then began to create splendid, but totally unprofitable, *livres d'art.* These books differ from most "luxury editions" because of the nature of the texts that Iliazd chose or wrote for them and because of the craftsmanship of the design, evident on every page, in every letter, indeed in the space between the letters. Adopting the most banal typeface in the standard French repertoire (Gill *baton demi-gras,* often 12-point, always in capitals), Iliazd completely altered the character of the type by varying the space between the letters in accordance with a carefully worked-out theory that took account of their individual forms. Iliazd called this process a *mise en lumière,* a "bringing to light" or "en-lightening," and the books that result from this artisanal passion for detail are exceptional in the way the text and the typography and images interact.[112]

For the latter part of his career, designing the interplay of the visual and the verbal became Iliazd's *primary* means of expression.

This allowed him to continue to balance, with a minimum of psychic strain, his own writing: critical and architectural studies in both French and in Russian; translations from various languages into French; studies on the relationship of the Georgian and Arabic alphabets; some French poems and some Russian ones; parts of novels in both French and Russian;[113] and, perhaps most interesting of all in our context, a final book that encompassed almost all Iliazd's artistic interests. This is *Boustrophédon au miroir* [The mirror of Boustrophedon], produced in 1972, just three years before his death.[114] *Boustrophédon* is an elegiac musing on Iliazd's past, on painters he had known (his brother Kiril Zdanevich; Niko Pirosmanashvili [Pirosmani], the Georgian primitive whom he and his brother had discovered; and Mikhail Ledentu) and on the authors of the texts he had "brought to light." *Boustrophédon* is written in French, but each line of the French verse is then repeated backward, with the word boundaries placed differently to produce a striking, clever, and touching French *zaum*.

Zdanevich-Iliazd's trajectory is marked not only by his bilingual writing and his activity in the field of visual arts, but also by the range of his other intellectual concerns—in particular, his efforts to resurrect the memory and reputation of the astronomer Ernst Guillaume Tempel and of certain forgotten explorers, as well as his own studies of exploration routes and architecture.[115] This breadth of interests would appear to be characteristic of many bilingual writers, and nowhere is this more striking than in the career of Vasily Yanovsky.

Vasily Yanovsky (Vasilii Semënovich Ianovskii)

Vasily Yanovsky's preoccupations span the spectrum from some of the most sordid areas of medicine (he was a physician whose activities ranged from anesthesiology to a stint in a New York venereal disease clinic) to philosophical and religious speculation. Because his primary purpose, especially in his later years, has been to address certain essentially spiritual experiences or to convey the texture of human relationships that occurred in a nonliterary professional context, Yanovsky somewhat belatedly became a bilingual writer in a language he acquired as an adult and in which he had no formal linguistic training.[116] The range of his concerns demanded, and psychically facilitated, a transformation that was not encouraged by a preexistent technical mastery of the second language (as had been the case for Nabokov). On the contrary, becoming a bilingual writer required Yanovsky to accept linguistic constraints far more severe than those of the "plaster corset" about which Triolet complained.[117] For Yanovsky, the use of English was not "bigamy" or "adultery," but essentially a marriage of convenience.

Vasily Yanovsky was born in 1906, the son of a civil servant in Poltava. His mother died when he was ten or eleven, and war, revolution, and civil war completed the disintegration of the family. For some time, the almost starving adolescent Yanovsky lived alone in an abandoned house, reading enormously: the Russian classics, as well as the *Confessions* of Rousseau, Guy de Maupassant, Edgar Allan Poe, and Jack London in translation. Tolstoi was of particular importance to him at this time, especially the postcrisis writings.[118]

Yanovsky's apprenticeship as a writer began with poetry at the age of thirteen or fourteen. Soon thereafter, he started a journal that served to prepare him for his first novel, *Koleso* [The wheel], which deals with the lives and relationships of unsupervised children like himself in the postrevolutionary period. *Koleso* was completed when Yanovsky was eighteen or nineteen, but publication did not come until some years after Yanovsky had settled in Paris.

Despite the disruptions of his adolescence, Yanovsky was able for a while to attend what passed for a *gymnasium* in those years. He was not a particularly assiduous student, however, and left Russia, his education incomplete, at sixteen. Like Poplavskii, whose schooling had been in French, and like a number of other younger writers whose education and family life had been disrupted by the chaotic events of history, Yanovsky belonged to a second generation of émigré writers who carried with them into exile only a haphazard linguistic baggage. Their frequently unconventional use of syntax and grammar—sometimes deliberate, at other times inadvertent—shocked and saddened the elder generation of Russian émigré writers, many of whom were old-fashioned in their literary tastes, and all of whom were genuinely concerned to preserve and protect the purity of the Russian language, which was all they had brought with them into exile.[119] Some of these writers were in fact only a few years older than the "younger generation," but they had been born in time to complete their linguistic and cultural formation before the Revolution.

During his Paris years, Yanovsky led what would at first seem to be a double, if not a triple, life. On the one hand, there was medical school and, subsequently, the actual practice of medicine; on the other, there was the life of the literary and philosophical circles of the Russian diaspora which Yanovsky has chronicled in his memoir *Polia Eliseiskie* [Elysian Fields].[120] Even within the latter context, however, Yanovsky seemed to some to incarnate diametrically opposed attitudes: he was something of a brawler, but he was also concerned with more spiritual questions.[121] Gleb Struve, in his *Russkaia literatura v izgnanii* [Russian literature in exile], sees in Yanovsky's work both a "crude naturalism" [grubyi naturalizm], which he attributes to Yanovsky's age and to "the times," and "elevated themes" [vysokie temy].[122]

Yanovsky himself does not consider that his dual involvement with medicine and literature has caused him to have a *mi-destin:* he does not assent to Chekhov's assertion that medicine was his lawful wife and literature his mistress.[123] Nor does Yanovsky see medicine and religion as being ultimately antagonistic. In fact, he has had not a *bi-destin* but a *tri-destin,* and his activities in all three domains— science and medicine, philosophy and spirituality, and the writing in two languages in which these activities are artistically embodied—have been complementary and interdependent.[124] His trajectory as a bilingual writer was determined primarily by his activity as a doctor. Unlike the majority of Russian writers in exile, who functioned in a relatively circumscribed linguistic and cultural milieu, the physician Yanovsky was obliged to live and work first in French and then in English. His clinical practice involved him daily, and in an immediate way, with a wide variety of people, and his relations with them were conducted in languages other than Russian. This is particularly true of Yanovsky's situation in the United States, despite the fact that he arrived here in 1942 with no active command of English.[125]

By the late 1940s and early 1950s, there was a dwindling audience for literature in Russian everywhere outside the Soviet Union. Nothing comparable to the critical mass of Russian émigrés in Paris in the 1920s and 1930s existed in the United States (even though

Yanovsky, Hélène Iswolsky, and a few others did establish *The Third Hour,* a magazine of ecumenical, philosophical, and religious character, in a brave effort to continue the spiritual activities of that earlier period).[126] Thus, Yanovsky was pushed toward writing in a second language when the context of his professional life made it the logical solution, even though the other language was far from being as fully developed as his Russian. It was, therefore, essentially an instrumental choice, rather than an inherent attraction to English or even "the desire to please a shadow."[127] This is not to say that the language Yanovsky used was unimportant to him; rather, his language was determined largely by the context of what he had to say.

This pattern had already begun to emerge in France, where he was preparing to write a novel in French, just before World War II. Looking back on this project, decades later, Yanovsky recalls that he already had the last line of the novel in his head: "Ça sent mauvais, les pieds d'un soldat" [Soldiers' feet stink]. As Raymond Federman and other bilingual writers have observed, the language in which a work is written is very often determined by a sentence that the writer "hears," either in reality or in his head. And one can speculate that, had Yanovsky's book come to fruition, it would have in large part been owing to this one French sentence that he still remembers. At any event, with his departure for the United States, Yanovsky's project for the French novel lapsed. Yanovsky describes the loss of his novel as a very late abortion, coming at a time when he had already decided on the name of the future child. One recalls Nabokov's comment that he feared *Solus Rex,* the novel *he* had been "carrying" when he emigrated to America, might "soon start to ooze from some part of my body if I go on keeping it inside."[128]

Yanovsky did not become a bilingual writer in English until he had spent a quarter of a century in America, although he realized after only a few years the absurdity of retransposing his *expérience vécue* back into Russian. This tension was already palpable in the aptly named *Amerikanskii opyt* [The American experience], which was serialized in the New York–based *Novyi Zhurnal* in 1944–1947. Yanovsky's first book written directly in English was *The Dark Fields of Venus.*[129] The striking title alludes to the dark-field microscopy test for early syphilis. *Dark Fields* illustrates

Yanovsky's ability to combine the poetic and the medical in a work based on the notes (recorded in English) of a rather distressing medical practice. In *Dark Fields,* Yanovsky's ear for colloquial speech is acute and accurate, and his psychological portrayals are subtle. No significant linguistic limitations are visible, but the form of the work does constrain him to a matter-of-fact vocabulary.

After *The Dark Fields of Venus,* Yanovsky wrote scientific and critical works directly in English. *Medicine, Science, and Life,* a kind of philosophy of science, also came to him naturally in English, as did some articles.[130] It was just as self-evident that his most recent work, *Elysian Fields,* about the Paris emigration, should have been written in Russian. What was not so obvious, however, was in what language his fiction should be written. Yanovsky's novels frequently combine erudite philosophical or spiritual speculation with a plot that evolves partly in a somewhat fantastic environment. In *No Man's Time,* for example, as W. H. Auden observed in his preface, "the story moves between two worlds, one fantasy-realist and the other fantasy-escapist."[131] The spiritually most significant part of *No Man's Time* occurs in a remote village on the Canadian border, which is more or less untouched by the modern world. For thirteen days in January, time stands still there, and the inhabitants can retrace their steps, correct their mistakes, change what has been into something that never was. As Richard Howard said in his review of another Yanovsky novel *(Of Light and Sounding Brass)* it, too, "attempts to chart, against all one-directional, irreversible 'laws' of time, place and memory, how a man's mind and his biography go their separate ways."[132] The second part of *Of Light and Sounding Brass,* which chronologically should precede the first, takes place in a peculiar, unidentified part of Europe separated from everywhere by a completely barren land, striated by deep ditches and faults. The villagers seem to continue to live in the eighteenth or nineteenth century, despite the arrival of a band of renegade Nazis still at large after the end of the war.

Both *No Man's Time* and *Of Light and Sounding Brass* were written in Russian. Their lyricism seemed to demand, and the surreality of their settings seemed to authorize, the continued use of Russian, which, though in some sense fading, was still Yanovsky's richest language. Part of *Of Light and Sounding Brass* (pp. 99–121) is in fact a complex meditation on the fate of language, memory, and personality in emigration. Nevertheless, Yanovsky could not find a publisher for these works in Russian, and so both practical feasibility of publication and Yanovsky's concern to transmit to readers the essence of his philosophical message led him finally to seek an English-reading audience for his novels as well as for his nonfiction.[133] The first step in this direction had been the translation of *No Man's Time* by Yanovsky's wife (Isabella Levitin) and Roger Nyle Parris; then Levitin and Yanovsky himself collaborated on the translation of *Of Light and Sounding Brass*. Because both these novels were published in English to considerable critical acclaim, the die seemed to be cast: Yanovsky wrote *The Great Transfer* directly in English, though regretting all the while the loss of the "lyricism" that had characterized his Russian texts. Yanovsky felt this greater spareness to be the result of a lack of "room inside oneself" caused by working in a second language, yet he also recognized that his novel in English goes more quickly to the point and has therefore become more highly charged with the essence of his ideas. Certainly the narrative structure of *The Great Transfer* as well as the syntax and vocabulary of its language are less complex than these had been in some of the Russian novels, and the essence of the author's message is more easily accessible than was the case with *No Man's Time;* but the novel is not without lyricism, especially in the quasi-mythic passages dealing with the hero's encounters with a great bull that roams the interior of an island where the hero has joined a spiritual retreat.

In *The Great Transfer,* Yanovsky successfully completed the transition to English that he had begun with *The Dark Fields of Venus.* Because he felt that he had something very important to say, he would use whatever artistic means he could—including a not entirely comfortable language, if necessary—to say it. Thus, Yanovsky's reasons for being a bilingual writer are diametrically opposed to Beckett's "nothing to express, nothing with which to express, and yet the obligation to express."[134] Yanovsky has a cause, and, as he has put it himself, he sees his change of language to be rather like the situation of a freedom fighter who, having lost a campaign, crosses the border to continue to fight with other weapons, in other conditions, perhaps even under a different standard. The changes are real, but there is also an underlying continuity.

Hélène Iswolsky (Elena Aleksandrovna Izvol'skaia)

It is obvious that many writers who change language move to do so under the impulsion of the *matter* of their works, whether this be provided by materialist social command or by the demands of spiritual conviction, especially if the latter is of the ecumenical kind espoused by Vasily Yanovsky and even more strongly by Helène Iswolsky (1896–1973). She was born in Bavaria, the daughter of a Russian diplomat, and as a small child spent time in Japan and in Copenhagen. Her father was Russia's minister of foreign affairs when she was ten, and he was then posted to Paris as (what turned out to be) the last imperial ambassador to France. Her parents communicated mostly in French (her mother, who was Danish, spoke little Russian), and Elena and her brother had also picked up a bit of German. As a result, she says, "our 'mother tongue' was a complete jumble until Nadezhda Vladimirovna [a governess who accompanied them on their return from Japan via the Trans-Siberian Railway] gave us large doses of excellent and highly refined Russian."[135]

Iswolsky remained abroad after the Revolution, and for many years she worked as a journalist in French for various Paris papers and translated works from Russian into French (including the Ivanov-Gershenzon letters[136] and several books by the religious thinker Nikolai Berdiaev). Her own major writing has more frequently been in French or English than in Russian—but this is not because, having grown up almost entirely abroad, Iswolsky was inadequate or uncomfortable in Russian. She notes: "I was often asked how I have preserved, through so many years of exile, the correct use of my native tongue. I would say that I did not as much 'preserve it' as perfect it, for during the twenties and thirties of my Paris period, I went through a thorough training which I could compare to postgraduate studies; the final polishing which I had missed in Russia. So that thirty years later, when I returned on a trip to Russia, my countrymen could not believe that I had been away so long."[137]

The fact that it was possible for Iswolsky to give herself such a "postgraduate" (but nonacademic) course in Russian, and that she should have perfected her Russian rather than lost it, despite her immersion in French culture and her own early writing in French, gives the lie to a number of frequently heard generalizations about the interactions of a bilingual's languages in exile or emigration. Without denying (or overemphasizing) the possible importance of class background, it is certain that the ease with which Iswolsky moved among Russian, French, and English was in large part the result of her overarching concern with the ecumenical Christian message. Thus, she seems to have been granted, or to have taken upon herself, the ability to "write in tongues," not in the sense of inspired speech incomprehensible to the uninitiated, but in the more pedestrian sense in which the Apostles were granted the ability to speak the tongues of men in order that they might preach to the unconverted. Iswolsky's Catholicism would also seem to have freed her from the attachment that Orthodox writers sometimes have to the Russian language as a privileged vessel of spiritual truth. Thus, Iswolsky began to write in French a panoramic overview of Russia's cultural and spiritual trends from early times to the present. Several chapters had been completed, but, these papers having been lost, Iswolsky began again in America, this time in English.[138] Similarly, she had written a few articles about her experiences in occupied France, but because they were destined for the American press, she switched from French to English. Her memoirs, *No Time to Grieve,* are in English, but she also worked in the United States on a book in Russian devoted to the lives of the American saints and of other outstanding Catholics in America.

The major foci of Iswolsky's writing were therefore either Russia (*La jeunesse rouge d'Inna* [Inna's Red youth], *La vie de Bakunine* [The life of Bakunin], *L'homme en Russie soviétique* [Man in Soviet Russia], and *Femmes soviétiques* [Soviet women]) or spirituality (*Light before Dark,* about the French spiritual revival of the 1930s), or a combination of Russia and spirituality (*The Soul of Russia Today* and *Christ in Russia*). She moved easily, and without emotional or spiritual fuss, among the various languages at her command.

Vladimir Pozner

If Yanovsky's and Izwolsky's linguistic trajectories have been influenced by their spiritual convictions, Vladimir Pozner's career seems to have been similarly determined, but by his pro-Soviet political beliefs. If one tried to make a table like the one I spoke about at the beginning of this chapter, Pozner would throw everything out of kilter, for his journey began and ended in Paris, where he was born in 1905. His mother had left Lithuania at the age of sixteen, her younger sister in tow, and had gone to Paris to study medicine. Despite her foreignness, her gender, her Jewishness, and the fact that she arrived knowing no French, she almost achieved her goal; she was within one final examination of becoming a doctor, but by then there were also two children to be nursed and reared, and she never did receive her degree. Pozner himself began his schooling in Paris in French. By the age of eight or nine he was writing poems in Russian (although his very first two had been in French).[139] The family then returned to Russia, where he and his brother went to Russian *lycées*.[140] Thus, unlike Boris Poplavskii, Pozner's higher education was in Russian, and the environment surrounding him in late boyhood and early adolescence was permeated by Russian literature.[141] He remembers, for example, that at the first New Year's Eve party he had ever been allowed to attend, in 1915 or 1916, Maksim Gor'kii and Mariia Fedorovna (and probably also Leonid Andreev, who "often came") were among the guests, as was Dem'ian Bednyi.[142]

Pozner himself became an active participant in Russian literature at a very early age—meeting Viktor Shklovskii, whose "literary pupil" Pozner became, when he was only fourteen. Pozner also hobnobbed with the other young writers who formally established themselves as the Serapion Brothers in 1921. He was their "Benjamin," and it was in one of the Serapion collections that his first published work ("Ballada," written when he was fourteen or fifteen) appeared.

In the spring of 1922, Pozner left the USSR, spending some time in Berlin, where he was close to Shklovskii and to Triolet (with whom he remained linked both by friendship and, subsequently, politics until her death). In Berlin, he published several pieces of prose and poetry, including "Vsia zhizn' gospodina Ivanova" [The whole life of Mr. Ivanov] in Andrei Belyi's magazine *Epopeia*.[143] After wandering around a bit, Pozner finally settled in Paris, where he continued at first to write in Russian, publishing in 1928 a book containing poems written between 1925 and 1928: *Stikhi na sluchai* [Circumstantial verse].[144] During the period from 1923 to 1929, when his first book in French was published, Pozner wrote stories and poems in Russian but increasingly worked in French for his critical and journalistic articles. This early use of a second language for "secondary" or "utilitarian" genres while maintaining for the nonce the first literary language for "serious" things is quite common among bilingual writers. Schakovskoy, as we have seen, also took this route. During the same period, Pozner also translated Tolstoi's 1853–1865 diaries into French.

Pozner's first book written in French was devoted to Russian literature: *Panorama de la littérature russe contemporaine* [The panorama of contemporary Russian literature].[145] It prominently featured his friends, the former Serapions, to whom he quite rightly gave pride of place among the prose writers of the first half of the 1920s. Pozner's own prose of this period was still very much influenced by Serapion tenets. One of the most interesting of these works is a story entitled "Chasy bez strelok" [The clock without hands].[146] He uses the complex plotting, narrative twists and revelations, and the mysterious, Hoffmannesque atmosphere so dear to the older Serapions (especially to Veniamin Kaverin),[147] to tell an updated romantic story about the difficulty of knowing someone else's true identity. What is particularly interesting in our context is the important role played by languages in this tale of incomprehension. In "Chasy bez strelok," language does not help to identify the major characters but, rather, obscures their true being.

A man, soon to be Narrator 2, arrives late one night in Narrator 1's room. He asks, in French, for a Russian doctor and assumes that he has found his man when Narrator 1, the occupant of the room, having first assumed that his visitor is American, recognizes his faint Russian accent and replies in Russian. Narrator 1 accompanies Narrator 2 on a weird journey in a horse-drawn carriage to see (and, he hopes, to help) a dying, deaf and dumb old man. During their journey, Narrator 2 explains to Narrator 1 that he has been obsessed with trying to establish the old man's identity, but it would seem that the old man's secret is forever unknowable. How can one learn the time from a watch whose hands have been broken off? The only clue is that the old man seems to be obsessed with phonograph records; his whole face lights up when Narrator 1 plays *Carmen,* even though, since he is deaf, he cannot hear it. After they finally arrive, Narrator 1 recognizes the old man and, after his almost immediate death, reveals that the nameless man was Battisto Angelini, once the world's most famous singer, who had dropped out of public sight some thirty years ago. This revelation is followed by another: Narrator 1 is not a doctor, but a writer. Narrator 2 and we the readers have been fooled all along by assuming that the presence or absence of a language can define a man. Because he spoke Russian, we and Narrator 2 have assumed that the writer was the Russian doctor for whom Narrator 2 was searching. Because the old man was now deaf and dumb, it did not occur to us that he might once have been a great singer.

Thus, Pozner observes, language is no clear guide to identity. The use of a given language may lead interlocutors into error, and the apparent lack of a tongue may lead to still graver misapprehensions. Worst of all is the possibility of being totally separated from oneself by being altogether deprived of voice. It is therefore no accident, as his Soviet colleagues like to say, that it should be the polyglot Pozner who gives back Battisto's identity by recognizing him and telling his story, thus allowing Battisto's tongue to be "set free"[148] one last time, even though the physical voice, lost to the man and barely audible even through the scratchy old recording, is gone forever. Nor, it seems, is it by chance that the polyglot Pozner, who could himself write in three languages and saw his fellow émigrés increasingly struggling with questions of language and identity, should have chosen to devote one of his last Russian artistic texts to the deathbed return of identity to a man who had become a deaf-mute, but who had once been "the greatest singer in the world."

Pozner's own subsequent writing was primarily in French but also in English during the Second World War, which he spent in the United States, turning out scenarios for Hollywood. (He was also awarded a Guggenheim Fellowship in the same year as Nabokov—which cannot have pleased Nabokov much.)[149] During his career, Pozner has translated English into French, Russian into French, and French into Russian (e.g., Louis Aragon's *Les cloches de Bâle* [The bells of Basel] and *Les beaux quarters* [The better part of town]), but he did not *self-translate* into Russian. Some of his French stories were, in fact, translated into Russian by Triolet.

Pozner was a member of the French Communist party for many years and thus maintained contacts with the Soviet Union and Soviet writers. During the Algerian War, which he opposed, his apartment in Paris was bombed by right-wing extremists, and he was gravely wounded. His literary activity has been much reduced since then.

Others

The idiosyncratic linguistic trajectories of the writers discussed in this chapter are just a sampling of the various paths followed by writers of the "first" Paris emigration. One could go on to detail the condescending and somewhat disgusted experiments of Dmitrii Merezhkovskii and Zinaïda Gippius with writing in French[150] or speak about the novels of Jacques Gorbof (Ia. N. Gorbov), some of which were written behind the wheel of his taxi.[151] One should note that the prolific historical novelist Mark Aldanov wrote a book in French about Lenin,[152] that Nina Berberova wrote one in French about Aleksandr Blok,[153] that D. S. Mirsky, a very minor poet in Russian, wrote the major popular history of Russian literature in English.[154] One could consider the trajectory of Dóvid Knut (1900–1955) who, while in Paris, wrote poems in Russian before emigrating again to Israel, where he became a Hebrew poet. And one must not forget at least to mention the two most influential critics of the emigration: Vladimir Weidlé (Veidle), like Mirsky, a minor Russian poet who also worked extensively in several disciplines and several languages,[155] and the greatest polyglot of them all, the theoretician, linguist, and critic Roman Jakobson.[156]

But even without a detailed consideration of these figures, the quantity and variety of the examples that we have discussed should be sufficient to illustrate why it is so difficult to make any generalizations about cultivated bilingualism. This is apparent even within my sample of bilingual writers drawn from a single emigration, all of whom left Russia between 1918 and 1923, and all of whom settled for a rather lengthy period in Paris, wherever else their destinies may subsequently have led them.

Conclusions and Projections

The bilingual writers whose careers I have been discussing are all reaching, or have already reached, the ends of their complex trajectories, but a new generation is preparing to take up their pens. Among the Russians of the "third" emigration, some are already experimenting with writing in English or French or Hebrew as well as in Russian. As I have mentioned, Joseph Brodsky, far and away the most important poet among them, has already written not only critical and autobiographical prose, but also some very impressive poetry in English. Brodsky has begun to self-translate,[1] and it is also interesting that he chose to write about his most intimate memories—childhood, home, and family—in English rather than in Russian.[2] Writing in English about his deceased parents, who tried vainly for twelve years to be allowed to visit him, grants them a "margin of freedom." For "to write about them in Russian would be only to further their captivity. . . . May English then house my dead.[3] In Russian I am prepared to read, write verses or letters. For Maria Volpert and Alexander Brodsky, though, English offers a better semblance of afterlife, maybe the only one there is, save my very self. And as far as the latter is concerned, writing this in this language is like doing those dishes: it's therapeutic."[4] Yet, in other respects, Brodsky knows that exile paradoxically ties him to Russian: "For one in our profession, the condition we call exile is, first of all, a linguistic event: an exiled writer is thrust, or retreats, into his mother tongue. From being his, so to speak, sword, it turns into his shield, into his [space] capsule. What started as a private, intimate affair with the language, in exile becomes fate—even before it becomes an obsession or a duty."[5]

It would therefore seem unlikely that Brodsky will ever abandon Russian, but it is not yet clear whether he will compartmentalize, as Nabokov did for a while, writing poetry in Russian and reserving English for prose, whether he will write poetry in both Russian and English, or whether, following Tsvetaeva, he will ultimately renounce English and cleave to Russian. One would hope that he will not choose the latter, drastic course, for he is not only the major Russian poet of his generation but also the one linguistically best equipped to become a great bilingual writer. Yet, as we have seen, linguistic competence is less important than emotion and affect in the decision to become or not to become a bilingual writer, and it is far too early to predict what Brodsky's linguistic solution will be. Other émigré poets are so far even more hesitant than Brodsky to commit themselves to writing in a language other than Russian, although there are some signs that Lev Loseff and Aleksei Tsvetkov may develop into bilingual writers.[6]

It is interesting that within the Soviet Union itself there are currently some actively bilingual prose writers, such as Chingiz Aitmatov, who has written in both Kirghiz and Russian, and Vasily Bykov, who has written in both Russian and Belorussian. There are also many writers from other countries and other cultures who are, or are becoming, bilingual as writers, José Donoso, Hector Bianciotti, Manuel Puig, Guillermo Cabrera Infante, Samuel Cioran, Milan Kundera, Stratis Haviaras, Leo Vroman, and Raymond Federman, to name only a few.[7] If we expand the rubric "writer" to include those bilinguals who write critical prose, rather than limiting it to authors of "poetry" and "fiction," then the number of currently practicing bilingual writers immediately jumps into the thousands. One might, therefore, hazard the admittedly polemical hypothesis that there are probably more bilingual writers in the world than there are writers *tout court* of any but the very largest national literatures. All the more reason to realize that it is a category mistake not to consider bilingual writers as a separate group!

While one of the findings that has emerged from studies of bilinguals is that they are significantly idiosyncratic and that one generalizes about them at one's peril, the evidence does allow one to maintain that active bilinguals are organized for language processing differently from monolinguals. This would be true whether or not the bilingual in question chooses to become bilingual *as a writer*. As we saw in Chapter 2 and in the case of Tsvetaeva, competent bilinguals or polyglots who attempt to become bilingual *as writers* have to struggle with a variety of emotional obstacles that are much more serious than the purely linguistic ones. It would also seem obvious that those bilinguals who *do* commit themselves to writing in more than one language usually share a general artistic trajectory. This trajectory cannot, of course, claim the status of a *law*. As is the case with measures of cognitive flexibility, it is not clear in which direction the causal arrow points: people who do not finally become bilingual writers may *therefore* not complete the trajectory; or, to the contrary, people who do not complete the trajectory may *therefore* not become fully bilingual writers. There can, however, be no doubt that an artistic trajectory such as the one outlined in Chapter 2 "likes to occur" with the successful long-term practice of bilingual writing.[8]

Samuel Beckett has quoted Marcel Proust as saying, "The duty and the task of a writer (not an artist, a writer), are those of a translator."[9] Surely bilinguals are even more constantly aware of their function as *transmitters* of a text than are most writers,[10] but that does not mean that there is no artist behind or below the artisan. In fact, the experience of bilingual writers (including Beckett, despite his statements to the contrary) leads to the conclusion that there is a core somewhere below the specific language. Whether the bilingual "translator" transmits it by saying *Ia* or *I* or *Je*, whether, as in Beckett's case, he says "I can't go on I'll go on" or "Je ne peux pas continuer je vais continuer," the text passes. The fact that it does, and that the voice is the same in two languages, would seem to promise that passing into *either* language from below is a self that is incontrovertibly, almost triumphantly, there.

Finally, it would behoove us to remember the variety of background and experience shown by even the relatively narrow sampling of bilingual Russian writers of the "first" emigration whom we have considered. The most salient characteristic of bilingual organization for language is in fact the (properly speaking) incalculable number of combinations of linguistic, affective, and other variables that make each bilingual a unique case. It is precisely this difference, and these anomalies, which constitute the norm for bilinguals and, *a fortiori*, for bilingual writers. And although our be-lated realization that they are not ugly (bigamous? monstrous?) ducks but a different kind of bird altogether cannot help those bi-lingual writers of the previous generation who struggled to come to terms with their (traitorous? abnormal?) practice of writing in more than one language, perhaps this knowledge (and an awareness of the physiological, psychological, and artistic characteristics of bi-lingual writing) will make the path easier for other potentially bi-lingual writers. For while being bilingual or polyglot *as a writer* is finally a choice and not a destiny, recognizing and accepting their bilingual difference is an essential step in the direction of full artis-tic individuation for those writers who do decide (despite warnings from some linguists and from at least one great poet) to undertake the lonely and difficult exploit [podvig] of "tempting alien tongues."

Samuel Beckett

There is no communication because there are no vehicles of communication.

—Samuel Beckett, *Proust*

... bribes d'une voix ancienne en moi pas la mienne.

—Samuel Beckett, *Comment c'est*

[... scraps of an ancient voice in me not mine.]

—Samuel Beckett, *How It Is*

Although this book concentrates on Russian writers, one of its primary concerns is to see what, if anything, can be safely said about bilingual writers in general. It is therefore very useful to consider at least one non-Russian bilingual writer of the same generation as the Russians who have been discussed here, a man who is probably Nabokov's only serious rival for the putative title of "greatest twentieth-century bilingual writer": Samuel Beckett. By comparing his trajectory with that of Nabokov, I will be able to correct for the purely Russian situation of the writers whom I have examined. Happily, such a comparison would seem to support my contention that thoroughly bilingual writers, regardless of national origin, have more in common with each other than with monolingual writers in any of the languages they use.

In his essay "Bilingual Playwright," Harry Cockerham asserts that with Beckett "we are faced, not with a writer who abandoned one language for another (a not infrequent occurrence), but with the possibly unique phenomenon of one who, throughout his career, has divided his efforts and his interests between two languages."[1] But Beckett is obviously not unique in his literary bilingualism. Nor has he really divided his efforts and interests between two languages. Like Nabokov or Triolet, he has *combined* his efforts, and, like them, Beckett has had a literary *bi-destin*. Like Nabokov, Beckett has created a large body of works in both languages. And, as with Nabokov, his fame is almost equal in both languages; his voice is immediately recognizable and unmistakable in either one. Both Beckett and Nabokov have devoted considerable creative energy to translations and, what is more significant, to self-translation, which would seem to be the key to the evolution of most bilingual writers. Like Nabokov and Triolet, Beckett has produced a tremendous *quantity* of works (one begins to wonder whether bilingualism is not conducive to a kind of creative logorrhea). Lastly, like Nabokov (and, to a slightly lesser extent, like Triolet), Beckett has provided the pretext for a daunting quantity of critical prose, so that my discussion of Beckett will be limited to an attempt to determine how his trajectory confirms or denies the patterns we have seen in the careers of bilingual Russian writers of the "first" emigration.[2]

The first evident difference between Beckett's career and those of the Russians is that, being Anglo-Irish, he was not pushed toward becoming a bilingual writer by forced exile and the destruction of the socioeconomic order into which he had been born. Beckett's exile was one of choice and was never made irrevocable by political circumstances over which he had no control. Much has been made of the Anglo-Irishman's perhaps inevitable concern with self-definition, and this has been offered as at least a partial explanation for Beckett's obsessive concern with problems of being, the identity of the self, and the "deep existential anguish that is the keynote of Beckett's work."[3] One might expect that Russian writers, deprived of a homeland, status, wealth, and the linguistic milieu that is the lifeblood of a writer, would share Beckett's "existential anguish." But while such problems do arise from time to time for *characters* in works by Nabokov or Schakovskoy, it is strikingly obvious that neither of these authors ever seriously suffered from the question "Who am I?" In fact, they present unusually powerful and coherent personalities. Theirs was a sense of self that was neither bound to a single language nor seriously jeopardized by a change of language.

Because polyglotism was a cherished part of Russian aristocratic culture, they were not betraying their background and values by also writing in another language, and the lack of a single linguistic identity did not ultimately endanger psychic identity. The search for the "real me" is not, therefore, a problem for aristocrats in forced exile.[4] It is a problem for the exile of choice, whose lack of psychic identity is often primordial and actually helps to bring about the shift of language and milieu.[5]

The forced exile worries about maintaining the purity and force of his mother tongue. This is not a problem that bothers Beckett. Beckett's acquisition of French and the choice of France as his linguistic and physical habitat are therefore significantly different from the patterns of polyglotism and involuntary exile that characterize twentieth-century Russian writers. His situation, in fact, resembles far more the ambiguous cultural self-hatred of the nineteenth-century *raznochinets* or of the twentieth-century American. Beckett learned French as a school language, and its acquisition was an element of class-cultural *ambition* rather than a matter of course. It was first an intellectual pursuit, not connected with home, French nannies, German tutors, or the language used by parents when they did not wish the servants to understand. Although Beckett's parents did expect him to learn French as part of his primary and secondary education, it was not a language they *used,* and his knowledge, once acquired, became an instrument of separation from parental values and Anglo-Irish life.

Not only did Beckett learn French at Earlsfort House School and at Portora, which would have been normal enough, but he also decided to take a degree in Romance languages at Trinity College. As Deirdre Bair observes, this was unusual, since modern languages were usually the special province of women.[6] It was definitely a *marked* choice, the choice of someone who was not entirely comfortable with his identity as part of the culture and milieu into which he was born, the choice of someone who is *mal dans sa peau,* or "uncomfortable in his skin," as the French so accurately put it. Thus, Beckett's decision to take a degree in Romance languages is already a (rather typical) attempt to find "me" elsewhere. In this respect, Beckett was not unlike the swarms of young Americans, uncomfortable with the brashness and poshness of the suburbs in which they were raised, who have discovered Culture through college French, and with it an identity that coincided more exactly, though not perfectly, with some putative essential self than with the milieu into which they were born.[7]

For Beckett, as for many others, the study of French, Italian, and German, which allowed him to grow beyond the Procrustean limits of Fatherland and Mothertongue, was the first step in psychic liberation; and one could maintain that he did not change languages because he had changed places but, rather, that he changed places in order to be able to change languages. His early prose works in French make it clear that among the things that French had freed him from were the constraints of proper English.[8] Mothers, even Mother Tongues, do not like swearing, and if one feels the need to do so, one can write "shit" and "fart" and "fuck" more freely in a foreign language. Here, too, the school-French syndrome seems to have played a role. As others have noted, the way Beckett learned French was fundamentally different from the way one learns a first language or even a second language that is part of family life.[9] The French that Beckett learned was doubly *formal:* a language learned in school and one that at first he used primarily to read "high literature." It is therefore not surprising that Beckett's initial efforts in French are in the "higher" genre of poetry, and that these first poems should be linguistically conservative and "correct."

As any professor of French in an Anglophone country knows, very few of one's otherwise highly competent colleagues have the slightest knowledge of street French, and those who do would certainly never use it in class. Thus, someone who has first learned a language in school and then begins to use it in its native context very often does not hear the different levels of which any native speaker is aware, and such a person will retain and use new expressions without any clear sense of whether they are acceptable idioms or vulgarisms. But Beckett's use of vulgarisms and colloquialisms cannot be explained away as "lack of ear," since he began to write prose in French only after a lengthy immersion in French life, including several years in an entirely French rural environment. His turning to French prose after the war is therefore doubly a new start: he has freed himself both from the inhibitions of the Mother Tongue and from the constraints of bookish French.[10]

This joyous *défoulement* (if anything in Beckett can rightly be called joyous) is possible only at the price of the abandonment of deep-seated restraints and strictures. No wonder then, that, as Erika

Ostrovsky has noted, the first French prose works are marked by the frequent use of words such as *jeter, abandonner, perdre* (throw away, abandon, lose).[11] Such pleasures, however, are psychically hard to admit, and these works are filled less with people deliberately casting things off than with people who lose things (e.g., *Mercier et Camier*) or with people who are themselves cast off or thrown out ("L'expulsé" [The expelled], "La fin" [The end]). Thus, the *transfuge* sees himself as expelled, and the blame, if blame there must be (and apparently there must), is projected onto what has been left behind.

Whatever the ambiguities of abandonment and rejection, Paris and exile were essential to the development of Beckett's writing—not only to the works in French, but to those in English. For all practical purposes, Beckett really began to write, even in English, only after his displacement to Paris. There he wrote poetry (from 1929 on), critical (?) prose ("Dante . . . Bruno. Vico . . . Joyce," in *Our Exagmination Round His Factification for Incamination of Work in Progress* [1929], and *Proust* [1930]), and short stories (e.g., "Assumption," published in *transition* in June 1929).[12] By 1930, he was also deeply involved in translation—first from Italian into English,[13] and then, more important, the translation of the Anna Livia Plurabelle section of Joyce's *Work in Progress* into French. Thus, almost immediately after he began to write in English, Beckett was using French as a target language—if not for his own work, then for that of Joyce, with whom he was intimately linked both artistically and personally at the time. Clearly, the relationship to Joyce was crucial to Beckett's development. If it is true, as Ralph Ellison says, that although one can do nothing about one's relatives, one gets to choose one's *literary* ancestors, then Beckett at first followed the beaten path of Stephen Dedalus into exile.[14] But he soon felt the need to reject Joyce as his literary ancestor, and with his rejection of Joyce he also renounced the style, the presence, the *plethora*.[15]

Throughout the 1930s Beckett continued to write in a variety of forms in English and to translate from French into English (most notably, twenty-one surrealist poems which he translated in 1932), but by the end of 1937 he was also beginning to write directly in French.[16] Between December 1937 and the fall of 1939 Beckett wrote twelve short, untitled poems in French.[17]

This plunge into French poetry was a concerted one—not mere dabbling, as were Eliot's four French poems.[18] The use of French was motivated by a variety of factors, some of which were exceedingly practical. The recently published *Murphy* had obtained only a very limited success, and Beckett began to think seriously of addressing himself to a French audience. All the more so, for in April 1938 he had finally found an acceptable apartment in Paris, the taking of which was of no mean symbolic significance. It was logical that he and his friend Alfred Péron should begin Beckett's attack on the world of French letters with several projects for the translation of works that Beckett had already written in English. They worked together on translating *Murphy* into French and Péron also tried to translate some poems from *Echo's Bones* on his own. Beckett's unhappiness with the latter effort may have been behind his comment to Thomas McGreevy that he wanted to see whether he could write poetry directly in French that was French in conception, not just English verse transferred to another language. Beckett also wrote to McGreevy at that time that he had the feeling that he would "probably write a great deal of poetry and that it would quite naturally be in French."[19]

It is important that Beckett worked into French gradually, and that his path led him from translation to poetry, then to critical prose, and only later into "major fiction." Bair notes that the early poems in French are direct and simple, with much less verbal ingenuity and convoluted phrasing than the poems of *Echo's Bones*.[20] This may be the result of an understandable artistic caution in a new language, but it is also an initial step in the retreat from the Joycean style, a retreat that was to characterize Beckett's later prose, though not the intervening early prose in French, much of which is highly colored and colloquial.[21]

There was, therefore, a rather lengthy period of flux, when Beckett was using both languages for different things and translating in both directions. There is every indication, however, that Beckett still reserved English for major prose—"anything that might evolve into a novel."[22] *Watt*, written in the Vaucluse, quite cut off from any English-language environment, was still in English, and it was not until after the war that Beckett committed himself to writing prose in French. That commitment, once made, was for a number of years, serious, and more or less exclusive, and it corresponds to the years when Nabokov tried to close his ears to his "ruddy Russian muse."

Yet the linguistic lines are already blurred in many ways, even at the beginning of this period of devotion to French prose. Ruby Cohn has noted that this is about the same time that Beckett begins the "series of self-translations [ultimately in both directions] that are unprecedented in the history of literature."[23] This juxtaposition is typical of bilingual writers. Triolet and Nabokov both pushed into writing prose in their second languages while still involved in, or having recently attempted, a difficult effort at self-translation.

Beckett's translation of *Murphy* is especially significant in this respect because the beginning of the translation coincides with Beckett's first attempts at writing poetry directly in French, while its belated completion coincides with the plunge into French prose. It is interesting that, as several scholars have remarked, the French version of *Murphy* is tainted by that heavy use of colloquialisms and vulgarity which characterizes the early French prose texts and which "corrupts the elegance of the English *Murphy*."[24] Because, as Cohn observes, most of the changes serve to heighten the comic tone, the vulgarization of *Murphy* may be attributed to that almost adolescent liberation of language which we have already seen to be characteristic of Beckett's early French prose and, therefore, to the general tone of Beckett's use of French at that period. Or, more simply, it may be seen as independent of language, the result of the revamping of an old text by an author who has grown during the interim. Cockerham has a still more interesting explanation. When the late plays are taken into account, he sees a clear pattern in the translations: "The truth of the matter is not that Beckett makes more use of coarseness in either the French or the English versions, but that in translating into whichever language, he is careful at least to maintain if not to increase the note of vulgarity."[25] This would seem to indicate that the freedom from formal language that Beckett finds when he turns to his second language remains, at least to some extent, a cherished quality of his use of that language for *dramatic* purposes even many years later.

Perhaps an even more important instance of the blurring of the lines between Beckett's English and early French prose is the fact, noted by Olga Bernal, that a development crucial to the subsequent French work of Beckett already appears in *Watt*, still written in

English. It is in *Watt,* she says, that "the world first splits in two with man and things on one side and words on the other [que le monde se scinde en deux, en l'homme et les choses d'un côté et les mots de l'autre]."[26] Because the capacity to separate names from things, which becomes an affliction and a torture to certain Beckett personages, is one of the primary psychophysiological character- istics of genuine bilinguals, the presence of this dichotomy in the English *Watt* may be seen as indicating Beckett's linguistic and psychological readiness to engage actively his second language. It signals the development that leads through *Mercier et Camier,* "L'expulsé," "La suite" [What follows], "La fin," and "Le cal- mant" [The tranquilizer] to the Trilogy.

Several critics have also remarked that Beckett's shift to French prose coincided with a shift from third-person narrators to first- person narrators, whereas the third-person narrator reemerged when Beckett returned to English.[27] These observations need quali- fication. There is still a third-person narrator in *Mercier et Camier,* although it is true that he is already sliding into the position of a participant in the action.[28] Nor must one forget that Beckett had already used the first person in his early English poems. Yet it is certainly important that, in his prose, Beckett should begin to speak in the first person only in his second language, where what he says is *Je,* not *I.* In Beckett's case, the emergence and dominance of the first-person narrator in the second language does not indicate an investment of psychic legitimacy in a new French persona. He has not been impelled to use French for the reason that Triolet was driven to do so: that the people and emotions and life about which she wrote no longer coincided with her mother tongue. Beckett nei- ther needs nor uses the background texture of the French language or of French life for his novels as Triolet did or as Nabokov used America in *Pale Fire* and *Lolita.* In this respect, Beckett never be- came a "French" novelist in the sense that Triolet did or that Nabokov was once an "American" one.[29]

Beckett's path to French is therefore deliberately the reverse of the ones followed by Triolet and Nabokov to their second languages. They ceased writing in Russian because of a need to invest the sec- ond language with psychic legitimacy. Beckett, on the other hand, is free to use the first person in the prose of his second language, precisely because it did *not* imply the investment of that everyday, culturebound psychic allegiance from which his whole work and life had been a flight. In France and in French, Beckett is not expected to belong completely. This is why he is more "at home" there—that is, nowhere. Such Beckett novels as *L'Innommable* [The Unnamable] do not attempt to render an intimate contact with external cultural complexity, but descend into an inner space without texture, a space as much as possible emptied of all objects and all being, except that of the core of self (if it exists) and the void that surrounds it. A remark that Beckett made in *Proust* in 1931 is therefore a program for *L'Innommable* and for others of his mature works: "For the artist, who does not deal in surfaces . . . the only possible spiritual development is in the sense of depth. The artistic tendency is not expansive, but a contraction."[30]

It is obvious that to anyone who defines the task of the artist in this way, to anyone who can say "L'artiste qui joue son être est de nulle part" [The artist who puts his being on the line isn't from anywhere],[31] nationality and language loyalty are among the first layers of psychic coverings that must be stripped away. Thus, the Unnamable revolts against the supposition that the use of a language (for him, language as such—the Unnamable is clearly monolingual) must mean integration into the group: "Ne pouvoir ouvrir la bouche sans les proclamer, à titre de congénère, voilà ce à quoi ils croient m'avoir réduit. M'avoir collé un langage dont ils s'imaginent que je ne pourrai jamais me servir sans m'avouer de leur tribu, la belle astuce. Je vais le leur arranger, leur charabia. . . . Il ne restera bientôt plus rien de leurs bourrages"[32] [Not to be able to open my mouth without proclaiming them, and our fellowship, that's what they imagine they'll have me reduced to. It's a poor trick that consists in ramming a set of words down your gullet on the principle that you can't bring them up without being branded as belonging to their breed. But I'll fix their gibberish for them. . . . Nothing will remain of all the lies they have glutted me with].[33] If a language is merely something *collé,* imposed from the outside, then it has no necessary connection with self. The bilingual Beckett therefore exercises an option unavailable to the monolingual Unnamable; he leaves *their* language behind and takes up the language of a tribe to which he does not belong. Having done this, being thoroughly detached, he can ultimately return to his first language without the original emotional servitude.

By deliberately ungluing himself from his mother tongue and choosing another language, Beckett has psychologically facilitated the utterance of that ontological homelessness which is the essence of his major work. As Vivian Mercier has so rightly observed, Beckett has learned that for him at least the secret of individuality lies not in being able to write in several languages at once or to parade characters belonging to half a dozen nationalities, but in presenting "the poor, bare, forked animal."[34]

Of course, Beckett is not content to stop there. He continues to peel away his characters, both from the inside and from the outside. In fact, they become progressively less "forked" until they are reduced, at least in one case, to a mere mouth.[35] His personages are never even sure they are themselves. The characters who speak through Beckett are not him, and the voices speaking through these characters are, so they maintain, not them. Thus, says the Unnamable: "Croient-ils que je crois que c'est moi qui parle? Ça c'est d'eux aussi. Pour me faire croire que j'ai un moi à moi et que je peux en parler comme eux du leur. C'est encore un piège, pour que je me trouve soudain, crrac pris parmi les vivants. . . . [p. 98] C'est parce qu'il dit je comme si c'était moi, j'ai failli le croire moi aussi. . . . [p. 195] Je dis je en sachant que ce n'est pas moi[p. 197]" [Do they believe I believe it is I who am speaking? That's theirs too. To make me believe I have an ego all my own, and can speak of it, as they of theirs. Another trap to snap me up among the living. . . . (p. 345) I seem to speak, that's because he says I as if he were I, I nearly believed him, do you hear him, as if he were I. . . . (p. 403) I say I, knowing it's not I (p. 404)].

It is somewhat surprising that the Unnamable does not take the obvious solution to the problem that all the words are *theirs* by inventing his own language. That way he would not have been colonized; if he invented the words, he would escape their *bourrage*. He *is* briefly tempted: "c'est comme ça que ça finira, par des gloussements, glouglou, aïe, ha, pah, je vais m'exercer, nyam, hou, plof, pss, rien que de l'émotion, pan, paf, les coups, na, toc, quoi encore, aah, ooh, ça c'est l'amour, assez, c'est fatigant, hi, hi, ça c'est les côtes, de Démocrite, non, de l'autre, en fin de compte, c'est la fin, la fin du compte, c'est le silence, quelques glouglous sur le silence, le vrai, pas celui ou je macère' (p. 202) [that's how it will end, in a chuckle, chuck, chuck, ow, ha, pa, I'll practice, nyum, hoo, plop, pss, nothing but emotion, bing bang, that's blows, ugh, pooh, what else, oooh aaah, that's love, enough, it's tiring, hee hee, that's the Abderite, no, the other, in the end, it's the end, the ending end, it's the silence, a few gurgles on the silence, the real silence, not the one where I macerate] (p. 408). But, finally, the Unnamable remains with his language (their language) and with known words: "il faut continuer, je ne peux pas continuer, il faut continuer, je vais donc continuer, il faut dire des mots, tant qu'il y en a, il faut les dire, jusqu'à ce qu'ils me trouvent, jusqu'à ce qu'ils me disent" (p. 213) [you must go on, I can't go on, you must go on, I'll go on, you must say words, as long as there are any, until they find me, until they say me] (p. 414).

One cannot help but pose the question once again. Why did Beckett, having already taken a second language, not go the route of the Russian Futurists and invent a *zaum*, or trans-sense language, if indeed he felt that there was nothing to express, nothing to express it with, yet the obligation to express? Beckett does not seem to be attracted by the rebaptized world and the grating consonants of an Aleksei Kruchenykh or the more Joycean and linguistically grounded creations of a Velimir Khlebnikov. For Beckett's purpose is not merely to fulfill the obligation to ex-press. Despite his denials as to the possibility of doing so, the purpose is to communicate; so Beckett continues to use known languages rather than creating his own.

To return for a moment to another aspect of the courageous, if hopeless, effort of the Unnamable to define a self free of all relationships and dependencies, consider Beckett's remark about the labors of Proust: "the heart of the cauliflower or the ideal core of the onion would represent a more appropriate tribute to the labors of poetical excavation than the crown of bay."[36] The Unnamable is therefore striving for the ultimate goal of art. Yet in his self-excavation, his attempt to find the core of self within the onion ("at the core of the eddy"),[37] the Unnamable has stumbled into a trap that had already closed on his Russian ancestor: the nameless and *innommable* Underground Man. If one could ever peel away the onion to a point where there were nothing left, then there would indeed be silence, but one can never get to that theoretical nothingness: the Mouth refuses to shut up; the Underground Man does not stop writing; the Unnamable goes on. So, although Beckett's onion image provides a key to the incessant jabber, it is a fallacious analogy to the problem of self. That there may be nothing at the center of the eddy or of the onion does not mean that there is no self or that one can never reach it. As Dostoevskii showed in *Bratiia Karamazovy* [The brothers Karamazov], an onion, unpeeled, whole, with all its layers, charitably given to another human being, may be enough to pull the soul of the giver out of purgatory. Beckett, of course, ostensibly refuses any definition of the self that involves relationship to others. If the self is not something within and separate from all external accretion and internal *bourrage,* then it is not. He will not conceive of the self as being created by the absorption of the Other into one's very stuff.

Yet his works belie their argument. Since the Trilogy (and sometimes even before), Beckett has tended to create works that function internally as binary systems. There is always an Other, if not a contrary, with whom one is held in an interminable, often senseless, dialogue—but by whom one is known, and whom one knows. One need merely consider the eternally symbiotic odd couples of the dramatic works. To exist at all, they need the Other with whom to interact. Even in *Krapp's Last Tape,* Krapp has as interlocutor the taped voice which resists him, which he cannot bend entirely to his will. His audition of his own recorded voices from previous periods of his life, and his violence to his tapes, are spiritually similar to the Underground Man's autocratic and pitiful relationship to his text, which provides him with the minimal contact with an Other that is requisite to life.

That more is going on than *expressing* is even clearer in *Not I,* where the Mouth's monologue involves a frequent response to a voice unheard by the audience. She is also heard by the hooded, onstage auditor, whose infrequent gestures of "helpless compassion" indicate that the Mouth is not only expressing but communicating, as well.[38] She is, of course also heard by the audience. It is a lot harder to maintain that what one is doing is expressing (against all odds and obstacles) the impossibility of expressing, when one chooses to write plays, all of which are conceived of as being presented before a live audience (or, in the case of the radio plays, an invisible audience which is, however, listening simultaneously and at a given time). It is also a lot harder to maintain that there is nothing with which to express when one has two languages, and one writes his works in both, creating a binary pair.[39] What possible excuse can there be for that?

All these considerations inevitably lead us back to the crucial matter of Beckett's obsessive commitment to self-translation. Why has Beckett bound himself to the servitude of writing each of his works twice? Does the fact that Beckett can and does write the same work in two languages confirm or deny that there is nothing with which to express? If you add two negatives, do you get a positive? Are two systems of nothing more, or less, than one system of nothing? And what determines which *charabia* should be used first for any given work? Why is one preferable to, or at least less inadequate than, another? Or is the choice random?

When pressed, Beckett has proffered a variety of explanations for his decision to write in French. The most convincing comments are those he made to Israel Shenker: "I just felt like it" and "It was more exciting for me, writing in French."[40] "I just felt like it" covers a number of factors, including some negative ones (e.g., the sense of blockage or dead end and the need for a new start to which Beckett has admitted in the periods before he began to write poetry in French, before he turned to French prose and, conversely, at the moment after the completion of the Trilogy when he turned back to English).[41] Certainly, in the beginning, it *was* "more exciting" in French: "the adventure," as Nabokov puts it, had shifted to Beckett's second language. After a while, though, it sometimes became "more exciting" to write in English again. In his later period, there seems to be very little internal inevitability for Beckett's choice of language.[42]

Beckett himself has observed, "I don't know, I never know in advance what language I will write in."[43] The fact of choice still mattered, but less and less, because Beckett knew that he would ultimately translate the work into the other language anyway. In fact, more and more the adventure would seem to be less in the original writing, whatever the language, than in the translation—despite the fact, or maybe because of the fact, that Beckett, like all bilingual writers, has declared that he hates self-translation.[44]

Ruby Cohn has called Beckett's obsession with self-translation "unprecedented." Perhaps it is. Nabokov did ultimately English most of his early Russian novels, and, as we have seen, he even Russianed *Lolita*, but Nabokov's use of self-translation is not entirely comparable. Except for a few early attempts, it is a late phenomenon. Beckett began to self-translate almost immediately and has continued to do so constantly through the years, often with little distance between the original writing and the translation. Nabokov, on the other hand, returned to the self-translation of an early Russian corpus that had lain untouched for years. Thus the fact that Beckett should have spent so much pain and energy on self-translation may be a key to his work, for his bilingualism seems to determine the nature of his work as a whole.

We have seen that an acute awareness of the difference and distance between self, words, and objects is specific to the idiosyncratic ways in which bilinguals process information. In Beckett's case, this awareness of the separation between expression and things becomes the subject and material of his works: "The only thing outside the self that the artist can hope to express is the space that intervenes between the self and the world of objects."[45] Concerted efforts at self-translation might be supposed to make the bilingual writer feel that one cannot even accurately grasp and project in words the *image* of the self. Sometimes, this is in fact the case (e.g., Triolet's comment: "You look at yourself as in a mirror, you try to find yourself there, and you don't recognize your reflection as your own" [On se regarde comme dans une glace, on s'y cherche, ne reconnaît pas son reflet] [*M en m*, 76]).

Self-translation causes the bilingual to be even more aware of the separation of the word, self, and objects than the practice of writing directly in two languages already does, because it makes it frustratingly clear that not even words can pass intact from one verbal system to another. Self-translation draws the author's attention (and ours) to what must be lost, to the need to abandon hard-won formulations. But a *successful* self-translation is therefore the ultimate triumph. It confirms the existence not only of the text, but of the self, and this may explain Beckett's peculiar devotion to the genre. The process of self-translation seems to have become for Beckett one of those "perilous zones . . . mysterious and fertile, when for a moment the boredom of living is replaced by the suffering of being."[46] It provides the Mephistophelian pleasure of creating two mutually orbiting works in dynamic equilibrium, works like the odd couples who people them, ostensibly independent, often in conflict, yet inextricably linked—almost, but not absolutely, mirror images.

Erika Ostrovsky draws a negative conclusion from the existence of these twin works: "These literary works that are capable of existing alternatively in two languages and that therefore lead a pseudo-life [show that] a work of literature could do without any language at all, could melt into the unnamable, could be based on nothing" [Ces œuvres littéraires] pouvant exister alternativement en deux langues et menant donc une pseudo vie [montrent que] l'œuvre littéraire pourrait se passer de toute langue, se fondre dans l'innommable, se fonder sur rien].⁴⁷ But it does not seem to me that this bilingual existence is a "pseudo-life," nor that works so conceived could "do without any language" and be founded on nothing. On the contrary. The existence of the twin works (whether Beckett consciously intended it or not) confirms not only the existence of something to express, but also the existence of something with which to express and, still more important, the existence of the somebody who is expressing.

In a successful self-translation, the writer finds alternatives and compensations in the two linguistic systems at his disposal, and *the text passes*.⁴⁸ The voice passes, and is unmistakably the same in both languages, and this very fact indicates that it emanates from a self which must exist *below* both languages, flowing up through the growth rings of the tree, manifesting itself in a bifurcating trunk and in separate systems of branches and leaves, all of which are in active balance. Here we return not only to Proust's image of the tree-man, but also to George Steiner's geological vision, and to his musings on the magma that must exist below the stratified, if constantly imbricated, linguistic layers of the mind. It is from this magma, beneath the bifurcation, that there emerges the voice that may say either *Je* or *I* or even *Ia*.⁴⁹

Notes

Introduction: Bilingual Trajectories

1. Elsa Triolet, *La mise en mots* (Geneva: Skira, 1969), 8.

2. Most bilingual writers are in fact polyglots. A few are even, at least tentatively, polyglot as writers. Most, however, write seriously in only two languages. I will use "bilingual" as my generic term, except in those circumstances where it is important to know that more than two languages are involved.

3. Nathalie Sarraute, Henri Troyat, Joseph Kessel, Zoé Oldenbourg, and Vladimir Volkov are French writers whose first language was Russian. Elias Canetti, Arthur Koestler, Jerzy Kosinski, Aharon Appelfeld, Jack Kerouac, among others, have also written in languages that were not their first.

4. Leonard Forster, *The Poet's Tongues* (London: Cambridge University Press, 1970). See also Jane Miller, "Writing in a Second Language," *Raritan* 2 (1982), 115–132.

5. R. Somerville Graham, "Widespread Bilingualism and the Creative Writer," *Word* 12 (1956), 369.

6. Věroboj Vildomec, *Multilingualism* (Leiden: A. W. Sythoff, 1963), 56–57.

7. André Martinet, preface to Uriel Weinreich, *Languages in Contact* (New York: Productions of the Linguistic Circle of New York, no. 1 [1953]), vii–viii.

8. Vildomec, *Multilingualism,* 32.

9. Macdonald Critchley, "Aphasia in Polyglots and Bilinguals," *Brain and Language* 1 (1974), 15–27, quoted in Martin Albert and Loraine K. Obler, *The Bilingual Brain: Neuropsychological and Neurolinguistic Aspects of Bilingualism* (New York: Academic Press, 1978), 106.

10. Albert and Obler, *The Bilingual Brain,* 106.

11. François Grosjean, *Life with Two Languages* (Cambridge: Harvard University Press, 1982), 288.

12. Osip Mandel'shtam: "Tempt not alien tongues, / rather try to forget them" [Ne iskushai chuzhikh narechii, no postaraisia ikh zabyt']. From a poem written in Staryi Krym, no. 270, in G. P. Struve and B. A. Filipoff, eds., *Sobranie sochinenii* (New York: Interlanguage Associates, 1966), I, 195.

13. The manuscripts of several of the writers whom I will treat, especially the early manuscripts, sometimes display copybook errors of grammar and spelling, but this does not in itself disqualify these writers from being considered bilingual. Nor has it prevented them from publishing and, in many cases, attaining considerable renown in their second languages.

14. The title of an essay by Brodsky and of the whole collection of essays of which it is a part: Joseph Brodsky, *Less than One* (New York: Farrar, Straus & Giroux, 1986).

Chapter 1. The Neurolinguistic Substrate of Bilingual Writing

1. For a historical overview of the clinical evidence for brain asymmetries, including Paul Broca's findings, see chap. 1 of Sally P. Springer and Georg Deutsch, *Left Brain, Right Brain*, rev. ed. (New York: W. H. Freeman, 1985). See also A. R. Lecours and F. L'Hermitte, *L'aphasie* (Paris: Flammarion, 1979), chap. 2.

2. Robert Zatorre, "La représentation des langues multiples dans le cerveau: Vieux problèmes et nouvelles orientations," *Langages* 72 (December 1983), 15–31; 15 (special issue: "La neurolinguistique du bilinguisme").

3. Among the recent and very informative books on the neurolinguistics of bilingualism are Martin Albert and Loraine K. Obler, *The Bilingual Brain: Neuropsychological and Neurolinguistic Aspects of Bilingualism* (New York: Academic Press, 1978); Jyotsna Vaid, ed., *Language Processing in Bilinguals: Psycholinguistic and Neuropsychological Perspectives* (Hillsdale, N.J.: Lawrence Erlbaum, 1986); and Sidney J. Segalowitz, ed., *Language Function and Brain Organization* (New York: Academic Press, 1983). See also the special issue of *Langages*, "La neurolinguistique du bilinguisme," ed. Michel Paradis and Yvan Lebrun, published in December 1983; and Loraine K. Obler, "Knowledge in Neurolinguistics: The Case of Bilingualism," in A. Z. Guiora, ed., *An Epistemology for the Language Sciences* (Detroit: Wayne State University Press, 1981), 159–191. For a more general overview of bilingualism per se, see François Grosjean, *Life with Two Languages* (Cambridge: Harvard University Press, 1982); and Kenji Hakuta, *Mirror of Language: The Debate on Bilingualism* (New York: Basic Books, 1986).

4. In a few extreme instances, the reverse pattern of lateralization holds true: e.g., in some left-handed persons and in cases where those portions of the left-hemispheric cortex which are usually specialized for language are defective or damaged in infancy and where it has proved possible for the right hemisphere to develop most of the essential language functions. Substitution of this magnitude does not, however, appear to be possible after puberty. For research on later abilities of early left-hemidecorticate children, see M. Dennis and B. Kohn,

"Comprehension of Syntax in Infantile Hemiplegics after Cerebral Hemidecortication: Left Hemisphere Superiority," *Brain and Language* 2 (1975), 472–482. On children with early left-hemisphere damage, see B. T. Woods, "Observations on the Neurological Basis for Initial Language," in D. Caplan, ed., *Biological Studies for Mental Processes* (Cambridge: MIT Press, 1980), 149–158. Woods indicates that, despite early hemispheric plasticity, there are some essential linguistic functions that only the left hemisphere can perform. See also M. Dennis, "Language Acquisition in a Single Hemisphere: Semantic Organization," in Caplan, ed., *Biological Studies for Mental Processes*, 159–186.

5. Michael C. Corballis and Ivan L. Beale, *The Ambivalent Mind: The Neuropsychology of Left and Right* (Chicago: Nelson-Hall, 1983), 135. What is known about the "location" of language(s) in the bilingual brain comes to us primarily through studies of the differential recovery of languages from aphasia (caused by stroke, traumatic injury, etc.), through tachistoscopic and dichotic listening tests, and, more recently, through procedures using sodium amytal or electrostimulation of various cortical areas. See Zatorre, "La représentation des langues multiples."

6. On left-handedness, see Springer and Deutsch, "The Puzzles of the Left Hander," *Left Brain, Right Brain,* 117–142; and S. F. Witelson, "Neuroanatomical Asymmetry in Left Handers: A Review and Implications for Functional Asymmetry," in J. Herron, ed., *Neuropsychology of Left-handedness* (New York: Academic Press, 1980), 79–113. For indications that females and children have greater language-learning ability than adult males, and that women, children, and bilinguals are less lateralized than the norm, see M. P. Bryden, *Laterality: Functional Asymmetry in the Intact Brain* (New York: Academic Press, 1982); S. J. Segalowitz and M. P. Bryden, "Individual Differences in Hemispheric Representation of Language," in Segalowitz, ed., *Language Function and Brain Organization,* 341–372; and Corballis and Beale, *The Ambivalent Mind.* L. K. Obler, R. Zatorre, L. M. Galloway, and J. Vaid cite conflicting findings in studies of cerebral lateralization for children, the elderly, women, and musicians ("Cerebral Lateralization in Bilinguals: Methodological Issues," *Brain and Language* 15 [1982], 40–54). Evidence that the standard pattern of lateralization is more characteristic of males than of females can be found in Jeanette McGlone, "Sex Differences in Human Brain Asymmetry: A Critical Survey," *Behavioral and Brain Sciences* 3 (1980), 215–263. Many studies on language and lateralization have not taken bilingualism into account or do so only minimally. Springer and Deutsch, for example, devote fewer than two pages to it in *Left Brain, Right Brain.*

7. Loraine K. Obler and colleagues have argued for a "stage" hypothesis, i.e., that right hemisphere processing is greater in the initial stages of second-language learning, particularly when the language is informally "acquired" rather than "learned" in a formal classroom situation; see Obler et al., "Right Hemisphere Participation in Second Language Acquistion," in K. Diller, ed., *Individual Differences and Universals in Language Aptitude* (Rowley, Mass.: Newbury House, 1981), 53–64. Also see Eta I. Schneiderman, "Leaning to the

Right: Some Thoughts on Hemisphere Involvement in Language Acquisition,"
in Vaid, ed., *Language Processing in Bilinguals*, 233–251. But see J. Vaid and
Fred Genesee, "Neuropsychological Approaches to Bilingualism: A Critical
Review," *Canadian Journal of Psychology / Revue canadienne de psychologie*
34 (1980), 417–445; Linda M. Galloway, "Bilingualism: Neuropsychological
Considerations," *Journal of Research and Development in Education* 15
(1982), 12–28; and L. Galloway and S. Krashen, "Cerebral Organization in
Bilingualism and Second Language Acquisition," in R. Scarcella and S.
Krashen, eds., *Research in Second Language Acquisition* (Rowley, Mass.: Newbury House, 1980), 74–80. H. Sussman, P. Franklin, and T. Simon, who used
a test of verbal-manual interference to establish hemispheric dominance, have
reported that bilinguals who acquired their second language before age six
show left-hemisphere dominance for both languages, whereas those who acquired a second language after that age had left-hemisphere dominance for the
first language and bilateral dominance for the second language ("Bilingual
Speech: Bilateral Control," *Brain and Language* 15 [1982], 125–142). Their
study supports the conclusion reached by Vaid and Genesee, who surveyed
forty-odd studies of lateralization in bilinguals, that the pattern of cerebral
dominance in bilinguals is most like that in monolinguals when the second
language has been learned early, but that late second-language acquisition en-
gages the two hemispheres differently ("Neuropsychological Approaches to Bilingualism," 435). See also J. Vaid, "Bilingualism and Brain Lateralization," in
Segalowitz, ed., *Language Function and Brain Organization*, 315–339.

8. Obler et al., "Right Hemisphere Participation in Second Language Acquisition." See also Galloway and Krashen, "Cerebral Organization in Bilingualism and Second Language Acquisition."

9. Vaid and Genesee, "Neuropsychological Approaches to Bilingualism,"
438–439.

10. C. Soares and F. Grosjean, "Left Hemisphere Language Lateralization in
Bilinguals and Monolinguals," *Perception and Psychophysics* 29 (1981), 599–
604; H. Gordon, "Cerebral Organization in Bilinguals," *Brain and Language*
9 (1980), 255–268.

11. See L. K. Obler, "Knowledge in Neurolinguistics: The Case of Bilingualism," in Guiora, ed., *An Epistemology for the Language Sciences*, 159–191;
176–177.

12. George Ojemann and Harry A. Whitaker, "The Bilingual Brain," *Archives of Neurology* 35 (1978), 409–412; H. A. Whitaker, Daniel Bub, and
Susan Leventer, "Neurolinguistic Aspects of Language Acquisition and Bilingualism," in *Native Language and Foreign Language Acquisition*, Proceedings
of Conference on Native and Foreign Language Acquisition, January 15–16,
1981, ed. H. Winitz, *Annals of the New York Academy of Sciences* 379,
(1981), 59–74; 71–73.

13. Whitaker et al., "Neurolinguistic Aspects of Language Acquisition," 71–
72; R. L. Rapport, C. T. Tan, and H. A. Whitaker, "Fonctions linguistiques et
troubles du langage chez les polyglotes parlant chinois et anglais," *Langages* 72
(December 1983), 57–78. Albert and Obler concur: "Taken as a group, studies

[in differential cerebral lateralization] argue forcefully in favor of the notions of cerebral ambilaterality of language representation in bilinguals, asymmetrical dominance for each language and influence of language acquisition circumstances on dominance" (*The Bilingual Brain*, 241). However, see Michel Paradis and Yvan Lebrun, "La neurolinguistique du bilinguisme: Représentation et traitement de deux langues dans un même cerveau," *Langages* 72 (December 1983), 7–13 and note their caveats (p. 9) about the general applicability of the research of Whitaker et al. See also Paradis, "Neurolinguistic Organization of a Bilingual's Two Languages," in *Seventh LACUS Forum*, ed. J. E. Copeland and P. W. Davis (Columbia, S.C.: Hornbeam Press, 1981). Here Paradis proposes a "dual system" hypothesis whereby two languages may be represented in overlapping but distinct areas of the brain, and he suggests that the weaker language occupies a wider area of the cortex.

14. The studies of Whitaker and colleagues, which used electrical stimulation of various sites in the cortex, are not subject to the same caveats as dichotic listening and tachistoscopic word-recognition tests. Dichotic listening tests present information to each of the subject's ears simultaneously, and the subject is supposed to report all the information that he or she remembers. Higher scores of correct responses are reported for the ear on the side opposite that of the cerebral hemisphere which is dominant for language. Tachistoscopic tests work on a similar principle for vision. Information is presented to the peripheral visual field at such high speed that the eyes cannot scan. Therefore, a written word presented to the right visual field of a "normal" subject will be processed faster and more accurately than the same information when it has to go first to the right hemisphere from the left visual field and then to the left hemisphere. These tests deal essentially with measures of *rapidity*, which may or may not have anything to do with normal processing of complex utterances in real language.

15. Whitaker et al., "Neurolinguistic Aspects of Language Acquisition and Bilingualism," 73. Albert and Obler agree (*The Bilingual Brain*, 241).

16. Paradis and Lebrun, "La neurolinguistique du bilinguisme," 7.

17. Harold W. Gordon and Robert Weide, "La contribution de certaines fonctions cognitives au traitement du langage, à son acquisition et à l'apprentissage d'une langue seconde," *Langages* 72 (December 1983), 45–56; 45. Gordon and Weide observe that determining the contribution of specialized functions of the right and left hemispheres to language acquisition, second-language acquisition, and language processing is not the same as "locating" languages in the left or right hemisphere. Comprehension and production of languages draw on many basic brain functions, such as pattern recognition, perception (both visual and auditory), temporal analysis, memory, and temporal production. They note that some stimuli essential to language processing may not be properly speaking linguistic and that some linguistic stimuli may be processed nontraditionally.

18. Vaid and Genesee, "Neuropsychological Approaches to Bilingualism"; Linda M. Galloway, "Études cliniques et expérimentales sur la répartition hémisphérique du traitement cérébrale du langage chez les bilingues: Modèles

théoriques," *Langages* 72 (December 1983), 79–113; 103.

19. Vaid and Genesee, quoting C. Tomlinson-Keasley and R. R. Kelley, "A Task Analysis of Hemispheric Functioning," *Neuropsychologia* 17 (1979), 345–351. Schneiderman, "Leaning to the Right," 234, cites the literature that documents the existence of distinct processing modes: e.g., J. E. Bogan, "The Other Side of the Brain II: An Appositional Mind," *Bulletin of the Los Angeles Neurological Societies* 34 (1969), 135–161; J. L. Bradshaw and N. C. Nettleton, "The Nature of Hemisphere Specialization in Man," *Behavioral and Brain Sciences* 4 (1981), 51–63; M. C. Corballis, *Human Laterality* (New York: Academic Press, 1983); Lecours and L'Hermitte, *L'aphasie.*

20. Gordon and Weide, "La contribution de certaines fonctions cognitives au traitement du langage," 50.

21. See Schneiderman, "Leaning to the Right," for an extremely interesting study of the role of right-hemisphere involvement and its application of holistic or "chunking" strategies to novel data in the target language.

22. Vaid and Genesee, "Neuropsychological Approaches to Bilingualism," 423. Corballis and Beale, for instance, have shown that the left hemisphere is generally more involved in production tasks and that reading seems to involve increased left-hemisphere processing, especially when the script in question is phonetic (*The Ambivalent Mind,* 133). Almost predictably, however, there is evidence that reading of logographic script involves relatively greater right-hemisphere participation. L. Obler, "La neuropsychologie du bilinguisme," *Langages* 72 (December 1983), 33–43; 35, cites T. Hatta, "Recognition of Kanji and Hirakana in the Left and Right Visual Fields," *Japanese Psychological Research* 20 (1978), 51–59; T. Nguy, F. Allard, and M. Bryden, "Laterality Effects for Chinese Characters: Differences between Pictorial and Non-Pictorial characters," *Canadian Journal of Psychology/Revue canadienne de psychologie* 34 (1980), 270–273; S. Sasanuma, M. Itoh, K. Mori, and Y. Kobashi, "Tachistoscopic Recognition of Kana and Kanji words," *Neuropsychologia* 15 (1977), 547–553; and, especially, R. Hasuike, O. Tzeng, and D. Hung, "Script Effects and Cerebral Lateralization: The Case of Chinese Characters," in Vaid, ed., *Language Processing in Bilinguals,* 275–288.

23. Albert and Obler (*The Bilingual Brain,* 243–244) predict that there will be more right-hemisphere involvement. Galloway and Krashen, Obler, Schneiderman and Wesche, Vaid, and others have found a variety of evidence for right-hemisphere processing: Galloway and Krashen, "Cerebral Organization in Bilingualism and Second Language Acquisition"; Obler et al., "Cerebral Lateralization in Bilinguals"; Eta Schneiderman and M. B. Wesche, "The Role of the Right Hemisphere in Second Language Acquisition," in K. Bailey, M. Long, and S. Peck, eds., *Second Language Acquisition Studies* (Rowley, Mass.: Newbury House, 1983), 162–174; Vaid, "Bilingualism and Brain Lateralization"; and Vaid and Genesee, "Neuropsychological Approaches to Bilingualism." Schneiderman, "Leaning to the Right," 237, lists studies that show no significant differences in lateralization patterns for the first and second languages—among them M. Barton, H. Goodglass, and A. Shai, "Differential Recognition of Tachistoscopically Presented English and Hebrew Words in

Right and Left Visual Fields," *Perception and Motor Skills* 21 (1965), 431–437; F. W. Carroll, "Cerebral Dominance for Language: A Dichotic Listening Study of Navajo-English Bilinguals," in H. Key, S. McCullough, and J. Sawyer, eds., *The Bilingual in a Pluralistic Society: Proceedings of the Sixth Southwest Area Language and Linguistic Workshop* (Long Beach: California State University Press, 1978), 11–17; L. Galloway and R. Scarcella, "Cerebral Organization in Adult Second Language Acquisition: Is the Right Hemisphere More Involved?" *Brain and Language* 16 (1982), 56–60; H. Gordon, "Cerebral Organization in Bilinguals," *Brain and Language* 9 (1980), 255–268; R. L. Rapport, C. T. Tan, and H. A. Whitaker, "Language Function and Dysfunction among Chinese and English-speaking Polyglots: Cortical Stimulation, Wada Testing, and Clinical Studies," *Brain and Language* 18 (1983), 315–341; C. Soares and F. Grosjean, "Left Hemisphere Language Lateralization in Bilinguals and Monolinguals," *Perception and Psychophysics* 29 (1981), 599–604; J. Walters and R. Zatorre, "Laterality Differences for Word Identification in Bilinguals," *Brain and Language* 2 (1978), 158–167. A few studies report greater *left* lateralization for the second language than for the first: F. W. Carroll, "The Other Side of the Brain and Foreign Language Learning," paper presented at the TESOL Conference, Mexico City, 1978; B. Kotik, "Lateralization in Bilinguals" (thesis, Moscow State University, 1973); L. Rogers, W. Ten Houghton, C. D. Kaplan, and M. Gordimer, "Hemispheric Specialization of Language: An EEG Study of Bilingual Hopi Indian Children," *International Journal of Neuroscience* 17 (1977), 89–92.

24. Galloway and Krashen, "Cerebral Organization in Bilingualism and Second Language Acquisition," 77–78.

25. Galloway, "Bilingualism: Neuropsychological Considerations," 22.

26. M. Moscovitch, "The Linguistic and Emotional Functions of the Normal Right Hemisphere," in Ellen Perecman, ed., *Cognitive Processing in the Right Hemisphere* (New York: Academic Press, 1983), 57–82. Schneiderman, "Leaning to the Right," 243, cites other studies as well; also see Eta Schneiderman and Chantal Desmarais, "A Neuropsychological Substrate for Talent in Second Language Acquisition," in L. K. Obler and D. A. Fein, eds., *The Exceptional Brain: The Neuropsychology of Talent and Special Abilities* (New York: Guilford Press, 1988), 103–126; 115–116.

27. E. Goldberg and L. D. Costa, "Hemisphere Differences in the Acquisition and Use of Descriptive Systems," *Brain and Language* 14 (1981), 144–173.

28. Schneiderman, "Leaning to the Right," 239. See also S. T. Witelson, "Early Hemispheric Specialization and Interhemispheric Plasticity: An Empirical and Theoretical Review," in S. J. Segalowitz and F. A. Gruber, eds., *Language Development and Neurological Theory* (New York: Academic Press, 1977), 149–158. Less-than-balanced bilinguals may process items in their two languages differently, and if the two languages are mixed in presentation (as they often are in experiments), people with greater proficiency in one language may process all the stimuli as if for that language (Obler et al., "Cerebral Lateralization in Bilinguals," 47). See also Beverly B. Wulfeck, Larry Juarez,

Elizabeth A. Bates, and Kerry Kilborn, "Sentence Interpretation Strategies in Healthy and Aphasic Bilingual Adults," in Vaid, ed., *Language Processing in Bilinguals*, 203–219.

29. Obler et al., "Cerebral Lateralization in Bilinguals," 52; C. Hardyk, "Hemispheric Differences and Language Ability," paper presented at Conference on the Neurolinguistics of Bilingualism: Individual Differences, Albuquerque, N.M., August 1980; F. Genesee, J. Hamers, W. E. Lambert, L. Mononen, M. Seitz, and R. Starck, "Language Processing in Bilinguals," *Brain and Language* 5 (1978), 1–12; S. Bentin, "Right Hemisphere Role in Reading a Second Language," forthcoming.

30. Schneiderman, "Leaning to the Right," 243; Moscovitch, "The Linguistic and Emotional Functions of the Normal Right Hemisphere."

31. Paradis and Lebrun, "La neurolinguistique du bilinguisme," 7. Consistent with this evidence is P. Ross-Kossak and G. Turkewitz's three-stage theory of hemispheric advantage in perceptual processing. According to this theory, "The initial stage of perceptual processing involves a holistic approach which is better performed by the right hemisphere. In the second stage, processing is more analytic and feature-oriented and favors the left hemisphere. During stage three, there is an integration of the former stages and synthesis of analytic and holistic approaches. This stage is better performed by the right hemisphere." Thus, Ross-Kossak and Turkewitz predict a shift in hemispheric advantage from the right to the left and back again to the right ("A Micro and Macro Developmental View of the Nature of Changes in Complex Information Processing: A Consideration of Changes in Hemispheric Advantage during Familiarization," in R. Bruyer, ed., *Neuropsychology of Facial Expression* [Hillsdale, N.J.: Lawrence Erlbaum, 1986], 125–145; 127).

32. Wulfeck et al., "Sentence Interpretation Strategies."

33. E. Bates and B. MacWhinney, "Second Language Acquisition from a Functionalist Perspective: Pragmatic, Semantic, and Perceptual Strategies," in Winitz, ed., *Native Language and Foreign Language Acquisition*, 190–214; Wulfeck et al., "Sentence Interpretation Strategies," 203.

34. Wulfeck et al., "Sentence Interpretation Strategies," 216 (also see 211 for examples).

35. See Elizabeth Peal and Wallace E. Lambert, "The Relation of Bilingualism to Intelligence," *Psychological Monographs* 76 (27, whole no. 546), 1962, 1–23, for a review of these studies. Also see Sandra Ben-Zeev, "The Influence of Bilingualism on Cognitive Strategy and Cognitive Development," *Child Development* 48 (1977), 1009–1018; L. K. Obler, M. Albert, and S. Lozowick, "The Aging Bilingual," in Vaid, ed., *Language Processing in Bilinguals*, 221–231.

36. W. E. Lambert, "The Effects of Bilingualism on the Individual: Cognitive and Sociocultural Consequences," in P. Hornby, ed., *Bilingualism: Psychological, Social, and Educational Implications* (New York: Academic Press, 1977). See also Hakuta, *Mirror of Language*, 35, for extensive references to studies in other settings that reconfirm Peal and Lambert.

37. W. E. Lambert, "Bilingualism and Language Acquisition," in Winitz, ed., *Native Language and Foreign Language Acquisition*, 10. See also evidence that bilingual children exhibit superior performance over monolinguals in "discover the rule" problems: Bruce Bain "Bilingualism and Cognition: Toward a General Theory," *Bilingualism, Biculturalism, and Education: Proceedings from the Conference at Collège Universitaire Saint Jean*, ed. S. T. Carey (Edmonton: University of Alberta, 1974).

38. Lambert, "Bilingualism and Language Acquisition," 11–12.

39. See Bruce Bain and Agnes Yu, "Cognitive Consequences of Raising Children Bilingually: 'One Parent, One Language,'" *Canadian Journal of Psychology / Revue canadienne de psychologie* 34 (1980), 304–313; L. Balkan, *Les éffets du bilinguisme français-anglais sur les aptitudes intellectuelles* (Brussels: Aimav, 1970); J. Cummins, "The Influence of Bilingualism on Cognitive Growth: A Synthesis of Research Findings and Explanatory Hypotheses," *Working Papers on Bilingualism* 9 (1976), 1–43; J. Cummins, "Metalinguistic Development of Children in Bilingual Education Programs," in M. Paradis, ed., *Aspects of Bilingualism* (Columbia, S.C.: Hornbeam Press, 1978), 127–138; and J. Cummins, "Bilingualism and the Development of Metalinguistic Awareness," *Journal of Cross-Cultural Psychology* 9 (1978), 131–149.

40. Schneiderman and Desmarais, "A Neuropsychological Substrate for Talent," 32.

41. Ben-Zeev, "The Influence of Bilingualism on Cognitive Strategy and Cognitive Development," 1009. This finding holds despite a lower vocabulary level. Because the bilinguals in Ben-Zeev's study have been confronted with a verbal environment of great complexity in which an underlying order is difficult to discover (since the rules belong to two structures rather than to one), they have "developed special facility for seeking out rules and determining which are required by the circumstances." These bilinguals demonstrate two characteristic strategies in relation to verbal material: (i) readiness to impute structure and (ii) readiness to reorganize verbal material in an effort to seek out underlying dimensions in the patterns they confront (1017).

42. Id. The superior performance of bilinguals in "discover the rule" problems was confirmed by Bain and Yu; see especially their "Cognitive Consequences of Raising Children Bilingually."

43. Hakuta, *Mirror of Language*, 40; and K. Hakuta and R. Diaz, "The Relationship between Bilingualism and Cognitive Ability: A Critical Discussion and Some New Longitudinal Data," in *Children's Language* 5, ed. K. E. Nelson (Hillsdale, N.J.: Lawrence Erlbaum, 1984). Hakuta and Diaz find this effect much stronger for the native language of Spanish-English bilinguals. See Ben-Zeev, "The Influence of Bilingualism on Cognitive Strategy and Cognitive Development"; Lambert, "Bilingualism and Language Acquisition"; and G. L. MacNab, "Cognition and Bilingualism: A Reanalysis of Studies," *Linguistics* 17 (1979), 231–55; 232.

44. B. Bain and A. Yu, "Towards an Integration of Piaget and Vygotsky," in Paradis, ed., *Aspects of Bilingualism*, 113–126; 125. A few researchers chal-

lenge these findings of cognitive enhancement, primarily for reasons having to do with the associational character of the studies and the self-selection of the samples (MacNab, "Cognition and Bilingualism," 232).

45. Hakuta, *Mirror of Language,* 35.

46. Ibid., 38. Hakuta quotes Peal and Lambert themselves on this point: "One may ask whether the more intelligent children, as measured by non-verbal intelligence tests, are the ones who become bilingual, or whether bilingualism itself has a favorable effect on non-verbal intelligence" ("The Relation of Bilingualism to Intelligence," 13).

47. See Obler, Albert, and Lozowick, "The Aging Bilingual." It may even be possible that early patterns can be reactivated.

48. See Edith Mägiste, "Selected Issues in Second and Third Language Learning," in Vaid, ed., *Language Processing in Bilinguals,* 97–122; 118; Cummins, "Bilingualism and the Development of Metalinguistic Awareness"; A. D. Ianco-Worrall, "Bilingualism and Cognitive Development," *Child Development* 43 (1972), 1390–1400; E. Mägiste, "Recall of Concrete and Abstract Sentences in Bilinguals," *Scandinavian Journal of Psychology* 20 (1979), 179–185; F. Genesee, G. R. Tucker, and W. E. Lambert, "Communication Skills of Bilingual Children," *Child Development* 46 (1975), 1010–1014; S. P. Cohen, G. R. Tucker, and W. E. Lambert, "The Comparative Skills of Monolinguals and Bilinguals in Perceiving Phoneme Sequences," *Language and Speech* 10 (1967), 159–168.

49. MacNab, "Cognition and Bilingualism," 237. Carringer and Lambert, using creativity tests, have also found greater originality in bilinguals than in monolinguals. See D. Carringer, "Creative Thinking Ability of Mexican Youth: The Relationship of Bilingualism," *Journal of Cross-Cultural Psychology* 5 (1974), 492–504; W. E. Lambert, "Cognitive and Attitudinal Consequences of Bilingual Schooling," *Journal of Educational Psychology* 65 (1973), 86–96. MacNamara and Ruke-Dravina have also discussed creativity in association with bilingualism. See J. MacNamara, "Nurseries, Streets, and Classrooms: Some Comparisons and Deductions," *Modern Language Journal* 57 (1973), 250–254; V. Ruke-Dravina, "Word Associations in Monolingual and Multilingual Individuals," *Linguistics* 74 (1971), 66–84; and V. Ruke-Dravina, "The Ability of Swedish-Latvian Teenagers to Describe Events," paper presented to Symposium on Child Speech, Belgrade, Yugoslavia, 1976.

50. Grosjean, *Life with Two Languages,* 271–273, citing, among others, Věroboj Vildomec, *Multilingualism* (Leiden: A. W. Sythoff, 1963). Vildomec concludes that active bilingualism is, in the main, an obstacle to literary expression (p. 32).

51. Obler, Albert, and Lozowick, "The Aging Bilingual," 227–228. Bilinguals performed better than monolinguals on a number of measures: they generated significantly more items on the animal list-generation test; they were faster and made fewer errors than monolinguals in naming colors in the congruent condition of the Stroop color-word interference test, and they scored higher than monolinguals on the time-constrained condition of the visual-closure test, a task that does not have any ostensible linguistic basis. The fact

that bilinguals were significantly faster than monolinguals in the timed condition of the visual-closure test suggests to Obler et al. that greater efficiency at making guesses about meaning is a by-product of mastery of two languages; see also Ben-Zeev, "The Influence of Bilingualism on Cognitive Strategy and Cognitive Development," for similar conclusions with respect to bilingual children. Obler et al. also note the need for further research concerning an apparent disinhibition in switching between the two languages (p. 229).

52. Schneiderman and Desmarais, "A Neuropsychological Substrate for Talent," 103.

53. Ibid., 115–116. Among the global strategies to look for in talented language learners are a reliance on more concrete or intuitive modes of operation, rather than on formal, superordinate types of organization; greater flexibility; superior memory for unfamiliar items; and a less left-lateralized than "normal" substrate for language. Schneiderman and Desmarais also propose that a type of flexibility similar to the one that underlies second-language learning may also underlie exceptional ease at adapting to novel sociocultural and belief systems (p. 119).

54. N. Geshwind and A. Galaburda suggest that there may be a "pathology of superiority," that is, compensatory growth leading to the superior development of some portions of the brain as a result of poorer development of others ("Cerebral Lateralization—Biological Mechanisms, Associations, and Pathology," *Archives of Neurology* 42 [1985]). Geshwind and Galaburda postulate a high coincidence of left-handedness, autoimmune disorders, learning disorders, and talent. They also suggest a causal relationship between some exceptional abilities and certain disabilities. While Schneiderman and Desmarais do not suggest that talent for language acquisition is the *result* of a previous lack of development of some part of the brain, they do point out that, because the talented language learner (particularly the polyglot) devotes a larger-than-average percentage of the cortex to language functioning, this may adversely affect performance in other tasks normally associated with the right hemisphere.

55. Schneiderman and Desmarais, "A Neuropsychological Substrate for Talent." See also Loriana Novoa, Deborah Fein, and Loraine Obler, "Talent in Foreign Languages: A Case Study," in Obler and Fein, eds., *The Exceptional Brain*, 294–302. Their "talented" subject, "C. J.," did not always rely on recognized superordinate categories to aid memory; he could establish other, equally effective access routes.

56. L. Selinker, "Interlanguage," *International Review of Applied Linguistics* 10 (1972), 209–231.

57. See G. G. Neufeld, "Language Learning Ability in Adults: A Study on the Acquisition of Prosodic and Articulatory Features," *Working Papers on Bilingualism* 12 (1977), 45–60; and id., "On the Adult's Ability to Acquire Phonology," *TESOL Quarterly* 14 (1980), 285–298. Neufeld notes that adult learners of a second language have lost neither their sensitivity to differences in sound, rhythm, and pitch nor their ability to reproduce those differences. Even those with strong foreign accents appear to have developed keen auditory dis-

crimination in their second language. C. Snow and M. Hoefnagle-Hohle, "Critical Period for Language Acquisition: Evidence from Second Language Learning," *Child Development* 49 (1978), 263–279, point out that some aspects of language may actually be learned better by adults than by children spending the same amount of time on them. See also studies which indicate that adults often surpass children as second-language learners in almost all aspects of language skills: e.g., B. McLaughlin, *Second Language Acquisition in Childhood* (Hillsdale, N.J.: Lawrence Erlbaum, 1978); and P. C. Smythe, R. E. Stennett, and R. C. Gardner, "The Best Age for Foreign-Language Training: Issues, Options, and Facts," *Canadian Modern Language Review* 32 (1975), 10–23.

58. On accents and ego-permeability in second-language learning, see A. Guiora, R. Brannen, and C. Dull, "Empathy and Second Language Learning," *Language Learning* 22 (1972), 111–130; A. Guiora, H. Buchtel, A. Herold, T. Homberg, and M. Woken, "Right 'Hemisphericity' and Pronunciation in a Foreign Language," paper presented at the TESOL Conference, Toronto, March 1983. On the relationship between social identity and accent, see S. J. Biondi, *The Italian-American Child: His Sociolinguistic Acculturation* (Washington, D.C.: Georgetown University Press, 1975); and W. Labov, *Sociolinguistic Patterns* (Philadelphia: University of Pennsylvania Press, 1972). As bilinguals know from experience, their accents are not fixed and unchanging. Some find them more pronounced when they are nervous, or when speaking to strangers or to answering machines. They can hear what they do wrong when they are recorded on tape (comments by Nancy Huston, in Leila Sebbar and Nancy Huston, *Lettres parisiennes* [Paris: Barrault, 1986], 15).

59. Schneiderman and Desmarais, "A Neuropsychological Substrate for Talent," 118.

60. Michel Paradis, "Contributions of Neurolinguistics to the Theory of Bilingualism," *Applications of Linguistic Theory in the Human Sciences* (East Lansing: Dept. of Linguistics, Michigan State University, 1980), 180–201; id., "Language and Thought in Bilinguals," in *Sixth LACUS Forum*, ed. W. McCormack and H. J. Izzo (Columbia, S.C.: Hornbeam Press, 1980); and id., "Neurolinguistic Organization of a Bilingual's Two Languages," in *Seventh LACUS Forum*, ed. J. E. Copeland and P. W. Davis (Columbia, S.C.: Hornbeam Press, 1981).

61. I. Taylor, "How Are Words from Two Languages Organized in Bilinguals' Memory?" *Canadian Journal of Psychology / Revue canadienne de psychologie* 25 (1971), 228–240.

62. See Grosjean, *Life with Two Languages*, 240–255; Paradis, "Language and Thought in Bilinguals"; and id., "Neurolinguistic Organization of a Bilingual's Two Languages" for a review of the situation.

63. Grosjean, *Life with Two Languages*, 247.

64. M. Paradis, "Bilingual Linguistic Memory: Neurolinguistic Considerations" (paper presented to the Linguistic Society of America, Boston, 1978), cited in Grosjean, *Life with Two Languages*, 247.

65. M. Preston and W. E. Lambert, "Interlingual Interference in a Bilin[gual] Version of the Stroop Color-Word Tasks," *Journal of Verbal Learning and [Ver]bal Behavior* 8 (1969), 295–301, cited in Albert and Obler, *The Bilin[gual] Brain*, 78. In a Stroop test, subjects must, as quickly as possible, label colors on cards that have color words written on them in inks of different colors (for example, the word "red" is written in green ink). For bilinguals, this test gets very complicated, and there are sometimes errors that take the form of saying the term in the wrong language. If they are supposed to answer in French, they may say "rouge" when they see the English word "red" written in green ink, when they are supposed to say "vert."

66. Albert and Obler, *The Bilingual Brain*, 93. See also L. Doob, "The Effect of Language on Verbal Expression and Recall," *American Anthropology* 59 (1957), 88–100.

67. Albert and Obler, *The Bilingual Brain*, 245.

68. Paradis, "Contributions of Neurolinguistics to the Theory of Bilingualism," 197. See also M. Paradis, "The Stratification of Bilingualism," in Paradis, ed., *Aspects of Bilingualism*, 165–175. Kim Kirsner maintains that lexical representation in bilinguals is governed by morphology rather than by language and that lexical representations may be defined in terms of the operations brought to bear on the stimulus input ("Lexical Function: Is a Bilingual Account Necessary?" in Vaid, ed., *Language Processing in Bilinguals*, 22–45; 42).

69. Obler, "Knowledge in Neurolinguistics," 183; Albert and Obler, *The Bilingual Brain*, 78.

70. Paul Kolers, "Bilingualism and Information Processing," *Scientific American* 218 (1968), 78–89; 82–83.

71. Grosjean, *Life with Two Languages*, 247, citing Paradis, "Bilingual Linguistic Memory." See also Paradis, "Language and Thought in Bilinguals"; and id., "Neurolinguistic Organization of a Bilingual's Two Languages." F. Grosjean and C. Soares, "Processing Mixed Language: Some Preliminary Findings," in Vaid, ed., *Language Processing in Bilinguals*, 145–179, appear to adopt the theory of two lexicons. However, in all fairness, also see P. D. McCormack, "Bilingual Linguistic Memory: The Independence-Interdependence Issue Revisited," in Hornby, ed., *Bilingualism*.

72. Allan Paivio and Ian Begg, *Psychology of Language* (Englewood Cliffs, N.J.: Prentice-Hall, 1981), 67, 70, 71.

73. Ibid., 296.

74. Paradis, "Bilingual Linguistic Memory," 2, cited in Grosjean, *Life with Two Languages*, 248.

75. Grosjean and Soares, "Processing Mixed Language," 149. As Grosjean observes, it is easy to translate words that share many conceptual features with their translation equivalents, and difficult to translate those which share few (*Life with Two Languages*, 248).

76. Paradis, "The Stratification of Bilingualism," 171.

77. Beneath or beyond the conceptual level, depending on whether the pro-

cess is one of input or output, there are also sememic, lexemic, morphemic, phonemic, and phonetic levels. In the decoding or encoding of a *written* text, graphemic and graphic strata are correlated with or substituted for phonemic and phonetic strata, depending on whether the writing system is phonetically based or ideographic (ibid., 172).

78. Ibid., 172–173.

79. Kolers, "Bilingualism and Information Processing," 79.

80. L. Obler and M. Albert, "A Monitor System for Bilingual Language Processing," in Paradis, ed., *Aspects of Bilingualism*, 156–164; 160. See also Grosjean and Soares, "Processing Mixed Language," for evidence of the residual activation of the second language when the bilingual is in a monolingual mode. It is interesting to note that the Spanish/English bilinguals in their study accessed real words in English as quickly as did English monolinguals but were substantially slower at responding to nonwords. This led the investigators to suppose that a nonword stimulus triggers a full search of the base-language lexicon *and* a (partial?) search of the other language before the bilingual classifies the stimulus as a nonword (p. 170).

81. S. Sridhar and K. Sridhar believe that code-switching requires that both languages be "on" at the same time. "They propose an interactionist model to account for switching: an 'assembly line' process in which individual components or constituents are put together separately and inserted into appropriate slots in the syntactic frame of the base language being spoken" (Grosjean, *Life with Two Languages*, 255, citing "The Syntax and Psycholinguistics of Bilingual Code-Mixing," *Canadian Journal of Psychology / Revue canadienne de psychologie* 34 [1980], 407–416).

82. M. Paradis, "Bilingualism and Aphasia," in H. A. Whitaker, ed., *Studies in Neurolinguistics* 3 (New York: Academic Press, 1977), 65–121; 91.

83. Paradis, "Neurolinguistic Organization of a Bilingual's Two Languages," 7, cited in Grosjean, *Life with Two Languages*, 267.

84. Paradis, "Bilingualism and Aphasia," 91.

85. Hakuta, *Mirror of Language*, 103.

86. Dostoevskii's Underground Man, the protagonist of *Zapiski iz podpol'ia* [Notes from underground], after a lengthy polemic with putative proponents of the idea of enlightened self-interest, proposes that *sometimes* what an individual may consider to be "the good" for himself is *not* his material self-interest. The individual may even go *against* this material self-interest in order to exercise his freedom—"his own sweet will." In Ralph E. Matlow's translation: "One's own free unfettered choice, one's own fancy, however wild it may be, one's own fancy, worked-up at times to frenzy—why that is that very 'most advantageous advantage' which we have overlooked, which comes under no classification and through which all systems and theories are constantly being sent to the devil" [Svoe sobstvennoe, vol'noe i svobodnoe khoten'e, svoi sobstvennyi, khotia by samyi dikii kapriz, svoia fantaziia razdrazhenniia inogda khot' by dazhe do sumasshestviia—vot eto-to vse i est' ta samaia, propushchennaia, samaia vygodnaia vigoda, kotoraia ni pod kakuiu klasifikatsiiu ne podkhodit i ot kotoroi vse sistemy i teorii postoianno razletaiutsia k chertu]

(*Zapiski iz podpol'ia*, in F. M. Dostoevskii, *Sobranie sochinenii* (Moscow: Iz-dat. Khudozhestvennaia literatura, 1956), *IV*, 153. This point is related to George Steiner's comment that "the human capacity to utter falsehood, to lie, to negate what is the case, stands at the heart of speech and of the reciprocities between words and world. . . . We are a mammal who can bear false witness" (*After Babel* [New York: Oxford University Press, 1975], 214).

87. See Zatorre, "La représentation des langues multiples dans le cerveau," on the frightening complexity of the question.

88. W. E. Lambert, "Psychological Approaches to the Study of Languages," reprinted in *Language, Psychology, Culture* [Stanford, Calif.: Stanford University Press, 1972], 186. Barry McLaughlin, in his more recent "Differences and Similarities between First and Second Language Learning," in Winitz, ed., *Native Language and Foreign Language Acquisition*, 23–32, takes this admission even further: "Since language balance is a very fragile phenomenon in bilingual children, we are dealing with a question of *degree of approximation.* . . . [T]he point at which acquisition of a second language becomes sequential is *difficult to demarcate with precision.* . . . [p. 24] Having said all this, what can one conclude about similarities and differences in first and second language learning? *It depends*, I have been arguing, *on the age of the learners, on their cognitive abilities, and on situational demands* [p. 30, emphasis added throughout]."

89. Uriel Weinreich, *Languages in Contact: Findings and Problems* (New York: Linguistic Circle of New York, 1953; repr. The Hague: Mouton, 1974), 80.

90. Grosjean and Soares, "Processing Mixed Language," 179.

91. George Steiner, "Extraterritorial," *Triquarterly* 17 (1970), 119–127; 125 (special Nabokov issue).

Chapter 2. The Mental Geology of Bilingual Writing

1. François E. Grosjean, "The Bilingual as a Competent but Specific Speaker/Hearer" (paper presented to Symposium on Bilingualism, 9th Annual Boston University Conference on Language Development, 1984), *Journal of Multilingual and Multicultural Development* 6 (1985), 467–477.

2. Kenji Hakuta, *Mirror of Language: The Debate on Bilingualism* (New York: Basic Books, 1986), 102.

3. François Grosjean, *Life with Two Languages* (Cambridge: Harvard University Press, 1982), 270–273. The only difference that bilinguals generally recognize is the obvious one—they can communicate with more kinds of people.

4. Grosjean, *Life with Two Languages*, 268–271. Those who do feel disadvantages frequently mention stress and fatigue in prolonged use of a weaker language. See Kim Kirsner, "Lexical Function: Is a Bilingual Account Necessary?" in Jyotsna Vaid, ed., *Language Processing in Bilinguals: Psycholinguistic and Neuropsychological Perspectives* (Hillsdale, N.J.: Lawrence Erlbaum, 1986), 21–45.

5. There are a few dissenting opinions. Raymond Federman, for example, has said that, rather than feeling *distance* between his languages, they seem to fornicate in one cell (personal communication).

6. George Ojemann and Harry A. Whitaker, "The Bilingual Brain," *Archives of Neurology* 35 (1978), 409–412; H. A. Whitaker, Daniel Bub, and Susan Leventer, "Neurolinguistic Aspects of Language Acquisition and Bilingualism," in *Native Language and Foreign Language Acquisition*, Proceedings of Conference on Native and Foreign Language Acquisition, January 15–16, 1981, ed. H. Winitz, *Annals of the New York Academy of Sciences*, vol. 379 (1981), 59–74, esp. 71–73.

7. Vladimir Nabokov, *Look at the Harlequins!* (New York: McGraw-Hill, 1974), 124–125. Hereafter, references to *LATH* will appear in parentheses in the text.

8. Jacques Hassoun, "Eloge de la dysharmonie," in *Du bilinguisme*, the proceedings of a conference at the University of Rabat, Morocco, November 26–28, 1981 (Paris: Denoël, 1985), 63–78; 65. He continues: "Right now, I am speaking to you in French, the language of distance, the language that authorizes me to evoke the ravine resulting from two languages that have gone underground . . . and that will allow me to understand the role of *repressed structuring elements* (as well as of affectivity and painful representations) flowing in these two languages, Arabic and Hebrew, which are not so much petrified as they are suspended in an achronological time" [Je vous parle en ce moment en français, langue de la distance, langue qui m'autorise à évoquer ce ravin comme la résultante de deux langues devenues souterraines . . . qui me permettront d'entendre la part de *refoulé structurant* (mais aussi la part d'affects et de représentations torturantes) qui court dans ces langues devenues rivières moins pétrifiées que suspendues à un temps achronologique: l'arabe et l'hébraïque] (p. 65).

9. George Steiner, *After Babel* (New York: Oxford University Press, 1975), 291. Hereafter, references to *AB* will appear in parentheses in the text.

10. Gordon Rattray Taylor, *The Natural History of the Mind* (New York: E. P. Dutton, 1979), 274.

11. Walter Benjamin, "The Task of the Translator," in *Illuminations*, trans. Harry Zohn (New York: Harcourt, Brace & World, 1968), 79–81.

12. Joseph Brodsky, "Footnote to a Poem," in *Less than One* (New York: Farrar, Straus & Giroux, 1986), 195–267; 234–235. Brodsky's essay is translated by Barry Rubin. Marina Tsvetaeva, "Novogodnee" [New Year's greeting]. As Brodsky points out, Tsvetaeva actually thinks of the postmortal world not as one where there is no more language, but as a world where one understands all earthly tongues: " 'Not tongueless but all tongues' goes much further, taking conscience back to its source, where it is relieved of the burden of earthly guilt" ["Ne bez a vse-iazychen" idet gorazdo dal'she, uvlekaia za soboi sovest' k ee istoku, gde ona osvobozhdaetsia ot gruza zemnoi viny] (p. 232). Later, he adds: "It is also remarkable that 'Angelic' testifies not to despair but to the height—almost literal, physical perhaps—of the spiritual flight precipitated not so much by the presupposed location of the 'next world' as by

the overall poetic orientation of the author. . . . It is a question of a height that is 'more native' i.e., not attainable by either Russian or German: a height that is supra-lingual, in ordinary parlance—spiritual" [Zamechatel'no takzhe, chto "angel'skii" svidetel'stvuet ne ob otchaianii, no o vysote—edva li ne bukval'noi, fizicheskoi—dushevnogo vzleta, prodiktovannogo ne stol'ko predpolagaemym mestonakhozhedeniem "togo sveta," skol'ko obshchei poeticheskoi orientatsiei avtora. . . . Rech' idet o vysote, kotoraia "rodnei," t.e. nedosiagaema ni dlia russkogo, ni dlia nemetskogo: o vysote nad—iazykovoi, v prostorechii—dukhovnoi] (p. 235). Both "Novogodnee" and Brodsky's article on it, "Ob odnom stikhotvorenii (vmesto predisloviia)," can be found in the original Russian in Marina Tsvetaeva, *Stikhotvoreniia i poemy v piatikh tomakh* (New York: Russica, 1980), *I*, 263–267 and 39–80, respectively, and the passages quoted here on pages 60 and 62, respectively.

13. Martin Albert and Loraine K. Obler, *The Bilingual Brain: Neuropsychological and Neurolinguistic Aspects of Bilingualism* (New York: Academic Press, 1978), 93; also see L. Doob, "The Effect of Language on Verbal Expression and Recall," *American Anthropology* 59 (1957), 88–100.

14. Michel Paradis, "Bilingual Linguistic Memory: Neurolinguistic Considerations" (paper presented to the Linguistic Society of America, Boston, 1978), cited in Grosjean, *Life with Two Languages*, 247; id., "Language and Thought in Bilinguals," in *Sixth LACUS Forum*, ed. W. McCormack and M. J. Izzo (Columbia, S.C.: Hornbeam Press, 1980); id., "Neurolinguistic Organization of a Bilingual's Two Languages," in *Seventh LACUS Forum*, ed. J. E. Copeland and P. W. Davis (Columbia, S.C.: Hornbeam Press, 1981).

15. See Kirsner, "Lexical Function," 21–45.

16. As Steiner has observed, "Reference to meaning or language 'beyond speech' can be a heuristic device, as at the end of Wittgenstein's *Tractatus*. It can be a conceit, often irritating, in epistemology or mysticism. But it can also serve as a metaphor, almost technical, through which to convey a genuine experience" (*AB*, 321).

17. Taylor, *The Natural History of the Mind*, 272; Taylor gives examples of what he means by "feelings" in this special sense of the word in chap. 9: "Traffic of the Mind."

18. Elsa Triolet, *La mise en mots* (Geneva: Skira, 1969), 55. Hereafter, references to *M en m* will appear in parentheses in the text.

19. Grosjean, *Life with Two Languages*, 276.

20. Vladimir Nabokov, *Strong Opinions* (New York: McGraw-Hill, 1973), 14. Hereafter, references to *SO* will appear in parentheses in the text.

21. When queried by the mathematician J. Hadamard in 1927 as to how *he* thought, Einstein replied that he thought in "more or less clear images and certain signs" (quoted in Taylor, *The Natural History of the Mind*, 271). Taylor adds: "His [Einstein's] images were visual and motor. Hadamard himself insisted that when he was engaged in thought words were absent; on the other hand, a lesser mathematician, George Polya, felt that the solution of mathematical problems was always verbal" (p. 271). Green writes: "When I was younger and knew even less about such matters than I do today, I used to be irritated

by a certain question. . . . The question was 'Do you think in English or in French.' My answer was: 'Tell me first if we think in words,' with the unexpressed assumption that we didn't." Green's (slightly) more mature judgment, however, was: "We may take it for granted that practically all our thinking is done in terms of a definite language" (Julien Green, "An Experiment in English," in *Le langage et son double* [Paris: Editions de la différence, 1985], 160). Leonard Forster devotes considerable attention to Yvan Goll (*The Poet's Tongues* [London: Cambridge University Press, 1970], 77–80, 81, 87). Goll's childhood language was French, but, as Forster notes, in pre-1914 Lorraine the language of education and culture was German, and it was in German that Goll wrote his first works. He went to France in 1919 and published in French, becoming associated with the Surrealists, although he used German for correspondence with his wife (who was also a bilingual and a writer) and for some poetry. Most of Goll's novels are in French; his plays are in German. He translated his own prose, but only rarely his poetry. His reputation as a lyric poet is largely owing to his French poetry (in particular, a lyric cycle with the appropriate title *Jean sans terre* [Homeless John]; yet, as Forster observes (p. 80), in his final months in the hospital in Strasbourg, Goll returned to German for the cycle *Traumkraut* [Dream-Cabbage]. It is also important to note that Goll, like many bilingual writers, was extremely prolific.

22. Forster, *The Poet's Tongues*, 79.

23. Of course, some of us may tend to think in images more (or less) than others. The late Dr. Grey Walter, an encephalographer who worked at the Burden Neurological Institute, estimated on the basis of his study of brain waves that 15 percent of the population think exclusively in visual terms, 15 percent think exclusively in verbal terms, and 70 percent employ a mixture (W. Grey Walter, *The Living Brain* [London: Duckworth, 1953], 153ff., cited in Taylor, *The Natural History of the Mind*, 214).

24. Vladimir Nabokov, *Speak, Memory: An Autobiography Revisited* (New York: E. P. Putnam, Wideview/Perigee, 1966), 34–35. Hereafter, references to *SM* will appear in parentheses in the text.

25. Raymond Federman, for instance: "I do my best writing mentally while driving or watching television. I hear sentences. Up there. In my skull, or wherever one hears sentences. Sometimes they are in French, and other times in English. Sometimes they get all mixed up in both languages . . . All my novels began with a sentence I heard in my head, and that sentence somehow contained the entire book. Lately, I hear more sentences in English than in French, and the tone, the movement is immediately established. But the other day, I heard this sentence (in French): 'Il ira vers le grand trou que sera sa vie.' (A rather nice sentence, don't you think? A whole novel could be written with such a sentence.) But right now I feel that the next book should be in English. To translate this sentence into, 'He will go towards the great hole which will be his life,' will not do the trick. No, doesn't work in English. So I have to wait for something else" (personal communication).

26. François Cheng, "Le cas du chinois," in *Du bilinguisme*, 227–235; 233.

27. One can see a similar movement in Nabokov's poem "On Translating *Eugene Onegin*" (written in English in 1955 and included in his *Poems and Problems* [New York: McGraw-Hill, 1970], 175): "O Pushkin, for my stratagem: / I travelled down your secret stem, / And reached the root, and fed upon it; / Then in a language newly learned [!—E.K.B.], / I grew another stalk and turned / Your stanza patterned on a sonnet, / Into my honest roadside prose— [roadside!—E.K.B.] / All thorn, but cousin to your rose." Also, this time descending within *himself* in his own translation of his 1942 Russian poem "Slava" [Fame]: "But one day while disrupting the strata of sense / and descending deep down to my wellspring / I saw mirrored, besides my own self and the world, / something else, something else, something else" [No odnazhdy, plasty razumen'ia drobia, / uglubliaias' v svoe kliuchevoe, / Ia uvidel, kak v zerkale, mir, i sebia, / i drugoe, drugoe, drugoe] (*Poems and Problems*, 112–113).

28. Benjamin, "The Task of the Translator," 74.

29. Giovanni Lucera, "Un Américain à Paris," preface to Green, *Le langage et son double*, 20.

30. For a discussion of Freud's self-analysis in its mythic/scientific context, see Frank J. Sulloway, *Freud: Biologist of the Mind* (New York: Basic Books, 1979), chap. 13: "The Myth of the Hero in the Psychoanalytic Movement," esp. 446–448, 476–480. On the archetypal voyage, see Joseph Campbell, *The Hero with a Thousand Faces*, 2nd ed. (Princeton: Princeton University Press, 1968).

31. "There is nothing to express, nothing with which to express, no power to express, no desire to express, together with the obligation to express," says Beckett ("Three Dialogues with Georges Duthuit," *transition* 49 [December 1949], 97–103).

32. See Lev Vygotsky, *Thought and Language*, trans. and rev. Alex Kozulin (Cambridge: MIT Press, 1986); chap. 7, "Thought and Word," contains a useful section on "inner speech" (210–256).

33. Joseph Brodsky's explanation of why he began to write in English (the shadow was the shade of W. H. Auden). See "To Please a Shadow," in Brodsky, *Less than One*, 358.

34. Nina Berberova, *The Italics Are Mine*, trans. Philippe Radley (New York: Harcourt, Brace & World, 1969), 321.

35. Hassoun, during a discussion transcribed in *Du bilinguisme*, 33. He refers to the notion of "infecte" as it is used by Italian painters to speak about a mixture of colors. One can paint a picture using primary colors, but Hassoun claims that the source of modern painting is precisely the ability to "mix" colors. The act of mixing colors is "infection" (pp. 32–33).

36. Elsa Triolet, preface to *Œuvres romanesques croisées* [Intertwined novels] (Paris: Robert Laffont, 1964), I, 26.

37. Nancy Huston, in Leila Sebbar and Nancy Huston, *Lettres parisiennes* [Paris letters] (Paris, Barrault, 1986), 74: "En même temps, j'ai peur quand je vois s'atrophier, comme un organe trop longtemps engourdi, ma langue maternelle."

38. Zinaïda Schakovskoy, *V poiskakh Nabokova* [In search of Nabokov] (Paris: La presse libre, 1979), 154.

39. This illegitimacy may be felt as *illegality*. Hassoun speaks of bilinguals who are "en rupture de langues, comme on peut dire en rupture de bans" ("Eloge de la dysharmonie," 64).

40. George Steiner considers the image of incest to be the master trope for Nabokov's bilingual creativity: "Incest is a trope through which Nabokov dramatizes his abiding devotion to Russian, the dazzling infidelities which exile has forced upon him, and the unique intimacy he has achieved with his own writings as begetter, translator and re-translator" ("Extraterritorial," *Triquarterly* 17 [1970], 119–127; 124 [special Nabokov issue]).

41. Sometimes, of course, the idea of the "mother tongue" is crucial. In *Lettres parisiennes,* Nancy Huston remarks: "I can make books and children only in an un-mother tongue" [Les livres, les enfants, je ne peux les faire que dans une langue non-maternelle]. See my discussion of Marina Tsvetaeva in Chapter 5; and consider the case of Elias Canetti, who writes in German. German is Canetti's fourth language, as English was Conrad's fourth language, but Canetti's situation is much more complicated than that of Conrad. Canetti's first languages were Ladino, Bulgarian (soon more or less forgotten), and English. German was a secret language between his mother and father which he was not allowed to learn: "Among the many intense wishes of that period, the most intense was my desire to understand their secret language. I cannot explain why I didn't really hold it against my father. I did nurture a deep resentment towards my mother, and it vanished only years later, after his death, when she herself began teaching me German" (*The Tongue Set Free* [New York: Seabury Press, 1979], 24). The actual lessons seem to have been anguishing: "It was only later that I realized that it hadn't just been for my sake when she instructed me in German with derision and torment. She herself had a profound need to use German with me, it was the language of her intimacy.... So, in a very short time, she forced me to achieve something beyond the strength of any child, and the fact that she succeeded determined the deeper nature of my German; it was a belated mother tongue, implanted in true pain. The pain was not all, it was promptly followed by a period of happiness, and that tied me indissolubly to that language" (p. 70).

42. Nabokov, *Poems and Problems,* 96–97.

43. Green, "An Experiment in English," 156.

44. Osip Mandel'shtam, "On the Nature of the Word" [O prirode slova], *The Complete Critical Prose & Letters,* ed. and trans. Jane Gary Harris (Ann Arbor, Mich.: Ardis, 1979), 119–120; G. P. Struve and B. A. Filipoff, eds. *Sobranie sochinenii* (New York: Interlanguage Literary Associates, 1966), II, 286. Wilhelm von Humboldt had said something similar: that every language traces a magic circle around the people to whom it belongs, a circle that one can escape only by entering another.

45. Elsa Triolet: "As for me, I am bilingual. I can translate my thought equally well into two languages. As a result, I have a double destiny. Or a half-destiny—a translated destiny" [Ainsi, moi, je suis bilingue. Je peux tra-

duire ma pensée également en deux langues. Comme conséquence, j'ai un bi-destin. Ou un demi-destin. Un destin traduit] (*M en m*, 8).

46. M. Adler, *Collective and Individual Bilingualism* (Hamburg: Helmut Buske Verlag, 1977), 38, 40, quoted in Grosjean, *Life with Two Languages*, 282.

47. Grosjean, *Life with Two Languages*, 282–283.

48. Einar Haugen, "The Bilingual Individual," in S. Saporta, ed., *Psycholin-guistics* (New York: Holt, Rinehart & Winston, 1961).

49. See my discussion of the cases of Schakovskoy (Chapter 5), Nabokov (Chapter 4), and Tsvetaeva (Chapter 5).

50. Green, "An Experiment in English," 180, 182. This essay, written in English in 1941, was translated by Green into French in 1943. Green makes similar comments in "My First Book in English" (1941), which he also trans-lated into French in 1943 and which was reprinted in *Le langage et son dou-ble:* "Having written about two dozen pages, I summoned up the courage to read what I had written. What struck me most, however, was how little these English sentences resembled the French sentences I had written on the same subject. Now, what I expected to read was a sort of unconscious translation from the French, or at least a very close equivalent, whereas what I saw might have been written by another hand than mine.

"I don't want to imply more than I mean. The subject was the same. The choice of details quite different. I did not say the same things in both lan-guages, because, when writing in English, I had the feeling that in some ob-scure way I was not quite the same person. . . .

"There is an Anglo-Saxon way of approaching a subject, just as there is a French way. The difference between the two is essential, although not easily defined. Also, the choice of words—I was about to say the choice of colors—varies considerably from one language to another. It has sometimes been de-nied, but I nevertheless think it true, that ideas are unconsciously suggested to us by words. . . . There are certain registers of thought which can be touched upon by the French language with greater felicity than by other languages, just as there are thoughts which seem to be provoked and brought to fullness and maturity more readily by English" (pp. 228, 230). Hereafter, references to "An Experiment in English," (*AEE*) and "My First Book in English" (*MFBIE*) will appear in parentheses in the text.

51. Green, speech to the Royal Belgian Academy, September 8, 1951, in *Le langage et son double*, 404.

52. Claude Esteban, "Traduire" [Translating], introduction to *Poèmes par-allèles* [Parallel poems] (Paris: Editions Galilée, 1980. Esteban uses the phrase "un étrange déchirement," a French expression for which it is not easy to find an English equivalent. For once, French and Russian are closer, and, in this context, the Dostoevskian *nadryv* would do quite well. (Nabokov once ob-served that translating Russian into English is a little easier than translating English into Russian, and ten times easier than translating English into French [*SO*, 36], but he unfortunately omitted characterizing the difficulty of translat-ing French into English.)

53. Esteban, "Traduire," 26, 29–30.

54. Tzvetan Todorov, "Bilinguisme, dialogisme, et schizophrénie," in *Du bilinguisme*, 11–26, and discussion, 29. Hereafter, references to *B, d & s* will appear in parentheses in the text.

55. This may be why, as Esteban notes, "balanced" bilinguals are not always good translators: "I am not sure, at least in my moments of uncertainty, whether knowing a language too intimately is the best situation for a translator. Too much knowledge may be more intimidating than encouraging" [Je ne suis pas sûr, du moins à certains moments d'irrésolution, que connaître trop intimement une langue soit la condition la meilleure pour traduire. Il est des savoirs qui intimident plus qu'ils n'encouragent] ("Traduire," 29).

56. Raymond Federman, born in Paris, came to the United States at nineteen, after escaping from a deportation train and spending the rest of World War II working and hiding on a farm in southern France. Although he did not start learning English until he came to the United States, four years in the U.S. Army, including a stint in the 82nd Airborne and six months on the front lines in Korea, vastly accelerated his acquisition of "colloquial" English. Federman writes in both French and English, and his own observations about his bilingualism frequently support the generalizations made in this chapter. When he began writing his novel *Amer Eldorado* (circa 1970), he worked, alternately, on the French and English versions—one day on the French version, the next day on the English, and so on. He kept that up for about six months: "It drove me crazy. The two languages were pulling apart, pulling together, encouraging one another, defying one another, feeding one another, or perhaps I should say devouring one another. Eventually I dropped the English text and finished the French which became *Amer Eldorado* (published in 1974 by The Editions Stock). Then I went back to the English text and worked on it for three more years. That became *Take It or Leave It*. But no longer the same book. *Amer Eldorado* is about 200 pages long. A first-person narrative. Though *Amer Eldorado* is contained, in a manner of speaking, in *Take It or Leave It* (which is about 500 pages long), it is there not as a translation but as a loose adaptation. Moreover, *Take It or Leave It* uses two narrative voices (first and third person)." Federman always feels a sense of incompleteness when his work exists in only one language. When he writes poems, he immediately does a version in the other language (whichever), because he has the feeling that the original text is not finished until there is a version in the other language. He usually abandons self-translation of his novels, however, "for reasons of time, laziness, etc.," but the result is that he feels his novels are never finished. Translations by other people do not do the trick. The only time Federman did an immediate translation of a prose text was for *The Voice in the Closet / La voix dans le cabinet de débarras*, where the two texts coexist in the same book, working from either end (the French text is rectangular, the English one, square). Federman says that his ambition is to write a book—admittedly, totally unreadable—in which the two languages would come together in the same sentence (there are a few such pages in *Take It or Leave It*). The cover would say "translated by the author," but would not indicate from which lan-

guage into which. (Federman did once publish a bilingual text ["D'une paren-thèse à l'autre" / "From One Parenthesis to Another"] wherein the English version says "translated from the French by the author" and the French version says "translated from the English by the author.") Behind the playfulness, there is a "need to abolish the 'original.' In fact, between the two texts translated by the author, there is no original, no possibility of origin" (personal communication).

57. Nabokov, quoted in Schakovskoy, *V poiskakh Nabokova*, 25.

58. Steiner, "Extraterritorial," 123: "I have no hesitation in arguing that this poly-linguistic matrix is the determining fact of Nabokov's life and art. . . ."

59. Benjamin, "The Task of the Translator," 72.

Chapter 3. Elsa Triolet

1. *Na Taiti* (Leningrad: Atenei, 1925); *Zemlianichka* (Moscow: Krug, 1926); *Zashchitnyi tsvet* (Moscow: Federatsiia, 1928). Part of a fourth book, *Busy*, was published in *Krasnaia Nov'*, no. 2 (1933), 160–180.

2. Lili Brik, *Avec Maïakovski* (conversations with Carlo Benedetti), trans. from Italian by F. Dupuigrenet-Desroussiles (Paris: Editions du sorbier, 1980), 10.

3. Elsa Triolet, *La mise en mots* (Geneva: Skira, 1969), 81–82. Elsa strongly resisted the idea that the letter *c* (Cyrillic *s*) before an *a* should be pronounced *k* in French. There was a family story about how Elsa had yelled, in her lim-ited French, that she wanted it to be her (Russian) way: "Et moi, je veux ça, et moi je veux ça!" [I want it *this* way! I want it this way!] (p. 82). Nabokov, too, was very sensitive to the relationship between letters, their sounds and their shape in various languages. See his *Drugie berega* [Other shores], the Russian version of his memoirs (Ann Arbor, Mich.: Ardis, 1978), 26–28.

4. Brik, *Avec Maïakovski*, 11–12; Ann and Samuel Charters, *I Love* (New York: Farrar, Straus & Giroux, 1979), 7.

5. Nabokov states: "I was bilingual as a baby (Russian and English) and added French at five years of age. In my early boyhood all the notes I made on the butterflies I collected were in English. . . . In other words, I was a perfectly normal trilingual child in a family with a large library" (Vladimir Nabokov, *Strong Opinions* [New York: McGraw-Hill, 1973], 5, 43). Elsewhere Nabokov adds: "In common with many other English children (I was an English child), I have always been very fond of [Lewis] Carroll" (interview with Alfred Appel, Jr., in L. S. Dembo, ed., *Nabokov, the Man and His Work* [Madison: University of Wisconsin Press, 1967], 34).

6. Triolet tells this story in her preface to the *Œuvres romanesques croisées*, in which her selected works are published "intertwined" with those of Louis Aragon (Paris: Robert Laffont, 1964), 15. Hereafter, references to the *Œuvres croisées* will appear in parentheses in the text. Gor'kii's comments can be found in *Letopis' zhizni i tvorchestva Maksima Gor'kogo*, ed. B. Mikhai-

lovskii, L. I. Ponomarev, and V. R. Shcherbina, 4 vols. (Moscow: Nauka, 1958–1960) III, 320–330.

7. "My dear, I'm sitting on the divan you don't like and thinking how very nice to be warm, comfortable, and in no pain. . . . The pile of books which I can read and don't read, the telephone into which I can speak and don't speak, the piano on which I can play and don't play, the people whom I can see and don't see and you, whom I should love and don't love. Yet without the books, without the flowers, without the piano, and without you, my own, my dear, I would cry. At this moment, I am all curled up like a true woman of the East. I'm meditating. . . . A very short time ago, I would have come home and undressed to try on this new nightgown, but now it lies there, wrapped in paper" (Viktor Shklovsky, *Zoo; or, Letters Not about Love*, trans. and ed. Richard Sheldon [Ithaca, N.Y.: Cornell University Press, 1971], 59–60). [Milyi, sizhu na tvoem neliubimom divane i chuvstvuiu, chto ochen' khorosho, kogda teplo, udobno i nichego ne bolit. . . . Kucha knig, kotorye ia mogu chitat' i ne chitaiu, telefon, v kotoryi ia mogu govorit' i ne govoriu, roial', na kotorom ia mogu igrat' i ne igraiu, liudi, s kotorymi ia mogu vstrechat'sia i ne vstrechaius', i ty, kotorogo ia dolzhna byla by liubit' i ne liubliu. A bez knig, bez tsvetov, bez roialia, bez tebia, rodnoi i milyi, kak by ia plakala. Svernulas' ia seichas kalachikom i, kak istinnaia zhenshchina Vostoka, sozertsaio. . . . Eshche ochen' nedavno ia prishla by domoi i razdelas' by, chtoby pomerit' novuiu nochnuiu rubashku, a seichas ona lezhit zavernutoi v bumagu (Victor Shklovskii, *Zoo*, in *Zhili-byli* [Moscow: Sovetskii pisatel', 1966], 173–256, 214–215). Sheldon has used the first (1923) Berlin edition, *Zoo, ili pisma ne o liubvi*, for his translation. The 1966 reprint is a slightly different version. The Russian passages I quote, however, are the same in both editions. The second subtitle of Shklovskii's book, *Tret'ia Eloiza* [The third Héloise], provides both an anagram of Elsa Triolet's name and a reference to Rousseau's epistolary novel *La nouvelle Héloise* [The new Héloise].

8. "Despite the peacefulness of my existence here [in Berlin], I miss London: the solitude, the measured life, the work from morning till night, the baths and the dances with attractive young men" (Shklovsky, *Zoo*, 12). [Nesmotria na pokoinoe zhit'e zdes'—toskuiu po Londonu. Po odinochestvu, razmerennoi zhizni, rabote s utra do vechera, vanne i tantsam s blagoobraznymi iunoshami (Shklovskii, *Zhili-byli*, 179).] Years later, Triolet's capacity for work amazed Sergei Iutkevich: "I was always struck by Elsa's astonishing capacity for work, inexhaustible, as regular as breathing, or the beating of a heart" [J'ai toujours été frappé de l'étonnante faculté de travail d'Elsa, inépuisable, régulière comme la respiration, comme les battements du cœur] (Serge Youtkévitch, "Les deux amours d'Elsa," in "Elsa Triolet," a special issue of *Europe*, 506 [June, 1971], 12–21; 19). Triolet actually seems more active in *Zoo* than does the heroine of her later novelistic re-creation of her Tahitian sojourn. Letter 21 of *Zoo* describes her life in Tahiti with André Triolet. It is primarily about a horse—Taniusha, which her husband had bought for her. She tells how she cared for it herself, groomed, fed, watered, and rode it. The letter also speaks of her husband's frequent absences on visits to other islands, and Elsa ruefully admits that she cried often in those days. When Triolet takes up her Tahitian experi-

ence again in her own first novel, the narrative attitude has shifted. The heroine depicts herself as being completely idle. Taniusha is spoken of, briefly, as a
horse bought by her husband which had then run away and was sold for its
"ingratitude." But there is no mention of the heroine's active relation to the
animal. Altogether she seems to move off her bed only to bicycle into town to
do the marketing, to go to the movies, or to dance to scratchy records at the
inevitable dinners of the European colony. She does not even cry much. Thus,
the heroine incarnates only the purposeless and passive part of Triolet, which
has in fact been overcome by the writing of the novel.

    9. Shklovskii, *Zoo,* in *Zhili-byli,* 188; Sheldon trans., 22.

    10. Elsa, of course, was not really alone. There was a large colony of Rus-
sian writers and artists, centered in Montparnasse, of which she was very
much a part. "Chance, which had guided me to Montparnasse, was wiser than
I was: It was certainly the only place in Paris where I could exist. I wasn't
alone in being alone there" [Le hasard qui m'avait conduite à Montparnasse
était plus malin que moi: c'était bien le seul endroit à Paris où je pouvais exister. Je n'y étais pas seule à être seule] (*OC, I,* 17).

    11. In 1919, when Elsa and André Triolet went to Tahiti, it took three
weeks to get there from San Francisco on the one boat a month serving Pap-
eete. The arrival of the mail seems to have been the only real "event" in the
lives of this European colony.

    12. "Back home" meant, more particularly, Moscow. Sergei Iutkevich says in
"Les deux amours d'Elsa" (p. 13), that the first question she asked him on his
first arrival at her apartment, and the first thing she asked every time he went
thereafter, was "What's new back home in Moscow?" [U nas v Moskve?]. Already in *Zemlianichka,* the heroine had complained of her longing for Moscow
as though it were a disease, like Triolet's bilingualism: "In the spring everything in me aches for Moscow. It's less like nostalgia than like rheumatism"
[Vot teper', vesnoi vse zanylo po Moskve, budto ne toska, a revmatizm] (p.
152). See Chapter 2 for a discussion of the "disease" of bilingualism.

    13. Triolet herself admits to this "cannibalization" in *OC, I,* 23.

    14. She left, much to the despair of a Moscow suitor who is modeled on
Roman Jakobson, a close childhood friend, on whose comments the opening
and closing passages of *La mise en mots* are based.

    15. These solitary wanderings are in some ways similar to those which fill
the novels of *flanerie* and *disponibilité* that were being written at the same time
by such French Surrealists as Philippe Soupault (*Les nuits de Paris*) [Paris
nights] and Louis Aragon (*Le paysan de Paris*) [The Parisian peasant]. This
shared taste for roaming, this susceptibility to "chance" (*le hasard*), to "encounters" (*la rencontre*), is surely one of the reasons why Elsa Triolet found *Le
paysan de Paris* so intimately "familar" and wanted to meet the author (*OC, I,*
7). Zemlianichka, however, takes to the streets in a flight from herself, and she
is therefore not in the spiritual state necessary for her wanderings to produce
any true "encounters," in the Surrealist sense of the word.

    16. "I was no longer on the same wavelength with my family and friends [in
Russia]: they had experienced the civil war, famine, deadly winters, while I had
been in a paradisiac Tahiti. Some made no bones about telling me so. The

wiles of destiny had led me elsewhere. As for tears . . . there is a terrible Russian saying: 'Moscow does not believe in tears . . . ' I no longer belonged in Moscow. I had lost my place there, and Paris was already in my blood. But wherever I was at the time, I always journeyed within my solitude" [Je n'étais plus de plain-pied avec les miens, famille ou pas: ils avaient vécu la guerre civile, la famine, les hivers-assassins, pendant que moi j'avais été dans quelque Tahiti paradisiaque. Certains ne me l'envoyaient pas dire. Les manigances du sort m'avaient entraînée ailleurs, quant aux larmes . . . il y a un terrible vieux dicton russe: "Moscou ne croit pas aux larmes . . . " Je n'avais plus de chez-moi à Moscou, j'y avais perdu ma place, et déjà j'avais Paris dans le sang. Mais ici ou là, à l'heure qu'il était, je ne voyageais jamais plus qu'à l'interieur de ma solitude] (*OC, I,* 15–16).

17. She added an additional note to herself: "when I finally decide that this fear is cowardice, I'll be so ashamed of it that I'll become brave" [quand j'aurai définitivement décidé que cette peur est de la lâcheté, j'en aurai tellement honte, que je deviendrai courageuse] (*OC, I,* 25). The Russian text of these diaries has not been published; the translations into French are Triolet's own.

18. André Thirion emphasizes this physical trait in his reminiscences of Elsa Triolet in *Révolutionnaires sans révolution* (Paris: Robert Laffont, 1972), trans. by Joachim Neugroschel as *Revolutionaries without Revolution* (New York: Macmillan, 1975). He comments that "André Triolet, who was not a one-woman man, had grown tired of Elsa's small white body" (p. 143). "Later, she appeared in Montparnasse in the group around Il'ia Erenburg. . . . [T]here was suddenly a small redhaired woman, with a full bust and a milklike complexion" (p. 141). [Mais André Triolet n'était pas l'homme d'une seule femme; il se lassa du petit corps blanc d'Elsa (p. 157). Dans le groupe des Ehrenbourg . . . il y avait une petite femme rousse, au corsage plein, à la peau de lait (p. 155).]

19. Triolet felt as though *Camouflage* had some kind of curse on it. First, the only corrected manuscript was burned in a hotel fire, then Soviet censorship delayed and defaced it, then critics said the novel was a failure, perhaps even a prelude to suicide. "And they were right" [et on avait raison], Triolet admitted (*OC, I,* 27).

20. During a particularly lean period (1931–1933), Triolet designed jewelry which she and Aragon peddled to high-fashion houses (*OC, I,* 29). She had great success with Schiaparelli, Molyneux, and Lelong. During the same period (1929–1933), Il'ia Zdanevich (Iliazd) supported *his* family by designing textiles for Chanel. He, too, wrote about the Paris fashion industry, in his *Posmertnye trudy* [Posthumous works], which is being published in *Novyi zhurnal* beginning with no. 168–169 (September-December 1987).

21. Part of *Busy* was published in *Krasnaia nov'*, no. 2 (1933), 166–180. The complete text, with photographs, was to have been published in Leningrad and was already set in proof when it was blocked.

22. "Suddenly I felt that their not wanting to publish my little book was a slap in the face. I didn't see that the reasons were non-literary, and that you and I were being given the cold shoulder in that country, which we loved. I felt myself becoming a literary prisoner of external and internal impossibilities, and I did not intend to give in. Since everything seemed to be trying to prevent

me from writing, I would write. You could have helped by taking sides, by telling me 'write!' But you didn't want to say it, you didn't know anything about what I was writing, you didn't know Russian and you feared the worst. You wouldn't give me the benefit of the doubt, and I resented that" [Et, soudain, qu'on n'ait pas voulu sortir ce petit livre, je l'ai reçu comme une gifle. Je ne voyais pas que les raisons de sa non-publication étaient extra-littéraires, qu'on nous faisait grise mine, à toi et à moi, dans ce pays que nous aimions. Je me sentais littérairement devenir prisonnière d'impossibilités extérieures et intérieures, et j'entendais ne pas m'y soumettre! Ecrire, puisque tout m'en empêchait. Tu aurais pu m'aider en prenant parti, en me disant: écris! Mais tu ne voulais pas le dire, tu ne savais rien de ce que j'écrivais, tu ne connaissais pas le russe, et tu craignais le pire. Tu ne me faisais pas confiance sur ma bonne mine, et je t'en voulais] (*OC, I*, 30). Aragon attributed Triolet's change of language to the banning of *Necklaces*, rather than to any lack of encouragement from himself: "In any event, the rejection of *Necklaces* was what brought Elsa to finally take the step of changing languages and writing for us, for the French in French" [En tout cas, c'est l'interdiction de *Colliers* qui devait amener Elsa à franchir le pas d'une langue à l'autre et à écrire pour nous, Français] (preface to *Fraise-des-bois* [Wild strawberry], trans. Léon Robel [Paris: Gallimard, 1975], xiii).

23. Triolet claims not to have a single style. While comparing two of her novels, *Les amants d'Avignon* [The lovers of Avignon] and *Le grand jamais* [Not if I can help it], Triolet exclaims: "One can't talk about my *style* . . . what nonsense! A writer does not have a single style. I have written somewhere that the style is not the clothing but the skin of a novel. It is as much a part of its anatomy as its entrails" [On parle de mon *style* . . . Eh bien, quoi! On n'a pas qu'*un* style. Où est-ce que j'ai déjà écrit que le style n'était pas le vêtement mais la peau d'un roman? Il fait partie de son anatomie comme ses entrailles] (*M en m*, 97).

24. Elsa Triolet, *Bonsoir, Thérèse* (Paris: Editeurs français réunis, 1938). "Bonsoir, Thérèse" may mean either "Good evening, Thérèse" (i.e., "hello") or "Good night, Thérèse" (i.e., "goodbye"). The phrase appears several times as a greeting (at the beginning of the fourth part of the novel) and as a farewell (in the novel's closing words).

25. Triolet's notebooks are now preserved in the archives of the CNRS in Paris.

26. The manuscript says *ranovar* or, perhaps, *ranovat*. Despite many queries, I have not found anyone who is familiar with either variant as a 1930s slang term. (As Nabokov said, one of the problems about being a bilingual writer is trying to keep up with the languages' ever-changing slang. [*SO*, 184]). One possibility *might* be that *ranovat* could be taken as the exact opposite of *pur sang* (i.e., a kind of recent, not to say upstart, nobility). The capital letters in the English translations of Triolet's notebook indicate the words written in Russian.

27. The mixing of Russian and French within a single sentence, even in violation of syntactic constraints, is, for example, a giveaway to the character of Anna Pavlovna Sherer in *Voina i mir* [War and peace], and it confirms one's

opinion that another character in the novel, Prince Ippolit, is a complete idiot. The usefulness of Leonora Timin's article on code-switching in *War and Peace* is seriously impaired by the author's apparent lack of concern for the fact that different kinds and degrees of code-switching had different levels of intellectual and social acceptability, both in the Russia of 1805 and in the Russia in which Tolstoi was writing. Her article misses the point that all code-switching is not alike, and that Tolstoi uses these distinctions as a primary device of characterization. See Leonora A. Timin, "Code-Switching in *War and Peace*," in M. Paradis, ed., *Aspects of Bilingualism* (Columbia, S.C.: Hornbeam Press, 1978), 302–315.

28. The yellow notebook also contains items, written in Russian, that did not become part of *Bonsoir, Thérèse*: e.g., a reply to a question from *Kommun* [The commune] that demanded to know, "Dlia kogo vy pishete?" [For whom do you write?]. Triolet's response includes the remark that she was being kept from her readers "back home" because the censorship had blocked *Busy*. There are also notations about such things as Maiakovskii's trips to Paris.

29. There is, for example, a report from Spain in 1936 which appeared, somewhat revised, in *Znamia* [The banner], no. 1 (1937), 163–184.

30. *Le rendez-vous des étrangers* (Paris: Gallimard, 1956) is set in a small Paris hotel inhabited by a sampler of emigrants from many countries. It is a novel full of bitterness, one that Triolet avoided reprinting even when almost all her other novels had become available in inexpensive paperback editions.

31. "About my novels in general I could say that, in one form or another, the theme of wandering recurs with the frequency of two lines of Pushkin which run through my head: 'He was seized by restlessness / The desire for a change of place,' and the style of the novels varies according to the different varieties of wandering" [Pourrais-je en dire (de ses romans—E.K.B.) globalement que le thême de l'errance sous des formes variées y revient avec la persistance en moi de ces deux vers de Pouchkine: "Il fut saisi par l'inquiétude / L'envie d'un changement de lieux . . . " et que le style en varie avec les diverses variantes de l'errance] (*M en m*, 98). Triolet cites Pushkin's lines in French without identifying them. They are the first two lines of book 8, stanza 13, of *Eugene Onegin:* "Im ovladelo bespokoistvo / Okhota k peremene mest." In Nabokov's Bollingen translation (Princeton University Press, 1975) these lines are rendered as "A restlessness took hold of him / the urge toward a change of places."

32. Triolet, *Ecoutez-voir* (Paris: Gallimard, 1963), 121.

33. Triolet, *Le rossignol se tait à l'aube* (Paris: Gallimard, 1969). The heroine is an aged actress attending an all-night party where she is the only woman.

34. In *La mise en mots*, she says again, "I could have gotten rid of my Russian accent. I preferred to keep it" [J'aurais pu me faire passer mon accent russe. J'ai préféré le garder] (p. 56). Whether Triolet *could* have gotten rid of her accent is doubtful, considering that she acquired it very early: "The young lady who taught me French had been born in Moscow to French parents, had been educated in a French school in Moscow, and had come away with a Russian accent which I faithfully caught in my turn!" [La jeune personne qui m'a

appris le français était née à Moscou de parents français, avait fait ses études dans une école française moscovite et en gardait un accent russe que j'ai fidèlement attrapé!] (p. 82).

35. Triolet's comment, "madness also has a nationality," recalls the title of a text by Julien Green: *Une langue est aussi une patrie* [A language is also a fatherland]. Triolet's "madness" is a rather sane one, however, as she herself admits: "Mine is a staid madness" [Ma folie est sage] (*M en m*, 26). One is tempted to agree with Jean Cocteau, whom Triolet quotes as having said that she was the most reasonable woman he had ever encountered (p. 25).

36. *M en m*, 62. *Motcréation* is a rather successful attempt at making a Khlebnikov transfer into French, involving as it does a punning combination of "pro-creation" and "word [mot] creation."

37. See Michel Paradis, "Language and Thought in Bilinguals," in *Sixth LACUS Forum*, ed. W. McCormack and M. J. Izzo (Columbia, S.C.: Hornbeam Press, 1980); and id., "Contributions of Neurolinguistics to the Theory of Bilingualism," *Applications of Linguistic Theory in the Human Sciences* (East Lansing: Dept. of Linguistics, Michigan State University, 1980), 180–201. It may be interesting to note (parenthetically) that Triolet wrote with her right hand. "Elsa thought left and wrote right" [Elsa pensait à gauche mais rédigeait à droite], as Michel Apel-Muller once put it (personal communication). Of course, Triolet, as well as all other Europeans until recently, would have been *forced* to write with her right hand, even if the left were her dominant one.

38. Semën Kirsanov was impressed by Triolet's demand for precision and clarity when he was working with her on the first translation of Aragon's poems into Russian in the early 1930s: "In the course of our work, I realized that Elsa would not tolerate the slightest approximation or fuzziness. She demands precision and clarity, both in literature and in human relations. She knows precisely who is her friend, who is a simple acquaintance, and also who does not deserve to have her shake his hand" [Au cours de ce travail, je me rends compte qu'Elsa ne tolère aucune approximation, aucun flou. En toute chose, elle exige l'exactitude, la netteté, elle l'exige et en littérature et dans les relations humaines. Elle sait exactement qui est son ami, qui une simple relation, et qui ne vaut pas qu'elle lui serre la main] ("Pour Elsa Triolet," trans. Léon Robel, *Europe*, 506 [June 1971], 23).

39. Triolet's taste for luxury and comfort is evident both in Shklovskii's *Zoo* and in the character of Lucille in *Camouflage*. André Thirion observed: "Elsa loved capitalist comfort. She preferred success to money as long as money wasn't lacking. In success she was modest. She depended mainly on her own self-approval, and since she wasn't fanciful and never tried to lie to herself, she needed other people's opinion only to objectify her own stance" [Elsa aimait le confort capitaliste, elle préférait le succès à l'argent sous la condition de ne jamais manquer d'argent; dans le succès elle était modeste. Elle tenait surtout à se donner à elle-même de bonnes notes et comme elle n'était pas chimérique et qu'elle essayait de ne jamais mentir, elle avait besoin de l'opinion des autres pour rendre cette notation objective]. He adds: "To get what she was after, Elsa never took anything from anyone or hurt another person. On the contrary she

was generous" [Pour obtenir ce qu'elle voulait, Elsa n'a rien pris de personne . . . elle n'a jamais fait de tort à quiconque. Au contraire, elle a été généreuse] (*Revolutionaries without Revolution*, 155, 157; *Révolutionnaires sans révolution*, 170, 171).

40. There does seem to be a pattern among Russian bilingual writers that those who were—and stayed—married to Russians found the psychic stresses of their bilingual practice to be less threatening and more manageable. Of course, like any other generalization about bilinguals, this one does not always hold. For example, as we shall see in Chapter 5, Tsvetaeva's indissoluble bond to Sergei Efron did not lead to a commitment to writing in French.

41. It is interesting that many modern artists who have worked in several media or in mixed media have also commanded several languages and, like Triolet, were expatriots (e.g., Zdanevich-Iliazd, Arp, Ernst, Kandinsky).

42. Aragon, preface to *Fraise-des-bois*, xvii.

43. Triolet may be right that a bird's song is determined by its species, but birds seem also to have marked *accents;* or, rather, there are "dialectal" differences between the songs of birds of the same species living in different geographical areas. For details, see Stephen J. Rothstein and Robert C. Fleischer in *Condor* (reported in the *New York Times*, February 24, 1987).

44. Roman Jakobson picked up this term in his obituary comments on Triolet's *La mise en mots:* "The book imperiously reminds excessively specialized exegetes of many dramatically complex phenomena, which are ordinarily neglected, such as the 'double destiny' or de-mi-destiny of bilinguals, and the dialectical tension between creation and translation" [Il rappelle impérieusement aux exégètes démesurément spécialisés maints phénomènes dramatiquement complexes, d'ordinaire méconnus, tels que 'bi-destin' ou 'de-mi-destin' des bilingues, tension dialectique entre création et traduction] (*Les lettres françaises*, June 20, 1970).

45. This is one of a series of statues by Mathias Braun von Braun (1684–1738) which stand in a park at Kuks, Czechoslovakia. Photographs of many of these statues appear in Triolet's *Ecoutez-voir.*

Chapter 4: Vladimir Nabokov

1. Nabokov's distaste for pigeonholes and pigeonholing appears in a number of interviews—for example, in his comment to Martin Esslin in 1968: "I've never been influenced by anyone in particular, dead or quick, just as I've never belonged to any club or movement. In fact, I don't seem to belong to any clear-cut continent. I'm the shuttlecock above the Atlantic, and how bright and blue it is there, in my private sky, far from the pigeonholes and the clay pigeons" (Vladimir Nabokov, *Strong Opinions* [New York: McGraw-Hill, 1973], 116–117). In response to Alfred Appel, Jr.'s question, "The painters you admire are for the most part realists, yet it would not be altogether fair to call you a 'realist.' Should one find this paradoxical? Or does the problem derive from nomenclature?" Nabokov replied: "The problem derives from pigeonhol-

ing" (*SO,* 170). And the French "New Novel," he declared, "does not really exist apart from a little heap of dust and fluff in a fouled pigeonhole"(173).

2. See, for example, Mikhail Osorgin's comment in his 1928 review of *Korol', dama, valet* [*King, queen, knave*]: "a talented novel that could have appeared in any language" (*Polslednie novosti* [*The latest news*], October 4, 1928, 3). Or Georgii Adamovich, speaking about *Zashchita Luzhina* [*The Defense*]: "*The Defense* is a Western, European, most of all French work. If it was published in, for example, the *Nouvelle revue française,* it would be perfectly at home there" (*Sovremennye zapiski* [Contemporary notes], no. 40 [1929], 2). In his *Russkaia literatura v izgnanii* [*Russian literature in exile*] (New York: Chekhov Press, 1956), Gleb Struve also stresses the émigré reaction to Nabokov's "un-Russianness."

3. He is unassimilable into the mainstream of American literature, unless, of course, one decides that the current mainstream (at least of prose) *is* the one fed by the tributaries of Eastern Europe—in particular, the Yiddish-influenced tonalities of Bernard Malamud, Philip Roth, Henry Roth, Saul Bellow, and the like. Murray Baumgarten suggests that what is enduring about these writers is precisely the interference between Yiddish and English, which the texture of their English preserves and reworks, giving back a new richness to English (cited in Michael M. J. Fischer, "Ethnicity and the Post-Modern Arts of Memory," in James Clifford and George Marcus, eds., *Writing Culture: The Poetics and Politics of Ethnography* (Berkeley: University of California Press, 1986), 232.

4. R. H. W. Dillard, for example, stressed the "Russianness" of Nabokov's English-language novels, finding in them a consistent focus on what he called "Russian fatalism" ("Not Text, but Texture: The Novels of Vladimir Nabokov," in R. H. W. Dillard, George Garrett, and John Rees Moore, eds., *The Sounder Few* [Athens: University of Georgia Press, 1971], 141, cited in Donald E. Morton, *Vladimir Nabokov* [New York: Frederick Ungar, 1974], 25).

5. It is interesting that despite Nabokov's assertions that he could not conceive of a Soviet regime to which his works would be *grata,* eleven years after his death *The Defense* and other short works were in fact published in the Soviet Union, with promise of more to come, including *Lolita.*

6. "Practically all the famous Russian writers of the nineteenth century have rambled here at one time or another. Zhukovski, Gogol, Dostoevski, Tolstoy—who courted the hotel chambermaids to the detriment of his health—and many Russian poets" (*SO,* 28). Or, again: "It's fitting for a *Russian writer* to settle in this region [emphasis added]. Tolstoy came here as a youth, Dostoevski and Chekhov visited, and Gogol began *Dead Souls* nearby" (quoted in Morton, *Vladimir Nabokov,* 21).

7. In the special Nabokov issue of the *Magazine littéraire,* no. 233 (September 1986), 39, John Updike observed: "I would say Nabokov is profoundly Russian. He was a writer of the Russian avant-garde who also became an American writer, because he loved America. His English is both extraordinary and very strange. For he could write things which Americans are unable to

write" [Je dirais que Nabokov, au fond, est profondément russe, c'était un écrivain de l'avant-garde russe qui est devenu aussi un écrivain américain, parce qu'il aimait l'Amérique. Son anglais est en même temps exceptionnel et très étrange. Car il pouvait écrire des choses que les Américains ne savent pas écrire] (interview with Gilles Barbedette; my retranslation from the French— E.K.B.).

8. Arizona appears to be a lepidopterist's paradise: "Late September in Central Europe is a bad season for collecting butterflies. This is not Arizona, alas" (*SO*, 60).

9. Exasperated by questions about his literary appurtenance, Nabokov remarked: "Nobody can decide if I am a middle-aged American writer or an old Russian writer—or an ageless international freak" (*SO*, 106).

10. George Steiner, "Extraterritorial," *Triquarterly* 17 (1970), 119–27; 123 (special Nabokov issue).

11. See, among others, Roy Judson Rosengrant, "Nabokov's Autobiography: Problems of Translation and Style" (Ph.D. diss., Stanford University, 1983); Joseph Michael Nassar, "The Russian in Nabokov's English Novels" (Ph.D. diss., SUNY-Binghamton, 1977); Jane Grayson, *Nabokov Translated: A Comparison of Nabokov's Russian and English Prose* (Oxford: Oxford University Press, 1977); Carl R. Proffer, "*Ada* as Wonderland: A Glossary of Allusions to Russian Literature," *Russian Literature Triquarterly* 3 (1972), 399–430, repr. in C. Proffer, ed., *A Book of Things about Vladimir Nabokov* (Ann Arbor, Mich.: Ardis, 1974), 249–279; Carl R. Proffer, *Keys to Lolita* (Bloomington: Indiana University Press, 1969); Carl R. Proffer, "Things about *Look at the Harlequins!* Some Marginal Notes," in *A Book of Things*, 295–301; Antonina Filonov Gove, "Multilingualism and Ranges of Tone in Nabokov's *Bend Sinister*," *Slavic Review* 32 (1973), 79–90; Alfred Appel, Jr., ed., *The Annotated Lolita* (New York: McGraw-Hill, 1970); Peter Lubin, "Kickshaws and Motley," *Triquarterly* 17 (1970), 187–208, repr. in Alfred Appel, Jr., and Charles Newman, eds., *Nabokov: Criticism, Reminiscences, Translations, and Tributes* (New York: Simon & Schuster, 1970), 187–208; Annapaola Cancogni, *The Mirage in the Mirror: Nabokov's "Ada" and Its French Pre-Texts* (New York: Garland, 1985); and Gennady Barabtarlo, "Phantom of Fact: Vladimir Nabokov's *Pnin* Annotated" (Ph.D. diss., University of Illinois at Urbana-Champaign, 1985).

12. *Sirin* is the *nom de plume* under which Nabokov published most of his Russian language works. In answer to Alfred Appel, Jr.'s question as to why he had chosen that pseudonym, Nabokov replied: "In modern times *sirin* is one of the popular Russian names of the Snowy Owl, the terror of tundra rodents, and is also applied to the handsome Hawk Owl, but in old Russian mythology it is a multicolored bird, with a woman's face and bust, no doubt identical with the 'siren,' a Greek deity, transporter of souls and teaser of sailors. In 1920, when casting about for a pseudonym and settling for that fabulous fowl, I still had not shaken off the false glamour of Byzantine imagery that attracted young Russian poets of the Blokian era. Incidentally, circa 1910 there had appeared literary collections under the editorial title *Sirin* devoted to the so-called

'symbolist' movement, and I remember how tickled I was to discover in 1952 when browsing in the Houghton Library at Harvard that its catalogue listed me as actively publishing Blok, Bely, and Bryusov at the age of ten" (*SO*, 161).

13. Quoted by Andrew Field in *Nabokov: His Life in Part* (New York: Penguin Books, 1978), 141. Nabokov has also said, "I am trilingual, in the proper sense of writing, and not only speaking, three languages" (*SO*, 111).

14. "Dazzling" seems to be the adjective of predilection to describe Nabokov's writing. Margaret Byrd Boegeman calls him "a stylist in English so dazzling that he is without peer" ("*Invitation to a Beheading* and the Many Shades of Kafka," in J. E. Rivers and Charles Nicol, eds., *Nabokov's Fifth Arc* [Austin: University of Texas Press, 1982], 105–121; 120). Steiner speaks of "the dazzling infidelities which exile has forced on him" ("Extraterritorial," 124). Robert Alter, rereading *Ada*, found it a "dazzling, but at times also exasperating, near masterpiece" ("*Ada;* or, The Perils of Paradise," in Peter Quennell, ed., *Vladimir Nabokov, a Tribute* [New York: William Morrow, 1980], 103–118; 104). "Perhaps the most dazzling prose ever written in English," says Douglas Fowler, in *Reading Nabokov* (Ithaca, N.Y.: Cornell University Press, 1974), 17. Nabokov himself applies the word to the "multicolored inklings" offered by Lubin in "Kickshaws and Motley," which Nabokov describes as "absolutely dazzling" (*SO*, 291).

15. One is reminded of the aplomb with which Vladimir Dmitrievich accepted the rather rough thanks of his peasants for some boon granted: "From my place at table I would suddenly see through one of the west windows a marvelous case of levitation. There, for an instant, the figure of my father in his wind-rippled white summer suit would be displayed, gloriously sprawling in mid-air, his limbs in a curiously casual attitude, his handsome, imperturbable features turned to the sky. Thrice, to the mighty heave-ho of his invisible tossers, he would fly up in this fashion, and the second time he would go higher than the first and then there he would be, on his last and loftiest flight, reclining, as for good, against the cobalt blue of the summer noon, like one of those paradisiac personages who comfortably soar, with such a wealth of folds in their garments, on the vaulted ceiling of a church while below, one by one, the wax tapers in mortal hands light up to make a swarm of minute flames in the mist of incense, and the priest chants of eternal repose, and funeral lilies conceal the face of whoever lies there, among the swimming lights, in the coffin [Glorious shades of Gogol'—E.K.B.]." In Vladimir Nabokov, *Speak, Memory: An Autobiography Revisited* (New York: E. P. Putnam, Wideview/Perigee, 1966), 31–32.

16. Field, *His Life in Part*, 84.

17. Andrew Field, *Nabokov: His Life in Art* (Boston: Little, Brown, 1967), 59–60.

18. Ibid., 56. In a letter to Edmund Wilson, Nabokov observed that his father had read every word Dickens had written, and wondered whether perhaps "his reading to us aloud, on rainy evenings in the country, *Great Expectations* (in English of course) when I was a boy of twelve or thirteen prevented me from rereading Dickens later on" (May 15, 1950, *The Nabokov-Wilson Let-*

ters, ed. Simon Karlinsky [New York: Harper & Row, Colophon, 1980], 246). Hereafter, references to *Letters* will appear in parentheses in the text.

19. In *Drugie berega,* the penultimate, Russian version of his autobiography (Ann Arbor, Mich.: Ardis, 1978), part of this passage appears in a slightly different version: " 'Eto, moi drug, vsego lish' odna iz absurdnykh kombinatsii v prirode—vrode togo, kak sviazany mezhdu soboi smushchenie i zardevshie-sia shcheki, gore i krasnye glaza, shame and blushes, grief and red eyes ... Tolstoi vient de mourir' vdrug perebil on samogo sebia drugim, oshelomlen-nym golosom" (p. 189). Hereafter, references to *Db* will appear in parentheses in the text.

20. In a letter to Wilson, Nabokov also recalls a nursery rhyme that he had kept in his head for thirty-seven years: "Paul-Montgomery-Vincent Green was the very best boy that ever was seen" (December 13, 1942, *Letters,* 91). In private, Nabokov even went so far in defense of his English as to admit that it was in fact his *first* language. (In response to a comment by his wife that, circa 1925, his English was a little shaky, Nabokov is reported to have protested, "No! No, no, no, no! It was as good as ever. It was my first language, let's not forget that. My *first* language. When I was two, three, four, my mother used to translate Russian words for me" (quoted in Andrew Field, *VN: The Life and Art of Vladimir Nabokov* [New York: Crown, 1986], 127).

21. Nabokov, interview with Willa Petchek, "Nabokov since *Lolita,*" *Observer Magazine,* no. 30 (May 1976), 118.

22. See Field's interesting remarks on why Nabokov could never think of himself as an Englishman—even of foreign birth, whereas he found himself much more comfortable in America (*His Life in Art,* 63–66).

23. Field estimates this library as containing around ten thousand volumes (*His Life in Part,* 94).

24. Many years later, Wilson met "your old roommate K[...] .... I tried to draw him out about your career at Cambridge, but all I could get out of him was that you were a queer fellow and that you had impressed him by writing English verse" (January 9, 1947, *Letters,* 180).

25. Nabokov's less intellectual pursuits at Cambridge included a lively amorous career and a passion for playing goalie at soccer.

26. Nabokov continued to be an adept and addict of dictionaries throughout his careers in English and Russian. A huge, open dictionary, like a friendly sleeping dog, graces a filmed interview with Nabokov in his study at the Montreux Palace Hotel as well as a photograph in *Triquarterly* 17. Only in the processs of self-translation did even the best dictionary become not a friend, but an opponent [ne drug, a vrazheskii stan] (Nabokov, letter quoted by Zinaïda Schakovskoy in *V poiskakh Nabokova* [In search of Nabokov] [Paris: La presse libre, 1979], 25).

27. In this respect, Nabokov at Cambridge is reminiscent of the early stages of development of Fëdor Godunov-Cherdyntsev, the poet-hero of *Dar* [The gift], whose early verses were also composed largely in response to technical challenges. For the mature poet, as Anna Maria Salehar observes, "the technical challenges of describing this world, specifically rhythm and rhyme, no

longer figure in the process of creation any more than writing down the words does. While a word may set in motion a chain of ideas . . . our mature poet is no longer preoccupied with words as the building blocks of expression. He thinks in images" ("Nabokov's *Gift*: An Apprenticeship in Creativity," in Proffer, ed., *A Book of Things*, 70–83; 81–82).

28. Rosengrant, "Nabokov's Autobiography," 6.

29. Carl Eichelberger, "Gaming in the Lexical Playfields of Nabokov's *Pale Fire*," points out examples of multilingual punning in *Ania*, in some cases even when Carroll's English is normal. For example, "Down the Rabbit Hole" becomes *Nyrok v krolich'iu norku*: "Literally, this reads 'A Dive into the Rabbit-Hole,' but the words chosen for 'dive' and 'hole' are also designations in Russian for two other animals: *nyrok* is a type of diving duck . . . and *norka*, a diminutive form of *nora*, 'hole' also means 'mink' " (in Phyllis A. Roth, ed., *Critical Essays on Vladimir Nabokov* [Boston: G. K. Hall, 1984], 176–184; 177).

30. Jane Grayson notes that, when translating his own work, Nabokov is always prepared to reverse the priorities announced in *Eugene Onegin* and that he frequently values the retention of the stylistic effect more highly than the retention of meaning. Especially in translation of alliteration and onomatopoeia, "he will often modify or change his meaning in order to give an equivalent auditive effect" (*Nabokov Translated*, 176).

31. Field, *His Life in Art*, 66.

32. Rolland was not a writer congenial to Nabokov. According to Field, Nabokov embarked on his translation of *Colas Breugnon*, a novel written in archaic, metered prose, because of a bet he had made with his father, who thought it could not be done (*His Life in Part*, 150).

33. Field notes, regarding sartorial matters, that it is characteristic of the way Nabokov behaved all his life to take an outsider's stance in whatever context in which he found himself, so that "while in England, he should adopt a double-dyed Russian air and then, in Berlin among the Russians, bear the characteristics of an English sportsman" (*VN*, 68).

34. According to Field, "Nabokov's cousin Peter de Peterson remembers visiting him in Berlin in the early 1920s and urging him to do something practical or at least to switch to writing in a language in which there might be a future for him. But in those years, his cousin said, Nabokov was determined to remain a Russian writer" (ibid., 71).

35. *Camera obscura* was translated into English by Winifred Roy (London: Long, 1936). Nabokov revised the translation, changing the title to *Laughter in the Dark* (New York: Bobbs-Merrill, 1938). Nabokov made other major changes for the 1961 edition.

36. Boegeman, "*Invitation to a Beheading* and Kafka," 118–119. As Grayson notes, the allusions are particularly to Shakespeare, Oscar Wilde, Arthur Conan Doyle, and James Joyce (*Nabokov Translated*, 175).

37. In his foreword to the English edition of *The Gift* (New York: E. P. Putnam, 1963), Nabokov declares that Russian literature is his heroine.

38. In his Paris period, not only was Nabokov writing short stories and poems in Russian and working on another novel, he also wrote several plays:

Sobytie [The event], in *Russkie zapiski*, no. 4 (1938); and *Izobretenie Val'sa* [The Waltz invention], in *Russkie zapiski*, no. 11 (1938). He published "Pouchkine ou le vrai et le vraisemblable" in *La nouvelle revue française* 48 (March 1937), 362–378. "Mademoiselle O" had already been published in Jean Paulhan's *Mesures*, no. 2 (April 15, 1936).

39. It was clear to Nabokov very early on that he could not rely on a third-person "professional translator," because he would still have to rework the results in maddening detail. In a letter to Wilson (January 9, 1942, *Letters*, 56), Nabokov complained that "the translation of my Russian works is in itself a nightmare. If I were to do it myself, it would obviously prevent me from writing anything new. Correcting the efforts of my present translators would take almost as much time." This situation improved when Nabokov became well known and could have the best translators available. His preferred collaborator was, however, his son Dmitri. Vadim Vadimich, the bilingual writer-hero of *Look at the Harlequins!* (New York: McGraw-Hill, 1974), also had some harsh words about the experience of third-person translations: "I received the typed translations of *The Red Topper* (sic) and *Camera Lucida* virtually at the same time, in the autumn in 1937. They proved to be even more ignoble than I expected. . . . Both made identical mistakes, choosing the wrong term in their identical dictionaries, and with identical recklessness never bothering to check the treacherous homonym of a familiar-looking word. They were blind to contextual shades of color and deaf to nuances of noise. . . . What struck me as especially fascinating, in a dreadful diabolical way, was their taking for granted that a respectable author could have written this or that descriptive passage, which their ignorance and carelessness had reduced to the cries and grunts of a cretin. . . . It took me several months to revise those atrocities" (pp. 118–119).

40. Schakovskoy, *V poiskakh Nabokova*, 25.

41. Vladimir Nabokov, "K Rossii" [To Russia], *Sovremennye zapiski*, 70 (1940), repr. in *Poems and Problems* with Nabokov's translation on the facing page (New York: McGraw-Hill, 1970), 97. I will, of course, follow Nabokov's translation, although he often takes considerable liberties with his own Russian, which would surely appall him if committed by other hands.

42. Nabokov's French was accented in the early 1960s when he was living in Montreux, to judge by interviews filmed there. He himself claimed a marked Saint Petersburg pronunciation in Russian [Nekotoraia nepriiatnaia dlia nepeterburgskogo slukha—da i dlia menia samogo, kogda slyshu sebia na plastinke—brezglivost' proiznosheniia v razgovornom russkom iazyke sokhranilas' u menia i do sei den'] (*Db*, 68). His spoken English in the Montreux period sounded (again, judging from filmed interviews) indistinguishable from that of a well-educated Swiss who had been to Anglican schools.

43. These lyrics appeared in the "Hommage à Pouchkine" issue of *Les cahiers du journal des poètes*, no. 28 (February 5, 1937). It is a curious fact of English usage that while one can say (as Nabokov did) that he "Englished" some of his works, and perhaps get away with saying that he "Russianed" others, "Frenched" simply will not do—even for Pushkin.

44. "One can translate only into one's mother tongue—at least this is true for poetry, because there is something primordial in poetry which cannot be captured in any other way" [. . . on ne peut traduire—traduire de la poésie du moins—que dans sa langue maternelle, car il y a dans la poésie quelque chose d'élémentaire qui ne peut pas être capté autrement] (my translation from the French original—E.K.B.). D. M. Thomas, remarks in *Actes des premières assises de la traduction littéraire, Arles*, 1984 (Arles: Actes Sud/Atlas, 1985), 162.

45. I would agree with Dmitri Nabokov's contention that Nabokov *might* have become a great French writer (translator's introduction to Vladimir Nabokov, "Pushkin, the Real or the Plausible," *The New York Review of Books* [March 31, 1988], 38), despite Field's assertions that Nabokov lacked a "historical umbilical cord to French culture" and that "a strong case could be put (to the detriment of neither) for a basic incompatibility between French literature and Nabokov's literary personality" (*His Life in Part*, 208), and despite Nabokov's evident spiritual discomfort during his years as a Parisian. For, paradoxical as it may seem, Nabokov was clearly *mal dans sa peau* in Paris: "Volodia simply could not acclimate himself to the French way of life. To us the family appeared profoundly miserable for the entire period of their Paris sojourn. It was with the greatest joy that they received all necessary permits and papers enabling them to leave for the United States" (Lucie Léon Noël, "Playback," *Triquarterly* 17 [1970], 209–219; 214).

46. As Vadim Vadimich puts it, suddenly lapsing into a Russian disdain for indefinite articles (*LATH*, 120).

47. Nabokov, *The Real Life of Sebastian Knight* (New York: New Directions, 1941), 83–84. As the narrator himself realizes, however, the real process is somewhat more complex than simply a "clothing" of thoughts in words (which sounds terribly much like some of Gor'kii's statements about "clothing thoughts in the best available words"). The narrator adds: "(to use a closer simile) the thought which only seemed naked was but pleading for the clothes it wore to become visible, while the words lurking far away were not empty shells, as they seemed, but were only waiting for the thought they already concealed to set them aflame and in motion" (p. 84). Hereafter, references to *RLSK* will appear in parentheses in the text.

48. At the end, the narrator declares: "Any soul may be yours, if you find and follow its undulations" (p. 204). Thus, he has coalesced with his half brother and cannot remove Sebastian's mask from his face: "I am Sebastian, or Sebastian is I, or perhaps we both are someone whom neither of us knows" (*RLSK*, 205).

49. See Lucie Léon Nöel's reminiscence, "Playback," 215, and Nabokov's response in *Strong Opinions*, where he adds that Sylvia Berkman checked the grammar of his first stories for *Atlantic Monthly* (*SO*, 292).

50. Nabokov adds: "what tortures me when I try to write 'imaginative prose' in English is that I may be unconsciously copying the style of some second-rate English writer [future shades of Vadim Vadimich—E.K.B.] although I know, theoretically, that 'form' and 'content' are one" (October 21, 1941, *Letters*, 51).

51. Grayson, *Nabokov Translated*, 207.

52. One of those "Ah rates," as the English twins of *Transparent Things* would call them (New York: McGraw-Hill, 1972), 89.

53. Tsvetaeva and Poplavskii, for example, about whom more in Chapter 5.

54. The words are in fact those of Vadim Vadimich. He, too, had decided that his shift of languages had to be draconian: "[The situation] was bad enough before I left Europe but almost killed me during the crossing. Russian and English had existed for years in my mind as two worlds detached from one another. . . . I was acutely aware of the syntactic gulf separating their sentence structures. I feared (unreasonably, as was to transpire eventually) that my allegiance to Russian grammar might interfere with an apostatical courtship" (*LATH*, 124–125). In his letter to Wilson of December 13, 1942, Nabokov said: "I envy so bitterly your intimacy with English words, tumbling them as you do, that it seems rather silly to send you the poem [in English—E.K.B.] you will find on a separate page" (*Letters*, p. 91).

55. Field, *His Life in Part*, 249.

56. Letter to George Hessen, quoted ibid.

57. "Slava," written in Wellesley in 1942, was published in *Novyi zhurnal* [New review] in 1942 and reprinted in *Poems and Problems*, 102–113, l. 115. One of Nabokov's richest and most complex Russian poems, "Slava" deals with, among other things, the fact that Nabokov will not be read in Russia, or, really, anywhere else, even though, as he is reminded, "furthermore, not without brio, /you happened to write in some quite foreign tongue. [A sluchalos' eshche, ty popisyval / ne bez bleska na vovse chuzhom iazyke] ("Slava," pp. 108–109, ll. 89–90).

58. Nabokov frequently distinguished himself from Conrad; for Conrad had written in his fourth language, but never in his first.

59. Poetry was a holiday, except for the extraordinary "Pale Fire," the writing of which was anything but (*SO*, 55). Bruno Jasienski also continued to write Polish verse after switching to Russian prose, and Sholom Aleichem did the same after switching from Hebrew to Yiddish.

60. Nabokov did, however, write all his numerous entomological papers in English, several of which he found of sufficient literary interest to reprint in *Strong Opinions* (viz., "The Female of *Lycaeides sublivens Nab.*," "On Some Inaccuracies in Klots' *Field Guide*," and "Butterfly Collecting in Wyoming, 1952"). Nabokov declares that the art of literature is essentially one in "L'envoi," *Lectures on Russian Literature* (New York: Harcourt Brace Jovanovich, 1981), 323.

61. Gove, "Multilingualism and Ranges of Tone," 82.

62. "Three centuries later, another man, in another country, was trying to render these rhythms and metaphors in a different tongue. This process entailed a prodigious amount of labour, for the necessity of which no real reason could be given. It was as if someone, having seen a certain oak tree (further called individual T) growing in a certain land and casting its own unique shadow on the green and brown ground, had proceeded to erect in his garden a prodigiously intricate piece of machinery which in itself was as unlike that or

any other tree as the translator's inspiration and language were unlike those of the original author, but which, by means of ingenious combinations of parts, light effects, breeze-engendering engines, would, when completed, cast a shadow exactly similar to that of individual T—the same outline, changing in the same manner, with the same double and single spots of suns rippling in the same position, at the same hour of the day. From a practical point of view, such a waste of time and material (those headaches, those midnight triumphs that turn out to be disasters in the sober light of morning) was almost criminally absurd, since the greatest masterpiece of imitation presupposed a voluntary limitation of thought, in submission to another man's genius. Could this suicidal limitation and submission be compensated by the miracle of adaptive tactics, by the thousand devices of shadography, by the keen pleasure that the weaver of words and their witness experienced at every wile in the warp, or was it, taken all in all, but an exaggerated and spiritualized replica of Paduk's writing machine?" (*Bend Sinister* [New York: McGraw-Hill, 1947], 119–120). Hereafter, references to *BS* will appear in parentheses in the text.

63. Nabokov, *Lolita* (New York, G. P. Putnam: 1958), 267.

64. Appel, ed., *The Annotated Lolita*, ix. It would seem safe to hazard the guess that the profound sense of play that unites Nabokov and Joyce is associated with their polyglotism. On the other hand, not all bilinguals are playful (witness Elsa Triolet).

65. Nabokov, "On a Book Entitled *Lolita*," in Appel, ed., *The Annotated Lolita*, 317: "There have been a number of wise, sensitive, and staunch people who understood my book much better than I can explain its mechanism here."

66. "After Olympia Press, in Paris, published the book, an American critic suggested that *Lolita* was the record of my love affair with the romantic novel. The substitution 'English language' for 'romantic novel' would make this elegant formula more correct" (ibid., 318).

67. Katherine O'Connor, "Nabokov and Dostoevsky: A Relationship Reconsidered," paper delivered February 14, 1987, at the Yale University Conference "The Legacy of Vladimir Nabokov," commemorating the tenth anniversary of his death.

68. Steiner, "Extraterritorial," 123. Field demurs, saying: "I don't think Steiner's case can be sustained as anything but opinion, because Nabokov said and believed firmly that he didn't think in any language but in images" (*VN*, 32). I would argue that, to the contrary, thinking in images is *precisely* a characteristic of polyglot writers; see Chapter 2 above.

69. Elizabeth Peal and Wallace Lambert, "The Relation of Bilingualism to Intelligence," *Psychological Monographs* 76 (27, whole no. 546), 1962, pp. 1–23; 20; K. Hakuta and R. Diaz "The Relationship between Bilingualism and Cognitive Ability," summarized in Hakuta, *Mirror of Language: The Debate on Bilingualism* (New York: Basic Books, 1986), 39–41; B. Bain and A. Yu, "Towards an Integration of Piaget and Vygotsky," in M. Paradis, ed., *Aspects of Bilingualism* (Columbia, S.C.: Hornbeam Press, 1978).

70. Věroboj Vildomec, *Multilingualism* (Leiden: A. W. Sythoff, 1963), 203; François Grosjean, *Life with Two Languages* (Cambridge: Harvard University

Press, 1982), 273. On tolerance of ambiguity, see R. Gardner and W. E. Lambert, *Attitudes and Motivation in Second Language Learning* (Rowley, Mass.: Newbury House, 1972).

71. Nabokov has expatiated on *poshlost'* in his *Nikolai Gogol* (New York: New Directions, 1944), and in *Strong Opinions* (all of p. 101). In part: "Corny trash, vulgar clichés, Philistinism in all its phases, imitations of imitations, bogus profundities, crude, moronic, and dishonest pseudo-literature . . . Freudian symbolism, moth-eaten mythologies. . . . "

72. D. Barton Johnson, "The Ambidextrous Universe of Nabokov's *Look at the Harlequins!*" in Roth, ed., *Critical Essays on Vladimir Nabokov*, 215.

73. Lambert, "Bilingualism and Language Acquisition," in *Native Language and Foreign Language Acquisition,* Proceedings of Conference on Native and Foreign Language Acquisition, January 15–16, 1981, ed. H. Winitz, *Annals of the New York Academy of Sciences* 379 (1981), 12.

74. It is important to remember in this connection that sense perceptions from either eye or ear must travel from the side on which they are received *across* to the opposing cerebral hemisphere for processing.

75. "Plexed artistry" is a phrase used by John Shade in his poem "Pale Fire": "Not flimsy nonsense, but a web of sense. / Yes! It sufficed that I in life could find / Some kind of link-and-bobolink, some kind / Of correlated pattern in the game, / Plexed artistry, and something of the same / Pleasure in it as they who played it found" (Canto 3, ll. 810–815). Michael Seidel speaks of "transforming the figure of rupture back into a 'figure of connection.' " (*Exile and the Narrative Imagination* [New Haven: Yale University Press, 1986], x).

76. In "word golf," a word or phrase is gradually transmuted into another by the replacement of one letter at a time. Lucie Léon Noël cites a palindrome that Nabokov contributed to her "memory book" and that he labeled "the only Russian poem that can be read from right to left" ("Playback," 218): "Ia el miaso losia, mleia . . . / Rval eol aloe, lavr . . . / te emu: Ogo! 'umeet / rvat'!' On im: 'ia—minotavr!' "

77. D. Barton Johnson, "Synesthesia, Polychromatics, and Nabokov," in Proffer, ed., *A Book of Things,* 84–103; 97. A particularly interesting aspect of this essay is the author's discussion of Nabokov's chromesthesia and, most specifically, the symmetrical opposition of the colors in Nabokov's Russian and English rainbows (pp. 93–97). See also the chapter on synesthesia in A. R. Luria, *The Mind of a Mnemonist,* trans. Lynn Solotaroff (New York: Basic Books, 1968). Gordon Rattray Taylor notes: "The late Dr. Grey Walter, the encephalographer who worked at the Burden Neurological Center near Bristol . . . estimated on the basis of the brain waves he studied, that fifteen percent of the population think exclusively in visual terms, fifteen percent exclusively in verbal terms, while the rest employ a mixture" (Taylor, *The Natural History of the Mind* [New York: E. P. Dutton, 1979], 214, citing W. Grey Walter, *The Living Brain* [London: Duckworth, 1953], 148ff.).

78. Interview in Quennell, ed., *Vladimir Nabokov, a Tribute,* 123.

79. Butterfly or moth drawings frequently punctuate Nabokov's letters and adorn copies of his books signed for friends. (For photographs of several spec-

imens, see the illustrations between pages 74 and 75 of Quennell, ed., *Vladimir Nabokov, a Tribute*.) In an interview, Nabokov remarked: "I think I was born a painter—really!—and up to my 14th year, perhaps, I used to spend most of the day drawing and painting" (*SO*, 17). "As a writer, I am half-painter, half-naturalist," he wrote to Alfred Appel, Jr., in 1966 ("Remembering Nabokov," in *Vladimir Nabokov, a Tribute*, 13).

80. The works produced in this period tend to be idiosyncratic in narrative structure, as well as in language, and they often belong no more to clearly defined genres than to a given "national" literature.

81. Ronald Hingley, "An Aggressively Private Person," *New York Times Book Review* (January 15, 1967), 16, quoted in William W. Rowe, *Nabokov's Deceptive World* (New York: New York University Press, 1971), 27–28.

82. Grayson, *Nabokov Translated*, 216.

83. Rowe, *Nabokov's Deceptive World*, 29.

84. Grayson, *Nabokov Translated*, 190.

85. Rowe, *Nabokov's Deceptive World*, 21.

86. Baumgarten, cited in Fischer, "Ethnicity and the Post-Modern Arts of Memory."

87. Rowe, *Nabokov's Deceptive World*, 21. By such bilingual transplants, says Rowe, Nabokov achieves a Russian emotional evocativeness in his English prose, even when the parodic character of this device sustains authorial detachment. One wonders, however, how often the nonbilingual reader recognizes the parodic quality. How much of it gets through to someone who is not aware of the source?

88. Alexander D. Nakhimovsky, "A Linguistic Study of Nabokov's Russian Prose," *Slavic and East European Journal* 21, 1 (1977), 78–87; 82, 85. Elsa Triolet did a good bit of this, too.

89. These verbal manipulations range from a "faint flavoring of older English to a heavy seasoning of word play" (Rowe, *Nabokov's Deceptive World*, 36–40; 37).

90. Proffer, *Keys to Lolita*, 82.

91. Nakhimovsky, "A Linguistic Study," 83–84.

92. Lubin, "Kickshaws and Motley," 194–196. Also see Rowe, *Nabokov's Deceptive World*, 26–27, for discussion of the "hold-off" effects produced by *tmesis*.

93. Rosengrant, "Nabokov's Autobiography," 138.

94. Ibid., 139.

95. Ibid., 54.

96. Ibid., 141.

97. Ibid., 104.

98. Ibid., 96.

99. Amateurs of *The Dare* are directed to Gennady Barabtarlo's translation, which attacks this problem by giving Pnin a stiffish Russian, riddled with Americanisms (*Pnin* [Ann Arbor, Mich.: Ardis, 1983]). Yakov (Jacques) Gorbov, reviewing a French translation of *Pnin*, in *Vozrozhdenie* [Renaissance], no. 134 (1963), declared that *Pnin* would have been more impressive had it

been written in Russian—thus missing a good part of the point, perhaps because the French translation did.

100. F. Grosjean and C. Soares, appendix to "Processing Mixed Language: Some Preliminary Findings," in Jyotsna Vaid, ed., *Language Processing in Bilinguals: Psycholinguistic and Neuropsychological Perspectives* (Hillsdale, N.J.: Lawrence Erlbaum, 1986), 179.

101. See Chapter 1 and Beverly B. Wulfeck, Larry Juarez, Elizabeth A. Bates, and Kerry Kilborn, "Sentence Interpretation Strategies in Healthy and Aphasic Bilingual Adults," in Vaid, ed., *Language Processing in Bilinguals*, 203–219.

102. Rowe, *Nabokov's Deceptive World*, 31. He adds: "Much of the pleasure from reading *Ada* with a knowledge of Russian derives . . . from the fact that the 'translations,' in parentheses, are so near and yet so far." *Ada* has spawned variegated and voluminous linguistically oriented criticism. See in particular those efforts cited in note 11 above and also Francis Bulhof, "Dutch Footnotes to Nabokov's *Ada*," in Proffer, ed., *A Book of Things*, 291.

103. Proffer, "*Ada* as Wonderland," 250.

104. Nabokov insisted on his artistic self-sufficiency: "I'm not interested in games as such. Games mean the participation of other persons; I'm interested in the lone performance—chess problems, for example, which I compose in glacial solitude" (*SO*, 117). Or: "The book I make is a subjective and specific affair. I have no purpose at all when composing my stuff except to compose it. I work hard, I work long, on a body of words until it grants me complete possession and pleasure. If the reader has to work in his turn—so much the better. Art is difficult" (p. 115). In "Nabokov's Kingdom by the Sea," *Sewanee Review* 83 (October 1975), 713–720, Kenneth Cherry claimed that Nabokov was more and more writing for himself and his "proven followers" (p. 715).

105. Steiner, "Extraterritorial," 125.

106. Robert Alter, "*Ada*; or, The Perils of Paradise," in Quennell, ed., *Vladimir Nabokov, a Tribute*, 104. For some readers, of course, what Alter objects to in *Ada* is a major attraction. Proffer says: "It is a world seemingly created by a bumbling brother of our God, an inept twin who has peeped over a galactic fence, but then hopelessly misarranged historical, geographical, and linguistic details when he patterned and peopled his new planet. For us, part of *Ada*'s wit and charm comes from adjusting these ultramundane distortions, clarifying obscurities, elucidating allusions" ("*Ada* as Wonderland," 249).

107. Steiner, "Extraterritorial," 124.

108. Johnson, "The Ambidextrous Universe," 211. It is only fair to note that "V. V." is, in this case, Vadim Vadimich, rather than his maker.

109. Steiner, "Extraterritorial," 124.

110. Proffer, "Things about *Look at the Harlequins!*" 295.

111. William Blake, "The Marriage of Heaven and Hell," the third Proverb of Hell; Steiner, "Extraterritorial," 124 ("In the main, this kind of disagreement is a matter of olives: one has the taste or one doesn't"). Nabokov declared: "*Ulysses* towers over the rest of Joyce's writings, and in comparison to its noble originality and unique lucidity of thought and style the unfortunate *Finnegans Wake* is nothing but a formless and dull mass of phoney folklore, a cold pudding of a book, a persistent snore in the next room, most aggravating

to the insomniac I am. Moreover, I always detested regional literature full of quaint old-timers and imitated pronunciation. *Finnegans Wake*'s façade disguises a very conventional and drab tenement house, and only the infrequent snatches of heavenly intonations redeem it from utter insipidity" (*SO*, 71). Or, again: "The real puns are in *Finnegans Wake*—a tragic failure and a frightful bore" (*SO*, 151).

112. "Translation is a cognitive task totally dissociable from understanding and speaking two languages" (Michel Paradis, "Contributions of Neurolinguistics to the Theory of Bilingualism," *Applications of Linguistic Theory in the Human Sciences* (East Lansing: Dept. of Linguistics, Michigan State University, 1980), 180–211; 201. See also Paradis, "Language and Thought in Bilinguals," in *Sixth LACUS Forum*, ed. W. McCormack and M. J. Izzo. (Columbia, S.C.: Hornbeam Press, 1980).

113. It was notoriously the case that writers felt that translation led to creative paralysis in the Soviet Union, from the 1930s through the mid-1950s, when many poets were forced to translate in order to eat. An additional impediment to their own writing was the fact that they were translating into their first language, which was also the language of their own creativity.

114. Rosengrant, "Nabokov's Autobiography," 6.

115. Its literary uncle (in the formalist sense) is certainly Chateaubriand's word-for-word translation of Milton's *Paradise Lost* (Paris, 1836), which Nabokov qualifies as "excellent" in his own commentary on *Onegin* (*Eugene Onegin: A Novel in Verse by Alexander Pushkin, Translated from the Russian with a Commentary by Vladimir Nabokov, in 4 vols.* [Princeton: Princeton University Press, Bollingen Series, 1975], *III*, 33). Nabokov uses Pushkin's own reaction to Chateaubriand's translation of Milton's masterpiece as an epigraph to *his* translation of Pushkin: "Nowadays—an unheard of case!—the foremost French writer is translating Milton word for word and proclaiming that an interlinear translation would be the summit of his art, had such been possible" (*I*, 1). Nabokov does not cite (out of uncharacteristic modesty or reverse arrogance?) the rest of Pushkin's comment—that such humility on the part of a French writer "who is artistically the Master of them all," must be a great shock to the partisans of "corrective" translation, and might just have an important effect on literature.

116. D. Barton Johnson, "Contrastive Phonoaesthetics; or, Why Nabokov Gave Up Translating Poetry as Poetry," in Proffer, ed., *A Book of Things*, 28–41.

117. Nabokov did once publish several stanzas of *Onegin* Englished into poetry in the American journal *Russian Review;* and one stanza, which he wrongly identified as being from *Onegin*, was translated into French in his "Pouchkine, ou le vrai et le vraisemblable."

118. Paul de St. Pierre, quoted in Brian T. Fitch, "The Status of Self Translation," in *Texte* (special issue: "Traduction/textualité: Text, Translatability") 4 (1985), 111–125; 119–120.

119. Walter Benjamin, "The Task of the Translator," in *Illuminations*, trans. Harry Zohn (New York: Harcourt, Brace & World, 1968), 79–81.

120. The Englished "Mademoiselle O" was published in *Atlantic Monthly* (January 1943), and other parts of the future *Conclusive Evidence* appeared in *The New Yorker, Partisan Review*, and *Harper's* (see Nabokov's foreword to *Speak, Memory*, 9–10).

121. Marcel Proust, *Le temps retrouvé* (Paris: Pléiade, 1956), 144–145.

122. Nabokov's explanation for the omission of this chapter raises more questions than it answers. If he cannot include biographical material in his autobiography because he has already used it as part of a novel, that would mean *Dar* is part of his autobiography. If so, the notion of "autobiography" ought to expand to include the material from other early novels such as *Mashen'ka*, which is also essentially autobiographical. But Nabokov does *not* leave out of *Speak, Memory* the material on "Tamara" that he had already used in *Mashen'ka*.

123. Grayson, *Nabokov Translated*, 141–154. Rosengrant goes further and maintains that the transformations of *Speak, Memory* "allow one to investigate . . . how the process of auto-translation may itself become an occasion for redefinition and remodeling of the self. It allows one, that is, to investigate by what means the literary self is shaped, and then to see to what extent that shaping is determined by the specific nature of the language medium in which it takes place" ("Nabokov's Autobiography," 17).

124. In his foreword to *Speak, Memory*, written in Montreux in January 1966, Nabokov said that he hoped someday to write a "Speak On, Memory," covering the years 1940–1960, spent in America: "The evaporation of certain volatiles and the melting of certain metals are still going on in my coils and crucibles" (*SM*, 14). There are other lacunae. Nabokov says that he has left out of *Speak, Memory* any real discussion of his European novels because his recent introductions to the English translations "give a sufficiently detailed, and racy, account of the creative part of my European past" (pp. 14–15). One could also make the case that *Look at the Harlequins!* is, in a sense, a continuation of *Speak, Memory*, insofar as it concerns the mechanisms of Nabokov's artistic creativity.

125. See, among other mostly negative reactions, Alexander Gerschenkron, "A Manufactured Monument?" review essay in *Modern Philology* 63 (May 1965), 336–347. "It has everything: artistic intuition and dogmatic stubbornness; great ingenuity and amazing folly; acute observations and sterile pedantry; unnecessary modesty and inexcusable arrogance. It is a labor of love and a work of hate" (p. 336). And, of course, there is the extended polemic between Edmund Wilson and Nabokov, the essential pieces of which can be found in Wilson's review in *The New York Review of Books* (July 1965), Nabokov's reply (August 1965), and his more detailed rebuttal in *Encounter* (February 1966). The sources of this quarrel of titans are already visible over the years of the Nabokov-Wilson correspondence.

126. "*Lolita* is a special favorite of mine. It was my most difficult book—the book that treated of a theme which was so distant, so remote, from my own emotional life that it gave me a special pleasure to use my combinational talent to make it real" (*SO*, 15).

127. It is amusing to envision Nabokov walking hand in hand in Writer's Paradise with, on the one side, his "ruddy Russian muse" and, on the other, his "little American" one. One assumes, however, that Paradise is polyglot and polygamous, and that the latter muse will not "avert her fierce young face," like the phantom of the second wife in canto 3 of Pale Fire (ll. 567–588). It was also to protect her from incompetents that Nabokov finally agreed to do the screenplay for *Lolita* himself.

128. Nabokov, postscript to the Russian edition of *Lolita* (New York: Phaedra, 1967), 296–297. The translation, by Earl D. Sampson, and approved by Vera Nabokov, was published in Rivers and Nichol, eds., *Nabokov's Fifth Arc*, 188–194; 190.

129. Vadim Vadimich, describing the English he hoped to acquire (*LATH*, 124).

130. Rosengrant, "Nabokov's Autobiography," 46.

131. Postscript to the Russian edition of *Lolita*, 296 (Sampson trans., 190–191).

132. Johnson, "Contrastive Phonoaesthetics," 39.

133. Ibid., 39, 41.

134. Eta Schneiderman and Chantal Desmarais suggest that exceptional second-language aptitude may be associated with a compromised visual-spatial system and mild-to-moderate deficiency in visual-spatial functions. Their subject ("J") had difficulty with mental rotation, a problem quite analogous to V. V.'s inability to complete a mental about-face that would transpose PH into HP. It is also important to note that J's facility with patterns obtained both in verbal and in visual realms, despite his otherwise relatively poor performance in visio-spatial tasks ("A Neuropsychological Substrate for Talent in Second Language Acquisition," in L. K. Obler and D. A. Fein, eds., *The Exceptional Brain: The Neuropsychology of Talent and Special Abilities* [New York: Guilford Press, 1988], 103–126). It is also interesting that Vadim Vadimich's "You" analyzes his problem as being the result of confusing a spatial (image system?) problem with a temporal (linguistic?) one—that is, confusing duration and direction and, in trying mentally to reverse space, actually trying to image the reversal of time, which is all right for old movies, but not for much else. It is not the visual but the verbal system that is specialized in making transformations on a sequential frame; and V. V. has no difficulty *describing* the maneuver that his image system will not allow him to execute.

135. In "The Ambidextrous Universe," Johnson notes images of left/right symmetries that provide a framework for *Look at the Harlequins!* The two symmetrical sets of Vadim Vadimich's Russian and English words are described in terms of two worlds, and Johnson reminds us that V. V.'s transition between languages and literary worlds resulted in "an extended period of madness for the writer coincident with his arrival in 'the new world,' a journey that physically duplicated his linguistic migration from Russian to English" (p. 210). After his attack, V. V. is "paralyzed in symmetrical patches" (p. 242). Of course, the initials of V. V. (as well as of H. H.!) are perfectly superimposable, not reversed like most mirror images. V. V. are also Nabokov's initials in English, but this does not mean that V. V. is a perfect clone of Vladimir Vladimirovich.

136. Robert Frost, "Directive," l. 62.

Chapter 5. Other Bilingual Writers of the Paris Emigration

1. W. E. Lambert, "Psychological Approaches to the Study of Languages," repr. in *Language, Psychology, Culture* (Stanford, Calif.: Stanford University Press, 1972), 186.

2. I will use the transliteration under which Schakovskoy published her non-Russian works.

3. Zinaïda Schakovskoy, *Lumières et ombres* [Lights and shadows] (Paris: Presses de la cité, 1964), 83. Hereafter, references to *L & o* will appear in parentheses in the text.

4. Schakovskoy's parents were separated in 1913, and her mother remarried Ivan Aleksandrovich Barnard, a Saint Petersburg lawyer whose estate, Pronia, was about twenty kilometers from Matovo. Ivan Barnard was killed by terrorists trying "to set an example" to the peasantry of the region in the summer of 1916 (*L & o*, 130–135).

5. She adds: "And I still remember with horror the disapproving, vertical finger that my German nurse wagged from right to left and from left to right in front of my face and which signified: 'Nein, nein, das ist ganz unmöglich.' That's not possible" [Et ce dont je me souviens encore avec horreur, c'est du doigt désapprobateur et vertical que ma nurse allemande balançait, de droite à gauche et de gauche à droite devant mon visage et qui signifiait "nein, nein, das ist ganz unmöglich." C'est impossible] (*L & o*, 20). There seems to be some confusion as to the semiotic significance of the vertically or horizontally wagged finger in Russian memories of this period. While Schakovskoy associates the vertical finger with her German nurse, Fedor Godunov-Cherdyntsev, the hero of Nabokov's *Dar* [The gift], sees the German wag as horizontal. Godunov-Cherdyntsev is secretly fulminating against a man he takes to be a hateful German who has jostled him in a tram car: "[he] knew precisely why he hated him: . . . for the Punchinello-like system of gestures (threatening children not as we do—with an upright finger, a standing reminder of Divine Judgment—but with a horizontal digit imitating a waving stick" (*The Gift* [New York: G. P. Putnam, 1963], 93). [Otchetlivo znal, za chto nenavidit ego: . . . za polishinelevyi stroi dvizhennii—ugrozu pal'tsem detiam—ne kak u nas stoikom stoiashchee napominanie o nebesnom Sude, a simvol kolebliushcheisia palki—palets, a ne perst] (*Dar* [Ann Arbor: Ardis, 1973], 93).

6. Schakovskoy says that, though well-off, they were not rich by Russian standards. The property consisted of about 1,000 desatines, half of which was rented out to the peasantry at low rates.

7. The most famous volumes of the *Bibliothèque rose*, such as *Le Général Dourakine* [General Durakin], were, as it happens, written by the Comtesse de Ségur, née Rostopchine, herself no slouch as a bilingual literary figure.

8. Schakovskoy also spent several weeks in a one-room village school and about a month or so in school in Kharkov after the family had fled the Soviet-controlled Tula area.

9. Many years later, the image of that horror resurfaced in a poem Schakovskoy wrote in 1939 (see *L & o,* 249–250).

10. Her father, who had remarried her mother after the murder of Ivan Barnard, remained behind in the Moscow area, where he died in 1918. The family, however, did not learn of his death until several years later.

11. Schakovskoy, *Une manière de vivre* [A way of life] (Paris: Presses de la cité, 1965), 31. Hereafter, references to *M de v* will appear in parentheses in the text.

12. Her brother, who at twenty-four had founded and become the editor of *Blagonamerennyi* [The well-intentioned one] which included among its contributors Ivan Bunin and Aleksei Remizov, provided an entrée into the Paris literary world and asked her to make certain contacts. It was in the second (and last) issue of *Blagonamerennyi* that Tsvetaeva published the article "Poet o kritike" [A poet on criticism], which set most of the émigré critics, whom she savaged, against her. For a detailed discussion of Schakovskoy's relationship with Paris-based Russian writers during this period, see *M de v,* 100–144. For reminiscences of other writers whom she knew in the 1930s, see Zinaïda Shakhovskaia, *Otrazheniia* [Reflections] (Paris: YMCA Press, 1975), and, of course, her somewhat controversial *V poiskakh Nabokova* [In search of Nabokov] (Paris: La presse libre, 1979).

13. According to Schakovskoy, the platform of the Eurasians proclaimed the primacy of the spiritual over the material (in opposition to the materialism of both communism and capitalism). They considered the territory of the former Russian Empire and its constituent peoples to be a distinct geographical unity with its own particular characteristics, separate both from the rest of Europe and from Asia. In the social domain, the Eurasians "rejected egalitarian theories, but posited a principle of obligatory justification of privilege." In economics, they advocated a conditional liberalism; in politics, they wanted "Soviets without communism" (*M de v,* 198–199). Simon Karlinsky opines that what initially attracted many astute minds to Eurasianism was "its claim that under Bolshevik rule, Russia was moving toward a harmonious co-existence between the European and Asian peoples which inhabit its territory, united by a strong, autocratic government similar to that of the medieval Mongol rulers. . . . Their insistence on Nationalism and on rule by an autocratic elite and their idealization of the Middle Ages left the Eurasians in an isolated position in the mostly liberal community of Russian exiles" (Karlinsky, *Marina Tsvetaeva—The Woman, Her World, and Her Poetry* [Cambridge: Cambridge University Press, 1985], 193; hereafter, *Tsvetaeva—WWP*). By the end of the 1920s, most of the original leaders had left the movement, and it became more and more closely identified with strongly pro-Soviet positions.

14. She contributed to *Le thyrse,* [The thyrsus], ed. Léopold Rosy, and then to *L'avant-garde* and to *Le rouge et le noir* [The red and the black].

15. Schakovskoy, *Vie d'Alexandre Pouchkine* (Paris: La Cité Chrétienne, 1937); id., *Insomnies, poèmes* (Paris: Journal des poètes, 1937).

16. The Jacques Croisé novels are *Europe et Valérius* [Europe and Valerius] (Paris: Flammarion, 1949), for which she received the Prix de Paris; *Sortie de secours* [Safety exit] (Paris: Plon, 1952); *La Parole devient sang* [And the Word

becomes blood] (Paris: Amiòt Dumont, 1955); and *Jeu de massacres* [The shooting gallery] (Paris: Grasset, 1956). The volumes of her autobiography, under the collective title *Tel est mon siècle* [Such is my century], were all published by the Presses de la cité. Both her histories of daily life in Russia, *La vie quotidienne à Moscou au XVII siècle* [Daily life in Moscow in the 17th century] (Paris: Hachette, 1963) and *La vie quotidienne à St. Pétersbourg à l'époque romantique* [Daily life in St. Petersburg in the Romantic era] (Paris: Hachette, 1967), received prizes from the Académie française. Her account of her return to Russia is *Ma Russie habillée en URSS* [My Russia dressed up as the USSR] (Paris: Grasset, 1958).

17. Letter to the author, January 21, 1981.

18. Her recent Russian books include *Pered snom: Stikhi* [Before sleep: Poems] (1970), *Otrazheniia* (1978), *V poiskakh Nabokova* (1979), and *Rasskazy, stat'i, stikhi* [Stories, articles, and poems] (Paris: YMCA, 1978).

19. Nabokov, who realized the critical difference a few years had made to him, once remarked to Andrew Field: "If I had been born four years later, I wouldn't have written all those books," implying that his participation as a young man in the "twilight of Russian literature and culture" had been crucial to his formation as a writer (Field, *VN: The Life & Art of Vladimir Nabokov* [New York: Crown, 1986], 35).

20. Schakovskoy also knew a good bit of German and some English.

21. The French uses the indeterminate pronoun *ça* (it), which is clearly pejorative in this case.

22. This is not common French usage. The normal word for "change" would be *monnaie*. Perhaps it is a Belgicism?

23. Karlinsky describes "the Paris note" of the disciples of [Georgii] Adamovich as "metaphysical despair and existential boredom, which went hand in hand with a distrust of technical brilliance and a lack of concern with the verbal aspects of literary art" (*Tsvetaeva—WWP*, 205).

24. The quotation is from Montaigne's essay "De la physionomie" [Of physiognomie], bk. 3, chap. 12. The translation is Donald M. Frame's from his *The Complete Essays of Montaigne* (Stanford, Calif.: Stanford University Press, 1965), 798.

25. Schakovskoy's reasons for believing that she was not "a genius" will be rather unpopular in the current climate of opinion: "Writing was my joy, but I couldn't help thinking that I could never attain the perfection of the writers whom I admire, all the more so as, not being a feminist, I am convinced that women cannot have genius, although they sometimes may come very close to it" [Ma joie était d'écrire, mais tout en écrivant je ne pouvais m'empêcher de songer que je ne pourrais jamais atteindre la perfection des écrivains que j'admire d'autant plus que, n'étant pas féministe, je suis persuadée qu'aucune femme ne peut avoir du génie, bien qu'elle puisse s'en approcher parfois de tout près] (*M de v*, 283). Schakovskoy seems to have frequently said things that interlocutors would not welcome. For example, she repeated to Poplavskii the French commonplace that "talent is a long patience" [le talent est une longue patience], hardly a precept he would have found congenial (*M de v*, 227).

26. Personal communication; letter to the author, January 21, 1981.

27. For Schakovskoy's brother's reminiscences, see Arkhiepiskop Ioann Sha-khovskoy, *Biografiia iunosti* [A biography of my youth] (Paris: YMCA, 1977).

28. Personal communication. Although the comparison would surely please neither of them, it would be interesting to compare Triolet and Schakovskoy in more detail than I can permit myself here. Suffice it to indicate the early sojourns in exotic places, the firmness of faith (albeit in quite opposing principles), and the images of early childhood and being the youngest.

29. In 1938, as she sorted her papers in preparation for following her husband back to the Soviet Union, Tsvetaeva came across a diary entry made in November 1917: "If God performs this miracle and leaves you among the living, I will follow you like a dog." She wrote in the margin: "And here I am, following him—like a dog (21 years later)" (quoted in Karlinsky, *Tsvetaeva—WWP*, 227–228).

30. Marina Tsvetaeva, letter to Rilke, July 6, 1926, in Boris Pasternak, Marina Tsvetaeva, and Rainer Maria Rilke, *Letters, Summer 1926*, ed. Yevgeny Pasternak, Yelena Pasternak, and Konstantin M. Azadovsky; trans. Margaret Wittlen and Walter Arndt (New York: Harcourt Brace Jovanovich, 1985), 169–170. Hereafter, this edition will be referred to as *Summer Letters*. Translations into English of the Rilke-Pasternak-Tsvetaeva correspondence are those of this edition, except for one or two disputable readings and some instances where the translator's choice of English obscures a point of particular interest. The German texts of Rilke's letters to Tsvetaeva and Pasternak, and of their letters to him, are available in Konstantin Asadowski, ed., *Rilke und Russland: Briefe Erinnerungen Gedichte* (Frankfurt am Main: Insel Verlag, 1986).

31. Karlinsky, *Tsvetaeva—WWP*, 3.

32. Ibid., 16–17.

33. See Tsvetaeva's answer to a questionnaire forwarded to her by Boris Pasternak, which was to be used by the Soviet Academy of Arts and Sciences in the preparation of a bibliographical dictionary of twentieth-century writers. The completed questionnaire also includes a great deal of biographical information and a select list of her favorite reading at various ages. It can be found in *Summer Letters*, 61–65.

34. Karlinsky, *Tsvetaeva—WWP*, 24.

35. Ibid., 27–28.

36. The younger daughter had died of malnutrition in February 1920, in a state-operated orphanage, where Tsvetaeva had placed her because she was unable to provide adequately for both children herself (ibid., 81–82).

37. Georgii's nickname "Mur" derives from the wise cat of E. T. A. Hoffmann's novel *Lebensansichten des Katers Murr*. Although Mur turned out to be far from wise, the signs at his birth were propitious. In the postscript of a letter to Anna Tesková, dated the day after his birth, Tsvetaeva wrote: "my son was born on Sunday at noon. In German he would be called a Sunday's Child [Sonntagskind], one who understands the language of animals and birds, and discovers buried treasure" [Moi syn rodil'ia v voskresen'e, v polden'. Po germanski eto—*Sonntagskind*, ponimaet iazyk zverei i ptits, otkryvaet klady]

quoted in Marina Tsvetaeva, *Neizdannye pis'ma* [Unpublished letters], ed. G. Struve and N. Struve [Paris: YMCA Press, 1972], 221; also see Tsvetaeva, *Pis'ma k A. Teskovoi* [Prague: Academia, 1969], 280.

38. Hélène Izwolsky's memoir, "Ten' na stenakh. O Tsvetaevoi," *Opyty* 3 (1954) 152–159, describes this poverty, as does Karlinsky, *Tsvetaeva—WWP,* 174–176. Karlinsky's earlier version of Tsvetaeva's life also includes quotations from Tsvetaeva's correspondence with Iurii Ivask, where she compares herself with Katerina Marmeladova "with her shawl, her children, her French dialect. That is myself—whether at home, in everyday life, with my children, in Soviet Russia, in emigration, myself in that all-too-real puddle of soapy dishwater which has been my life since 1917 and from which I judge and threaten [*suzhu i grozhu*]" (Karlinsky, *Marina Tsvetaeva: Her Life and Art* [Berkeley: University of California Press, 1966], 82). Tsvetaeva appears to have compared herself several times with Marmeladova. See the letter to O. E. Chernova-Kolbasina, January 25, 1925, in *Neizdannye pis'ma,* 120–121: "Do you remember Dostoevskii's Katerina Ivanovna—That's me, exhausted, embittered, indignant, in a kind of frenzy of self-abasement, as well as its contrary. The same hatred, falling upon innocent heads. To me the whole world is like the landlady, Amaliia Liudvigovna; *everyone* is to blame. But my fury does not dull my good judgment, and that's the hardest thing to bear. Sharing Katerina Ivanovna's feelings, looking at the world through her eyes, I can still judge her honestly—i.e., no one is to blame, one can never get corners really clean, so then I'm justified (out of sheer rage) in not taking the dustpan in my hands. And I always burn myself, so my black and blistered hands have only themselves to blame, and there's no point complaining" [Vy pomnite Katerinu Ivanovnu iz Dostoevskogo?—Ia—zagnannaia, ozloblennaia, negoduiushchaia, v kakom-to isstuplenii samounichizheniia i obratnogo. Ta-zhe nenavist', obrushivaiushchaiasia na nevinnye golovy. Ves' mir dlia menia—kvartirnaia khoziaika Amaliia Liudvigovna,—*vse* vinovaty. No iarostnost' chuvstv ne zamutniaet zdravosti suzhdeniia, i eto samoe tiazholoe. Chuvstvuia, kak K. I., otzyvaias' na mir kak ona, suzhu ego zdravo, t.e.—nikto ne vinovat, ugly vsegda pachkaiutsia, vol'no zhe mne ikh, minuia (iz chistoi iarosti!) sovok, brat' rukami.—I vsegda zhguts'ia.—posemu, chernota i ozhogi ruk moikh—delo ikh zhe i nechego roptat'].

39. As Karlinsky remarks (*Tsvetaeva—WWP,* 207), writing *Le gars* demanded that Tsvetaeva learn the principles of French versification which she found uncongenial, later declaring to Pasternak that French was the language least hospitable to poetry (January 1, 1927, *Summer Letters,* 209). Tsvetaeva also translated other Russian poets into French, among them Maiakovskii and Pushkin. See Efim Etkind, "Marina Cvetaeva, Franzosische Texte," in *Marina Cvetaeva: Studien un Materialien* (Wiener Slavistischer Almanach, Sonderband 3, 1981), 195–206.

40. Iswolsky, in her *No Time to Grieve* (New York: Winchell, 1985), 199–200, describes the reading Tsvetaeva gave at one of Natalie Clifford Barney's Fridays.

41. Karlinsky, *Tsvetaeva—WWP,* 118.

42. Natalie Clifford Barney, an American heiress from Dayton, Ohio, spent most of her adult life in France and wrote in French. Tsvetaeva's "Lettre à l'Amazone," addressed to her, was revised and recopied by Tsvetaeva in November 1934 "avec un peu plus de cheveux gris" [with a few more gray hairs]. Tsvetaeva's comment refers to the penultimate paragraph: "Weeping willow, tearful willow, willow, the body and soul of woman. Mournful willow's neck. Grey hair thrown over the face so as to see no more. Grey hair sweeping the face of the earth" [Saule pleureur! Saule éploré! Saule, corps et âme des femmes! Nuque éplorée du saule. Chevelure grise ramenée sur la face, pour ne plus rien voir. Chevelure grise balayant la face de la terre]. Translation obscures Tsvetaeva's play on the radical *pleurer/éploré*. The choice of the final image of the *saule pleureur,* the weeping willow, may have been partially determined by its phonetic resemblance to *seule,* "alone." This engendering of imagery through sound is a typical Tsvetaeva device, in Russian as well as in French. "Lettre à l'Amazone" has been published several times, first as Marina Zvétaieva, *Mon frère féminin,* ed. Ghislaine Limont (Paris: Mercure de France, 1979) and then in *Lettera all'Amazzone,* ed. Serena Vitale (Milan, 1981). The French text is also included in Vitale's edition of *Les nuits florentines* [Le notti fiorentine] (Milan, 1983).

43. See Serena Vitale, "Su tracce a rittroso," in Marina Cvetaeva, *Lettera all'Amazzone;* Karlinsky, *Tsvetaeva—WWP,* and Tsvetaeva's poem (dated December 5, 1921) "Amazonki" [Amazons].

44. Like Nabokov and later Schakovskoy, Tsvetaeva therefore turned to her non-mother tongue (at least partially) for memoirs of her childhood. Several of these prose pieces have survived only in French. The Russian texts are posthumous translations from the French by Tsvetaeva's daughter, Ariadna.

45. In "Charlottenburg," Tsvetaeva and her sister are given the opportunity to choose two plaster casts for their own. Asia quickly chooses casts of a boy's head and of an angel, but it is not so easy for Marina to find what she wants: "I want something very much *my own,* not selected, but beloved from the first glance, *predestined.* What's no less hard to find than a husband-to-be" ("Charlottenburg," in Marina Tsvetaeva, *A Captive Spirit: Selected Prose,* ed. and trans. J. Marin King [London: Virago, 1983], 193). [Khochu chego-to ochen' *svoego,* ne vybrannogo, a poliublennogo s pervogo vzgliada, *prednachertannogo.* Chto ne menee trudno, chem naiti zhenikha] (Marina Tsvetaeva, *Sochineniia v dvukh tomakh* [Moscow: Khudozhestvennaia literatura, 1980], II, 20). Because she knows that she will not be able to find a head of Bonaparte among the Greco-Roman casts, she continues her search among the statues of women: "And—here she is! Here—a head thrown back towards the shoulders, brows twisted in suffering, not a mouth, but—a cry. A living face among all those soulless beauties. Who is she? I don't know. I know one thing—she's *mine!*" (p. 193). [I—vot ona! Vot—otbroshennaia k plechu golova, skruchennye mukoi brovi, ne rot, a—krik. Zhivoe litso mezh vsekh etikh bezdushnykh krasot! Kto ona?—Ne znaiu. Znaiu odno—*moia!* (II, 20). Although Tsvetaeva's bust seems to be one of a maenad, the director of the casting works identifies it as "the Amazon." The Russian text of "Charlottenburg" was

translated from Tsvetaeva's French by her daughter, Ariadna Efron. The French original has not been published.

46. Karlinsky, *Tsvetaeva—WWP*, 222–223.

47. Shortly before her departure, Tsvetaeva said that she could not abandon Sergei Efron when he was in trouble and needed her: "I had no choice, one can't abandon a person in trouble, that's how I was born" (letter to Tesková, quoted ibid., 224).

48. Tsvetaeva frequently made enemies by saying the wrong thing at the wrong time to the wrong people. Thus she defended Germany during World War I, and the tsar after his death; she read poems from the pro-White collection *Lebedinyi stan'* [Demesne of the Swans] to Soviet audiences and praised the "strength" of Soviet poetry to the émigrés.

49. "Yet every language has something that belongs to it alone, that *is* it. That is why you sound different in French and in German—that's why you wrote in French, after all! German is deeper than French, fuller, more drawn out, darker. French: a clock without resonance; German, more resonance than clock (Chime). German verse is reworked by the reader, once more, always, and infinitely, in the poet's wake; French is there. German *becomes*. French *is*. Ungrateful language for poets—that's of course why you wrote in it. Almost impossible language! German—infinite promise (that *is* a gift, surely!); French—gift once and for all. Platen writes French. You (*Vergers*) write German, i.e., yourself the poet. For German surely is closest to the mother tongue. Closer than Russian, I think, closer still" [Doch jede Sprache hat etwas nur ihr Gehörendes, was *sie* ist. Darum klingst Du Französisch anders als Deutsch,— deswegen hast Du doch Französisch geschrieben! Deutsch ist tiefer als Französisch, voller, gedehnter, *dunkler*. Französisch: Uhr ohne Nachklang, Deutsch—mehr Nachklang als Uhr (Schlag). Deutsch wird noch einmal, noch immer, unendlich vom Leser nachgedichtet, Französisch ist da. Deutsch—*wird*, Französisch *ist*. Undankbare Sprache für Dichter—deswegen schriebst Du sie ja. Fast unmögliche Sprache! Deutsch—unendliche Versprechung (das *ist* doch Gabe!), Französisch—endgültige Gabe. Platen schreibt Französisch. Du ("Vergers") schreibst Deutsch, d.h.—Dich, den Dichter. Denn Deutsch ist doch der Muttersprache am nächsten. Näher als Russisch, glaub ich. Noch näher] (Tsvetaeva to Rilke, July 6, 1926, *Summer Letters,* 170; *Rilke und Russland,* 410).

50. "(though German is more native than Russian / For me, the most native is Angelic!) . . . " [(pust' russkogo rodnei nemetskii / Mne, vsekh angel 'skii rodnei!) . . .] ("Novogodnee" [A New Year's greeting], in Marina Tsvetaeva, *Stikhotvoreniia i poemy v piati tomakh* (New York: Russica, 1980), I, 264.

51. Karlinsky, *Tsvetaeva—WWP*, 204. Tsvetaeva also became emotionally attached to a variety of other young men who she felt *needed* her, among them the critic and journalist Aleksander Bakhrakh and the poet Anatolii Shteiger (p. 216). During an interruption in her correspondence with Rilke, she told Pasternak that it was too painful to write to Rilke because he did not *need* her—or anyone else for that matter (*Summer Letters,* 120).

52. Karlinsky, *Tsvetaeva—WWP*, 42. He also says that "Voloshin was nothing less than prophetic when he wrote in his review of *Vechernii al'bum* [The

evening album] that the essence of Tsvetaeva's poetry was encompassed in the following quatrain: 'I love women who knew no fear in battle, / Who were able to handle a sword and a spear. / But I know that only in the cradle's prison / Is my ordinary feminine happiness' " [Ia zhenshchin liubliu, chto v boiu ne robeli, / umevshikh i shpagu derzhat', i kop'e,— / No znaiu, chto tol'ko v plenu kolybeli / Obychnoe — zhenskoe—schast'e moë!] (p. 41). These lines come from a poem called "V liuksemburgskom sadu" [In the Luxembourg Gardens], which is about the children playing there and about Tsvetaeva's adolescent desire to have children: "On the shady paths, children, children everywhere / O children in the grass, why are you not mine?" [V tenistykh alleiakh vsë detki, vsë, detki . . . /O detki v trave, pochemu ne moi?] This last line is doubtless romanticized: children were *not* allowed on the grass in the Luxembourg Gardens. (Children in the grass, alas!)

53. In a conversation with Simon Karlinsky, Dmitrii Sezeman described it as "the love of a female beast for her cub" (Karlinsky, *Tsvetaeva—WWP*, 203). To Rilke, Tsvetaeva declared: "I only believe in mother's boys. You too are a mother's boy, a man taking after the female line—and therefore so *rich* (duality)" [Ich glaub nur an Muttersohne. Sie sind auch ein Muttersohn. Ein *Mann* nach der weiblichen Linie—darum so *reich* (Zweifaltigkeit)] (May 9, 1926, *Summer Letters*, 83; *Rilke und Russland*, 382). After his death, Tsvetaeva addressed even Rilke as her "darling grown-up boy" (December 31, 1926, *Summer Letters*, 210). *Rilke und Russland* does not include this letter.

54. Letter to O. E. Chernova-Kolbasina, April 25, 1925, in Tsvetaeva, *Neizdannye pis'ma*, 170–171. Nevertheless, as though predicting his sojourn in France, Tsvetaeva notes that upon awakening, Mur says: "heureux, heureux" [happy, happy] [Murka, prosnuvshis', dobr, povtoriaet: "heureux, heureux"] (p. 175).

55. Letter to Chernova-Kolbasina, May 10, 1925, *Neizdannye pis'ma*, 175–176.

56. Karlinsky comments: "As her subsequent poems and letters show, 'Verses to my Son' reflected a transient mood" (*Tsvetaeva—WWP*, 214), but while this is true of the pro-Soviet content of the poems, the anti-French attitude was long-standing and unchanging. Tsvetaeva wrote to Vera Bunina in 1934, for example, that her favorite people were the Chinese and the Blacks; the ones she most disliked—the Japanese and the French (*Neizdannye pis'ma*, 467). Incidents that reflect badly on the French are recounted earlier in the same letter and in another one, dated November 3, 1934 (p. 479).

57. Tsvetaeva, "Stikhi k sinu," *Sochineniia v dvukh tomakh*, I, 306–307.

58. Tsvetaeva, "Lettre à l'Amazone" (as *Mon frère féminin*), 25.

59. Ibid., 21–22.

60. Jane Taubman, " 'Ne byt' tebe frantsuzom': Tsvetaeva's 'Stikhi k synu' and the Lyrics of her Paris Period," paper delivered at the Annual Convention of the MLA, New York, December 1983.

61. Tsvetaeva, "Toska po rodine" [Longing for one's native land], quoted and translated in Joseph Brodsky, "Footnote to a Poem," *Less than One* (New York: Farrar, Straus & Giroux, 1986), 200. For some interesting speculation on the "(m)other tongue," see Jane Gallop, "Reading the Mother Tongue: Psy-

choanalytic Feminist Criticism," *Critical Inquiry* (special issue: "The Trial(s) of Psychoanalysis") 13 (Winter 1987), 314–329; and, by extension, Shirley Nelson Garner, Claire Kahane, and Madelon Sprengnether, eds., *The (M)other Tongue: Essays in Feminist Psychoanalytic Interpretation* (Ithaca, N.Y.: Cornell University Press, 1985).

62. Karlinsky, *Tsvetaeva—WWP*, 19.

63. Ibid., 20.

64. Letter to Anna Tesková, January 26, 1937, quoted ibid., 175: "Now, taking stock, I can say: I've lived my life in captivity. And, strange as it may seem, a freely chosen captivity, because, after all, no one forced me to take everything so seriously. It was in my blood, in its German component" [Teper', podvodia itogi, mogu skazat': Ia vsiu zhizn' prozhila—v nevole, ibo nikto menia, v kontse kontsov, ne zastavlial tak vsë primat' vser'ëz,—eto bylo v moei krovi, v nemetskoi eë chasti]. For the "puddle," see her letter to Ivask, quoted in note 38 above.

65. Letter to Tesková, February 15, 1936, quoted in Karlinsky, *Tsvetaeva— WWP*, 224.

66. Among the German sources for Tsvetaeva's works is Gustav Schwab's *Die schönsten Sagen des klassischen Altertums* [The most beautiful myths of classical antiquity], which Karlinsky says is the sole source for her Theseus trilogy (only two plays of which were completed) (*Tsvetaeva—WWP*, 181–182). Tsvetaeva requested that Rilke send her a Greek mythology in German, preferably the one she had in her childhood (August 22, 1926, *Summer Letters*, 203–204). Her "Krysolov" [pied piper] draws on various German versions of *Der Rattenfänger von Hameln* [The Pied Piper of Hamelin] (see Karlinsky, *Tsvetaeva—WWP*, 44). Tsvetaeva also frequently borrowed German terms and cited German poetry in her letters to various correspondents, none of whom was German.

67. Letter to Leopold von Schlözer, 1920, epigraph in P. P. Brodsky, *Russia in the Works of Rainer Maria Rilke* (Detroit: Wayne State University Press, 1984). The translation is Tsvetaeva's.

68. I.e., "Les quatrains valaisans" [Quatrains from Valais], "Les fenêtres" [The windows], and "Tendres impôts à la France" [Tender duties to France]. See K. A. J. Batterby, *Rilke and France* (Oxford: Oxford University Press, 1966), for a discussion of Rilke's French connections and output. Batterby's analysis includes observations of considerable interest to anyone who would study Rilke as a bilingual writer.

69. Rilke had written to Pasternak's father, the painter Leonid Pasternak, an old acquaintance, to tell him how much he had enjoyed reading several of Boris's poems that he had seen published in translation. Leonid wrote to Boris, who replied to Rilke (whom he had always considered a kind of poetic guardian angel) with an enthusiastic letter beginning "Great, most beloved poet" [Grosser, geliebtester Dichter!] (April 12, 1926, *Summer Letters*, 53: *Rilke and Russland*, 371). It is characteristic of Pasternak's generosity that, having belatedly discovered Tsvetaeva's genius, he wanted Rilke to know her too (and her to know Rilke), rather than keeping Rilke's admiration for himself.

70. In preparation for and during his trip to Russia in 1900, Rilke undertook a crash course in Russian, as a result of which his Russian was "far from perfect, but sufficient to enable him to read widely in Russian literature, write letters and a few marred but recognizably Rilkian poems in the language" (Brodsky, *Russia in the Works of Rainer Maria Rilke*, 9). Asadowski, ed., *Rilke und Russland*, includes letters written by Rilke entirely in Russian to Spiridon Droshchin, Sofiia Schill, and Leonid Pasternak as well as a half-and-half letter to Aleksandr Benois and some letters with a good deal of code-switching in and out of Russian. The all-Russian letters date from 1900–1901. By the time of his correspondence with Tsvetaeva, Rilke's Russian had deteriorated, and he found her poetry very difficult to read (so, after all, did many Russians). See his letter to Tsvetaeva of May 17, 1926, wherein he declares that he had been led to overestimate himself with respect to Russian (*Summer Letters*, 100). On Rilke and Russian, see also Sophie Brutzer, *Rilkes russische Reisen* [Rilke's Russian journeys] (Darmstadt: Wissenschaftliche Buchgesellschaft, 1969).

71. Tsvetaeva to Rilke, May 12, 1926, *Summer Letters*, 89; *Rilke und Russland*, 388–389.

72. If one is reading the correspondence in translation, the French edition is much more helpful in indicating these *jeux de mots* than is the English translation. In a revealing passage, Tsvetaeva tells Rilke something of her poetic practice: "Not to sweep anymore—of that is my kingdom of heaven. Plain enough? Yes, because my soil is poor enough! (Rainer, when I wrote in German *fegen—Fegfeuer*—that magnificent word—sweeping here, purgatory there, swept right into the middle of purgatory, etc., *that's* how I write, from the word to the thing, re-creating the words poetically. This is how you write, I think" [Nicht mehr fegen—so heisst mein Himmelreich. Schlicht genug? Ja, weil mein Erdreich—schlecht genug! (Rainer, schrieb ich deutsch: fegen—Fegfeuer (das herrliche Wort), fegen hier, Fegfeuer da, bis ins Fegfeuer hineingefegt, etc. *So* schreib ich, vom Worte zum Ding, die Worte nachdichtend. So schreibst Du, glaub ich] August 22, 1926, *Summer Letters*, 202; Rilke und Russland, 423).

73. Rilke to Tsvetaeva, May 17, 1926, *Summer Letters*, 99; *Rilke und Russland*, 401).

74. Tsvetaeva tells Rilke that he is a phenomenon of nature, a force, an impossible task for the poets who come after him: "A Master (like Goethe) one overcomes, but to overcome you—means (would mean) to overcome poetry itself" [Was nach Ihnen ein Dichter noch tun kann? Einen Meister (wie Goethe z. B.) überwindet man, aber Sie überwinden—heisst (würde heissen) die Dichtung überwinden] (May 9, 1926, *Summer Letters*, 82; *Rilke und Russland*, 380). With his *Book of Hours*, Rilke has "done more for God than all the philosophers and priests taken together. . . . You alone have said something new to God" [. . . hast Du mehr für Gott gemacht als alle Philosophen und Prediger zusammen. . . . Du allein hast Gott etwas Neues gesagt] (May 12, 1926, *Summer Letters*, 88, 89; *Rilke und Russland*, 388).

75. Tsvetaeva to Pasternak, January 1, 1927, *Summer Letters*, 209. *Summer Letters* translates "iazyk svoego rozdeniia" as "native tongue," and "delo oka-

zalos' ne v nemetskom a v chelovecheskom" as "the trouble, it seems, was not in the language but in the man," and "progovorilsia" simply as "speaks." The original Russian texts of Tsvetaeva's letters to Pasternak can be found in *Neizdannye pis'ma;* this one is on page 318.

76. Earlier, Tsvetaeva had praised Rilke's boldness in choosing to love God the Father, because He was lonelier and more impossible to love than the Son (Tsvetaeva to Rilke, May 12, 1926, *Summer Letters,* 89).

77. Brodsky, "Footnote to a Poem," 231.

78. In her first letter to him, Tsvetaeva had begged Rilke "that you should allow me to spend every moment of my life looking up at you—as at a mountain that protects me (one of those guardian angels of stone!)" [Was ich von Dir will, Rainer? Nichts. Alles. Dass Du mir es gönnst, jeden Augenblick meines Lebens zu Dir aufblicken—wie auf einen Berg, der mich schützt (so ein steinerner Schutzengel!)] (May 9, 1926, *Summer Letters,* 84; *Rilke und Russland,* 383).

79. Brodsky notes that Tsvetaeva uses *du Lieber* in a supra-lingual fashion—as an attempt to approximate "the original" language of poetry in essence—rather than in its strictly German meaning ("Footnote to a Poem," 234). But one should note that she also uses the English "nest."

80. Note the dedication (dated May 1926) of a copy of Rilke's *Duineser Elegien* [Duino elegies] sent by the poet to Tsvetaeva. This dedication serves as the epigraph to the French edition of the *Summer Letters* and is reproduced in autograph facsimile in the English edition: "We touch one another. How? With wings that beat, / With very distance touch each other's ken. / One *poet* only lives, and now and then / Who bore him, and who bears him now, will meet" [Wir rühren uns, womit? Mit Flügelschlagen, / mit Fernen selber rühren wir uns an. / *Ein* Dichter einzig lebt, und dann und wann / kommt, der ihn trägt, *dem* der ihn trug, entgegen] (*Summer Letters,* 81; facsimile between pp. 84 and 85). See, too, Tsvetaeva's response (May 12, 1926, *Summer Letters,* 93; *Rilke und Russland,* 393). Rilke also replied to Pasternak that he had initiated a correspondence with Tsvetaeva: "In the very hour in which your direct letter to me wrapped me about like the beating of wings, your wish was fulfilled" [Ihr Wunsch ist in derselben Stunde, da Ihr unmittelbarer Brief mich, wie ein Wehen von Flügelschlägen, umgeben hatte, erfüllt worden] (letter received by Pasternak on May 18, 1926, *Summer Letters,* 102; *Rilke und Russland,* 379).

81. Tsvetaeva sees the sign of Rilke's election in his given name—*Rainer,* the root of which *rai,* means "Paradise" in Russian (Tsvetaeva to Rilke, May 9, 1926, *Summer Letters,* 81; *Rilke und Russland,* 379).

82. Rilke to Tsvetaeva, May 17, 1926,(*Summer Letters,* 100; *Rilke und Russland,* 401).

83. Quoted in Brodsky, "Footnote to a Poem," 236.

84. Anthony Olcott, "Poplavsky: The Heir Presumptive of Montparnasse," in Simon Karlinsky and Alfred Appel, Jr., eds., *The Bitter Air of Exile: Russian Writers in the West, 1922–1972* (Berkeley: University of California Press, 1977), 274–288; 275.

85. See the biography of Poplavskii by his father, Iulian Poplavskii, in Karlinsky and Appel, eds., *The Bitter Air of Exile,* 321.

86. Simon Karlinsky, "In Search of Poplavsky: A Collage," in Karlinsky and Appel, eds., *The Bitter Air of Exile,* 317.

87. Nina Berberova remarked that "he spoke Russian, when he spoke, somehow poorly and muddily, and sometimes like an illiterate. In his writings one senses this, an unsurmounted awkwardness, clumsiness, an unintended but organic paleness of syntax" (*The Italics Are Mine,* trans. Philippe Radley [New York: Harcourt, Brace & World, 1969], 274). Temira Pachmuss remarks on his vulgarisms in expression, his stress on normally unstressed syllables, and his awkward rhymes and poor word choice (*A Russian Cultural Revival* [Knoxville: University of Tennessee Press, 1981], 296–297). Irina Odoevtseva writes that Poplavskii could not write any language correctly and that his manuscripts were peppered with monstrous errors [Gramotno pisat' on ne na odnom iazyke tak i ne vyuchilsia, i rukopisi ego pestreli prosto chudovishchnymi oshibkami] (*Na beregakh Seny* [On the banks of the Seine] [Paris: La presse libre, 1985], 145). It is, however, extremely difficult to attribute Poplavskii's twisting of Russian usage exclusively to linguistic incompetence *or* to the desire to *épater* and deform characteristic of modernist poetic techniques.

88. E.g., "Paysage d'enfer" [Landscape of hell], "Diabolique," "Dolorosa," "Hommage à Pablo Picasso," "Lumière astrale" [Astral light]. Poplavskii's poem to Arthur Rimbaud, however, is titled in Russian.

89. Vladimir Padunov, "Boris Poplavskii's Narcopoetics," paper delivered to the Annual Convention of the MLA, New York, December, 1983.

90. Olcott, "Poplavsky: The Heir Presumptive," 275.

91. The letter was found by Schakovskoy between the pages of a book, borrowed by Poplavskii from Aldanov, which subsequently came into her hands (*Otrazheniia,* 51).

92. Olcott, "Poplavsky: The Heir Presumptive," 284. Olcott is quoting from Poplavskii's "O misticheskoi atmosfere molodoi literatury v emigratsii" [On the mystical atmosphere of young émigré literature], *Chisla* [Numbers] 2/3 (1930), 309.

93. Berberova thinks that, had he not died so young, Poplavskii "would have ended by settling into French literature (as Arthur Adamov did), leaving the Russian language completely" (*The Italics Are Mine,* 274).

94. Schakovskoy, *Otrazheniia,* 51.

95. See Iulian Poplavskii's biography of his son (n. 85 above) and a section on Iulian Poplavskii from P. A. Puryskin, *Moskva kupecheskaia* [Mercantile Moscow] (New York, 1954), 256–257, appended to Karlinsky, "In Search of Poplavsky," 318–322.

96. Schakovskoy, *Otrazheniia,* 52.

97. Vasily Yanovsky, who knew Poplavskii well, opines that Popslavskii's somewhat mysterious death cannot have been a suicide: "I do not believe Boris was aware of his forthcoming journey. He was, after all, a professional, and would, at the last minute, have remembered his diaries and unfinished manu-

scripts and left them in some sort of order" (*Elysian Fields: A Book of Memory*, trans. Isabella and V. S. Yanovsky [DeKalb: Northern Illinois University Press, 1987], 24). Poplavskii died of an overdose of drugs, apparently deliberately administered by his companion, who wanted to commit suicide but was afraid to die by himself.

98. Anthony Olcott, "Poplavsky's Life," in Poplavskii, *Sobranie sochinenii* (Berkeley, Calif.: Berkeley Slavic Specialties, 1980), I, xvii. Poplavskii's father states that Boris also frequented the academy at La Grande Chaumière (Iulian Poplavskii, biography of Boris Poplavskii, in Karlinsky and Appel, eds., *The Bitter Air of Exile*, 321).

99. Karlinsky, "In Search of Poplavsky," 328. Il'ia Zdanevich (Iliazd), who was close to Poplavsky, remarked that, in many ways, things were easier for the émigré painters, who could become full-fledged members of the Paris School. Refugee literary and publishing circles, in contrast, were closed and unwelcoming and, in their turn, unacceptable to Zdanevich and Poplavskii. This was, said Zdanevich, the reason why Poplavskii, Aleksandr Ginger, and Boris Bozhnev were drawn to the artists and to Montparnasse, and it explains the creation of Cherez, the literary section of the Union of Russian Artists. Zdanevich observed that he, Poplavskii, and the others spent five years in that milieu—writing and reading out loud for painters, enjoying painting more than poetry, and going to exhibits of painting more frequently than to libraries. Zdanevich adds that this poetic seclusion permitted Poplavskii to develop as a poet far from the *poshlost'* of refugee literary circles, and in this sense it protected Poplavskii, while, however, confirming his pessimism and the theme of death which continued to pervade his poetry. See Il'ia Zdanevich, "Boris Poplavskii" (a manuscript found in Zdanevich's archives), *Sintaksis*, no. 16 (1986), 164–169; 167.

100. Olcott, "Poplavsky: The Heir Presumptive," 281.

101. Karlinsky, "In Search of Poplavsky," 317.

102. "A sky-blue horse dashed out, / a blue-glass carriage" [Vybezhala golubaia loshad' / Siniaia kareta iz stekla] ("Dolorosa," in Poplavskii, *Sobranie sochinenii*, I, 39). For G. Struve's discussion of Poplavskii's imagery, see *Russkaia literatura v izgnanii* (New York: Chekhov Press, 1956), 339.

103. E.g., "Under the spangled sky ships leave port. / Spirits wave handkerchiefs from the bridge, and sparkling in the dark air / a locomotive chants on the viaduct" ("The Rose of Death," trans. Ron Loewinsohn, in Karlinsky and Appel, eds., *The Bitter Air of Exile*, 290). [Korabli otkhodiat v nebe zvezdnom, / Na mostu platkami mashut dukhi, / I sverkaia cherez temnyi vozdukh / Parovoz poet na viaduke] ("Roza smerti," in Poplavskii, *Sobranie sochinenii*, I, 40).

104. Karlinsky, "In Search of Poplavsky," 328.

105. See, for example, Wassily Kandinsky's *Klange*. A recent English translation by Elizabeth R. Napier, *Sounds* (New Haven: Yale University Press, 1981), containing the German text in an appendix, is available. Hans Arp also wrote poetry in both French and German. There is a major study of his German poetry: Reinhard Dohl, *Das literarische Werk Hans Arps, 1903–1930* [The literary work of Hans Arp] (Stuttgart: J. B. Metzler, 1967), and an informative

article on his French works, which were collected and published by Marcel Jean under the title *Jours effeuillés* [Plucked days]. See Armine Kotin, "Jean Arp, Poet and Artist," *Dada/Surrealism* 7 (1977), 109–120; W. Hoffmann, "Les écrivains dessinateurs [Writers who draw]: Introduction," *Revue de l'Art* 44 (1979), 7–18; Philippe Souppault, "Hans Arp," in his *Ecrits sur la peinture* [Writings on painting] (Paris: Lachenal & Ritter, 1980); and Renée Riese Hubert, *Surrealism and the Book* (Irvine: University of California Press, 1987). Although Rilke did not himself "do" painting and sculpture, his preoccupation with them (especially with the work of Rodin and Cézanne) was formatively crucial and may have been a balancing factor in his developing bilingualism. See Batterby, *Rilke and France*.

106. The nineteen-year-old Zdanevich was instrumental in the formation of the theory of *Vsechestvo*, or "All-ism," and wrote with Mikhail Larionov the 1913 manifesto *Pochemu my raskrashivaemsia* [Why we paint our faces], repr. in English in John E. Bowlt, ed., *Russian Art of the Avant-Garde: Theory and Criticism* (New York: Viking, Documents of 20th-Century Art, 1976), 79–83. Larionov later cannibalized (not to say plagiarized) Zdanevich-Eganbiury's *Natalia Goncharova/Mikhail Larionov* (Moscow: Editions Tz. A. Munster, 1913) for his prefaces to his exhibitions. "Eganbiury" is the name "Zdanevich" written in longhand, in the dative case, in Cyrillic, as it would be interpreted by a French letter carrier who knew no Russian.

107. The *dras* are *Janko Krul' Albanskai* [Janko, King of Albania] (Tiflis: 41°, 1918); *Asël naprakat* [Dunkey for rent] (Tiflis: 41°, 1919; *Ostraf Paskhi* [Easter eyeland] (Tiflis: 41°, 1919); *Zga iakaby* [As if Zga] (Tiflis: 41°, 1920); and, the most extraordinary of them all, *Lidantiu faram* [Ledentu as lighthouse] (Paris: Le degré 41, 1923). For studies and interpretations of Zdanevich's *dras*, see Françoise Le Gris-Bergmann, "Iliazd, ou d'une œuvre en forme de constellation" [About Iliazd; or, Works in the form of a constellation], in *Iliazd, maître d'œuvre du livre moderne* [Iliazd, master creator of the modern book], catalogue of the exhibition at the Gallery of the Université du Quebec à Montréal (September 5–28, 1984), 25–84; and Gerald Janecek, *The Look of Russian Literature: Avant-Garde Visual Experiments, 1900–1930* (Princeton: Princeton University Press, 1984), 164–188. Some elements of Janecek's analysis of the principles of Zdanevich's *zaum* are subject to caution, because Janecek did not have available to him the text of Zdanevich's lecture "Le degré 41 sinapisé," delivered at the Paris Academy of Medicine in February 1922, wherein Zdanevich speaks of the "pearly disease" [Zhemchuzhnaia bolezn'] and outlines his conception of *zaum*. The Russian text of this lecture has been reprinted in Marzio Marzaduri, ed., *L'avanguardia a Tiflis* [The avant-garde in Tiflis] (Venice: University of Venice, 1982), 294–308. See also Olga Djordjadzé, "Ilia Zdanévitch et le futurisme russe" [Il'ia Zdanevich and Russian Futurism], in *Iliazd*, catalogue of the exhibition at the Centre Georges Pompidou, Paris (May 10-June 25, 1978), 9–22.

108. *Il y a Zd*(anevich), or "There is Zd(anevich)."

109. For a discussion and brief analysis in English of *Voskhishchenie*, see my introduction to the Russian facsimile re-edition (Berkeley, Calif.: Berkeley

Slavic Specialties, 1983), v-xxiii. A French translation, *Le ravissement,* by Régis Gayraud has recently been published (Paris: Alinéa, 1987).

110. Iliazd, *Afat. Semdesiat' shest' sonetov* [Afat. Seventy-six sonnets] (Paris: Le degré 41, 1946).

111. "Brigadnyi" was published posthumously by Hélène Iliazd as a *mise en lumière* of a translation of the poem into French by Guillevic with a facsimile of the autograph Russian text appended and with a *mise en page* and engravings by Staritsky (Paris: private publication, 1982).

112. For a description of these books, see the bibliography established by François Chapon and reprinted, in a corrected version, in *Iliazd* (1978 catalogue) and *Iliazd, Maître d'œuvre du livre moderne* (1984 catalogue).

113. Iliazd wrote some prefaces directly in French. The one for his book on the Georgian primitive painter Niko Pirosmanashvili (whom he and his brother had discovered) exists in five slightly different versions, all dating from 1972. The changes are careful variations for purposes of rhythm or style. Iliazd also wrote prefaces to some of the books he had "brought to light"—e.g., the preface to Iliazd's *Le frère mendiant* [The mendicant friar] (Paris: Le degré 41, 1959)—and wrote polemical texts in French such as "Après nous le Lettrisme" [After us, Lettrism]. The most extraordinary product of this polemic was Iliazd's *Poésie de mots inconnus* [The poetry of unknown words] (Paris: Le degré 41, 1948). Among his architectural studies, one written in French was "L'itinéraire géorgien de Ruy Gonzales de Clavijo et les églises aux confins de l'Atabégat" [The Georgian itinerary of Clavijo and the churches of the Atabegat region] (Trigance: Le degré 41, 1966). Other studies of Byzantine architecture remain unpublished. Among the many notebooks full of unpublished material, one chosen almost at random for 1937 contains a mixture of exercises toward the creation of a French *zaum,* which led to "La chasse sous-marine" [Underwater fishing] of 1948, drafts of letters in French, and Russian poems. Of particular interest to us is the rough draft of a good part of a novel in French which takes place on the Manchurian border in 1932. The text is peppered with linguistic inaccuracies (verb endings that sound the same being written the same; *ais, er, ait* often interchanged), but this is a very rough draft, and Triolet's notebooks for the same period were only slightly better.

114. Iliazd, *Boustrophédon au miroir* (Paris: Le degré 41, 1972).

115. The fruits of this effort are *Maximiliana; ou, L'exercice illégal de l'astronomie* [Maximiliana; or, The illegal exercise of astronomy], including thirty-four etchings by Max Ernst (Paris: Le degré 41, 1964), and an essay by Iliazd that retraces the vicissitudes of the life of the unjustly forgotten astronomer: *L'art de voir de Guillaume Tempel* [Guillaume Tempel's art of vision], which appeared·as a pamphlet simultaneously with *Maximiliana. Le frère mendiant,* with engravings by Picasso, is a *mise en lumière* of extracts from the *Libro del conocimiento,* the record of the African voyages of an anonymous fourteenth-century Franciscan friar (originally published in 1877), as well as extracts from *l'Histoire de la première découverte et conqueste des Canaries faite dès l'an 1402 par Messire Jéhan de Bethancourt . . . éscrite . . . par P. Boutier . . . et Jean Le Verrier* [The history of the first discovery and

conquest of the Canary Islands in 1402 by Messire Jehan de Bethencourt, recorded by Brother Pierre Boutier (a Franciscan) and Father Jean Le Verrier], originally published in 1896. Iliazd did much research on the great voyages of the fourteenth through the sixteenth century, although few of his studies were ever published. He also discovered the sixteenth-century tomb of Simon Begnius on the tiny island of Ulian. Another product of Iliazd's own voyages was "Ruy Gonzales de Clavijo en Géorgie: Observations sur son chemin d'Avnik à Trébizonde du 5 au 17 septembre 1405" [Ruy Gonzales de Clavijo in Georgia: Some observations on his route from Avnik to Trebizond, September 5–17, 1405], a paper prepared for the Twelfth International Congress of Byzantine Studies, Belgrade, September 1961. In the summer of 1964, Iliazd traveled around the Peloponnesus of Greece, following the itinerary of Cyriacus of Ancona as well as the route of the Fourth Crusade.

Iliazd's interest in architecture was lifelong. In May 1917, having returned to Tiflis after completing his legal studies in Saint Petersburg, he joined an expedition to Turkey, the purpose of which was to study medieval architecture. According to Annick Lionel-Marie, about a third of the plans and architectural drawings that resulted from the voyage were Iliazd's work ("Iliazd, facettes d'une vie" [Iliazd, facets of a life], in *Iliazd* [1978 catalogue], 50). Iliazd prepared a paper "La construction géométrique du plan byzantin" [The geometric construction of Byzantine plans] for the Eighth International Congress of Byzantine Studies at Palermo, April, 1950. In 1965, he went to Crete in search of the episcopal church of Kessamos, which had been described by the Italian Byzantine archaeologist Gerola at the beginning of the century. Iliazd recorded the measurements and established the plan of this church, as well as those of many others, in the course of his voyages into isolated and little traveled regions.

116. Yanovsky is one of those adults about whom G. Neufeld has noted that they may achieve excellent control of syntax, grammar, and vocabulary (although in Yanovsky's case there are occasional gallicisms) while retaining a heavy accent in the spoken language.

117. Elsa Triolet, *Œuvres romanesques croisées* (Paris: Robert Laffont, 1964), I, 32.

118. Personal communication. All biographical facts about Yanovsky not otherwise attributed were told to the author by Yanovsky or by his wife, Isabella Levitin, in several conversations between spring 1986 and spring 1987.

119. Gleb Struve took Yanovsky to task for what he considered to be cardinal sins against the Russian language, greater even than those of Gaito Gazdanov, to whom he otherwise compared Yanovsky favorably in his *Russkaia literatura v izgnanii* [Russian literature in exile] (New York: Chekhov Press, 1956), 296: "With all his crude naturalism, with all his sins against the Russian language (and they are much cruder and much more numerous than Gazdanov's lapses), there is genuine strength in Yanovsky's works, which are more moving than the smoother, more polished novels of Gazdanov" [Pri vsem ego grubom naturalizme, pri vsekh ego grekhakh protiv russkogo iazyka (i gorazdo bolee grubykh i bolee mnogochislennykh, chem liapsusy Gazdanova) u

Ianovskogo byla kakaia-to podlinnaia sila, veshchi ego bol'she zadevali chem bolee gladkie, bolee vyloshchennye romany Gazdanova]. Adamovich took Gazdanov to task for obvious grammatical errors or French calques, which he referred to as "a mixture of French with the Nizhegorodsky dialect, or ultra-French influences combined with those from the Soviet language" (Georgii Adamovich, "Literaturnye besedy," [Literary conversations], *Zveno* [The link], no. 5 [1928], cited in Pachmuss, ed. and trans., *A Russian Cultural Revival*, 313). While Gazdanov never became a bilingual writer, the first part of his *Vecher u Kler* [An evening with Claire] contains a good deal of French. For an illuminating discussion of the (strictly speaking) nonlinguistic sources of tension between the two generations, see Marc Raeff's preface to the English version of Yanovsky's memoir, *Elysian Fields*, ix-xv.

120. Richard Howard remarks on the back cover of *Elysian Fields:* "At eighty, Yanovsky has preserved every last drop of the émigré's venom, unsweetened by a magnificent old age in America, by the translation into English of three luminous visionary novels, and by a volume of medical memoirs unique in the literature: no, his account of the Russian literary émigrés in France in the twenties and thirties ('we lay like moss-covered stones, not moving but manifesting an enormous strength in our inertia') must be read as a concoction *at full strength* of that historically traduced cluster of geniuses and fakes, thrust upon the thorns of life: there is blood on every page."

121. The only actual fistfight in which he was involved was with Poplavskii (*Polia Eliseiskie* [New York: Serebrianyi vek, 1983], 20–21; *Elysian Fields*, 15).

122. Struve, *Russkaia literatura v izgnanii*, 296. The more spiritual element of Yanovsky's earlier works is best represented by his *Liubov' vtoraia* [The other love] (Berlin: Parakhvla, 1935) and by *Portativnoe bessmertie* [Portable immortality], the novel that Yanovsky himself considers a key to his spiritual concerns, which was written in 1935–1936 but published only much later (New York: Chekhov Press, 1953).

123. Anton Chekhov to A. S. Suvorin, September 11, 1888, in Anton Chekhov, *Letters on the Short Story, the Drama, and Other Literary Topics,* ed. Louis S. Friedland (New York: Dover, 1966), 42. In the 1960s Yanovsky had prepared a book of texts by physician-writers and about physicians as they appear in literature, but could not find a publisher "because there was too much about death."

124. It is interesting to compare Yanovsky with Leo Vroman, a bilingual Dutch-English poet, prose writer, artist, and blood physiologist, who has written love poetry to the same woman for forty years, but many of whose most striking poems have to do with physiology. See, for instance, his "Love Greatly Enlarged" (on the idea that no matter how horrible something might be at normal scale, if you look closely enough, it is beautiful). He also sees a connection between writing and the study of proteins: the twenty amino acids are like an alphabet that has to be read across a surface by their fellow proteins.

Some of Vroman's works exist only in one language or the other. "In vitro, in vivo, in toto," exists only in English (despite its Latin title), as does *Blood* (a scientific work). He also claims to be the first poet in any language to have written a love poem in computer language. His poetry (thus far) is collected in *Gedichten 1946–1984* (Amsterdam: Querido, 1985), the early prose in *Proza* (Amsterdam: Querido, 1960). Several of Vroman's earliest English poems, written almost immediately after his arrival in the United States, were published in *Poetry 75* (March 1950), 320–325, but some of the poems he wrote in America are in Dutch. Vroman would rather translate his own poetry than have someone else do it, because he can allow himself to break it apart and rebuild it around a skeleton that remains the same. He finds that reading his own poems, when translated by someone else, is "like meeting a dead friend" (remark made in answer to a question at a reading at the CUNY Graduate Center, May 1, 1987). Whatever the language, Vroman feels, the poet has something in him, and when he finds the right words for it, he has a poem. But this is not simply "clothing thought," for the form the poem takes is serendipitous: you go where the words lead you, and you frequently come to one thought or another through rhyme. Vroman also says that he feels the same satisfaction whether the product of his activity is a poem, a drawing, or a discovery in the lab (May 1, 1987).

125. Yanovsky had learned some French in the *Gymnasium*, but he could not speak it before he arrived in Paris. As for English, he had acquired enough to read scientific texts for his dissertation, but he could not speak it before his arrival in the United States.

126. See Iswolsky, *No Time to Grieve*; and Yanovsky, *Polia Eliseiskie*.

127. It is interesting that W. H. Auden, whom Brodsky so admires and under whose influence he claims to have begun writing in English ("To Please a Shadow," *Less than One*, 358), should have been interested enough in Yanovsky's work to write a foreword for his *No Man's Time*, trans. Isabella Levitin and Roger Nyle Parris (New York: Weybright & Talley, 1967).

128. Nabokov to Wilson, April 29, 1944, in *The Nabokov-Wilson Letters*, ed. Simon Karlinsky, (New York: Harper & Row, Colophon, 1980), 44.

129. Yanovsky, *The Dark Fields of Venus: From a Doctor's Log Book* (New York: Harcourt Brace Jovanovich, 1973).

130. Yanovsky, *Medicine, Science, and Life* (New York: Paulist Press, 1978).

131. W. H. Auden, foreword to Yanovsky, *No Man's Time*.

132. Yanovsky, *Of Light and Sounding Brass*, trans. V. S. Yanovsky and Isabella Levitin (New York: Vanguard, 1972); review by Richard Howard, *New York Times Book Review*, Feburary 25, 1973, quoted in the *Contemporary Authors* article on Yanovsky, vols. 97–100 (Detroit, Mich.: Gale Research Co., 1981), 577–579; 578.

133. *No Man's Time* has only recently been published in Russian as *Po tu storonu vremeni*, in *Novyi zhurnal*, nos. 167–169 (1987–1989). *Of Light and Sounding Brass* remains unpublished in Russian. *The Great Transfer* was published in New York by Harcourt Brace Jovanovich, 1974.

134. Samuel Beckett, "Three Dialogues with George Duthuit," *transition* 49 (December 1949), 97–103.

135. Iswolsky says that when her father was foreign minister, he wrote to ambassadors abroad in French, although he preferred to write in Russian to

his contemporaries. Other affairs were conducted in bilingual style, but his tendency was to use Russian (Iswolsky, *No Time to Grieve*, 10).

136. This correspondence between the philologist-philosopher Mikhail Gershenzon and the poet-scholar Viacheslav Ivanov was written when they were both ill in the same hospital ward in 1920. Thus its title: *Perepiska iz dvukh uglov* [Correspondence between two corners].

137. Iswolsky, *No Time to Grieve*, 172.

138. Ibid., 231.

139. Vladimir Pozner, personal communication.

140. Vladimir Pozner, *Mille et un jours* [A thousand and one days] (Paris: Julliard, 1967), 21: "It was there that I learned to pronounce and write Russian correctly with a teacher who must have been barely twenty-one" [C'est là où j'ai appris à mieux prononcer et à bien écrire le russe chez une maîtresse qui devait être à peine majeure].

141. Not that the brothers forgot their French side either. Pozner tells of his first ride in an open carriage with his younger brother, during which they were heartily singing the "Marseillaise" in French. They were stopped at the crossing of the Nevskii and Liteinyi Avenues by Saint Petersburg's largest policeman, who demanded to know why they were singing a revolutionary song. Pozner recalls having replied, in French, that France and Russia were allies (ibid., 14).

142. Ibid., 39.

143. Vladimir Pozner, "Vsia zhizn' gospodina Ivanova," *Epopeia* 4 (1923), 9–16. Pozner also published poetry in Russian in *Volia Rossii* [Russia's will] and in *Sovremennye zapiski* [Contemporary notes].

144. Pozner sent a copy of *Stikhi na sluchai* (Paris: Imprimerie de la societé nouvelle d'éditions franco-slaves 1928) to Pasternak and received in return a lengthily dedicated copy of *Poverkh bar'erov* [Over the barriers] and a long letter that, rather than speaking in detail about *Stikhi na sluchai*, starts out with Pasternak's declaration that he finds it very difficult to judge poetry, that he understands nothing about it. He goes so far as to say that the book was agreeable to read, but he admits to a certain "reticence of judgment" before the letter veers away from Pozner's book to the relationship of the author (in general) to his readers (in general) and to a discussion of Khodasevich (in particular). See *Vladimir Pozner se souvient de* [Vladimir Pozner remembers . . .] (Paris: Julliard, 1972), 158–162.

145. Vladimir Pozner, *Panorama de la littérature russe contemporaine* (Paris: Kra, 1929).

146. Vladimir Pozner, "Chasy bez strelok," *Zveno* [The link], no. 226 (1927), 7–80.

147. One thinks as well of the Hoffmannesque works of Aleksandr Chaianov, written in the 1920s. Chaianov's stories have been republished in *Istoriia parikmakherskoi kukly i drugie sochineniia botanika kh* [The tale of the hairdresser's dummy and other writings of Botanist X] (New York: Russica, 1982).

148. *Die gerettete Zunge* [The tongue set free] is the title of the first volume of Elias Canetti's autobiography. It comes from his earliest memory: a smiling man who tells him, "Show me your tongue" and who then brings the blade of

a jackknife up to it, saying, "Now we'll cut off his tongue." At the last minute, the man pulls back the knife saying, "Not today, tomorrow." This scene was repeated frequently. The purpose was to get the child to "hold his tongue" about the relations between the man and the boy's nursemaid. The threat worked, says Canetti, and the child "held his tongue" about the matter for ten years (*The Tongue Set Free,* trans. Joachim Neugroschel [New York: Seabury Press, 1979], 3–4).

149. It was Edmund Wilson who brought to Nabokov's attention the fact that Pozner, too, had been awarded a Guggenheim (April 1, 1943, *Letters,* 98).

150. In a letter to Nikolai Berdiaev, Gippius explained: "Almost imperceptibly D. S. and I began to incline toward French circles. These are superficial, of course, because the French people in general are superficial; but what is even worse, is that, wishing to escape this *humanité,* we have managed to get into the *beau monde* where . . . you can picture yourself what it is like. Moreover, for money, we are forced to involve ourselves with French literature, to associate with French publishers and journals. Translators consume half our income; therefore D. S. sometimes writes in French for the French journals. I am also indulging in this vice, however absurd it may appear. Or I do the translating myself—adjusting everything to Frenchmen" (quoted in Temira Pachmuss, *Zinaida Gippius: An Intellectual Profile* [Carbondale: Southern Illinois University Press, 1971], 234).

151. I. N. Gorbov (1896–1982) was trained in a military academy in Russia and, at eighteen, participated in World War I and subsequently in the civil war that followed the 1917 Revolution. He first wrote novels in French, one of which, *Le Second Avènement* [The Second Coming] (Paris: Editions Pierre Horay, 1955), which he later self-translated into Russian and published in *Vozrozhdenie* [Renaissance] is particularly striking. As Jacques Gorbof, he also published *Les chemins de l'enfer* [Hell's paths] (Paris: Editions Lardanchet, 1947); *Les condamnés* [The condemned] (Paris: Editions Pierre Horay, 1954); *Madame Sophie* (Paris: Emmanuel Vitte, 1957); and several collections of short stories. Gorbov continued to be active in the literary life of the Paris Russian emigration and, in 1961, became the editor of *Vozrozhdenie,* subsequently publishing both criticism and fiction in Russian (e.g., *Asunta* and *Vse otnosheniia* [All respects], [Paris: Editions de Flore, 1964]).

152. Mark Aldanov (writing under the name M. A. Landau-Aldanov), *Lénine* (Paris: J. Povolozky, 1919); also see his *Deux révolutions: La révolution française et la révolution russe* [Two revolutions, the French and the Russian] (Paris: Imprimerie union, 1920).

153. Nina Berberova, *Alexsandre Blok et son temps* [Aleksandr Blok and his time] (Paris: Editions du chêne, 1947).

154. Dmitri S. Mirsky, *A History of Russian Literature from the Earliest Times to the Death of Dostoevsky (1881)* (New York: Alfred A. Knopf, 1926) and *Contemporary Russian Literature (1881–1927)* (New York: Alfred A. Knopf, 1927).

155. Vladimir Weidlé (1895–1979) was an art historian as well as a literary critic. He wrote poetry and much criticism in Russian, but his *Les abeilles d'Aristée: Essai sur le destin des lettres et les arts* [The bees of Aristaeus: An

essay on the fate of the arts and letters] (Paris, 1954) and other works were written in French. A few works of criticism were also written in English and Italian.

156. Roman Jakobson (1896–1982), one of the most influential literary and linguistic theorists of the twentieth century, spoke and read an indeterminate, but considerable, number of languages. Founder of the Prague Linguistic Circle, intimate associate of the Russian Futurists, Jakobson was a rather early polyglot but was not bilingual from infancy. His parents were, he said, typical examples of the Russian Jewish intelligentsia. He began to learn French when he was six, from a "young person," and considered that in many ways his early linguistic experience was comparable to that of his childhood friend Elsa Triolet: "I share and recognize what Elsa has said about the influence that the absence of borders between French and Russian, between French and Russian literature, French and Russian poetry have had on her whole life. It has been the same for me" [Ce que dit Elsa sur l'influence qu'a eu pour elle, pendant toute sa vie, cette absence de frontières entre le français et le russe, les lettres françaises et les lettres russes, la poésie française et la poésie russe, c'est exactement le même cas avec moi] (Jakobson, "Réponses," *Poétique* 57 [February 1987], 5). Jakobson notes that, because of his weak eyesight, his parents restricted his reading; they were less strict about French books, however, because these presented the added utility of helping him acquire French more rapidly. Therefore, as a child he mainly read French books and, as a result, throughout his life until old age, whenever he was tired or ill, he preferred to read French books rather than Russian ones. In the 1930s, when he had to write (in German) a major study on the Russian case system and on the general significance of case systems, he asked his mother to come and actually *write* it for him: he dictated and she transcribed, for her German was better than his. In the same *Poétique* interview, Jakobson makes several interesting comments about the linguistic differences between the great (Russian) linguists Baudoin de Courtenay and Aleksei Shakhmatov: "Baudoin de Courtenay belonged to an entirely different school than did Shakhmatov. He was French, and when he was asked where he was from, he replied, 'I am a Polonized Frenchman and a Russified Pole' " [Baudoin de Courtenay appartenait à une toute autre école que Chakhmatov, c'était un français. Lui-même disait, quand on lui demandait d'où il venait: "Je suis un Français polonisé et un Polonais russifié"] (p. 18).

Conclusions and Projections

1. Brodsky's self-translations appear with some regularity: e.g., "Kelomyakki," *The New Yorker* (January 26, 1987), 26–27; and "North Baltic" (1978), *The New York Review of Books* (February 18, 1988), 16.

2. Joseph Brodsky, "In a Room and a Half," *Less Than One* (New York: Farrar, Straus & Giroux, 1986), 447–501.

3. Brodsky remarks that what he writes in "In a Room and a Half" is what his deceased parents would remember about him, unless they now have the gift of omniscience and observe him as he sits and writes in a language that they did not understand "although now they should be pan-glot" ("In a Room and

a Half," 457). Shades, doubtless not accidental, of Tsvetaeva's vision of the "Angelic" Rilke.

4. Brodsky, "In a Room and a Half," 460–461.

5. Joseph Brodsky, "The Condition We Call Exile," written for a conference on exile sponsored by the Wheatland Foundation, Vienna, December 1987, in *The New York Review of Books* (January 21, 1988), 16–20; 18. Brodsky indulges in some almost Nabokovian polyglot punning—e.g., his comment that if exiles "decide to remain effects and play at exile in an old-fashioned way, that shouldn't be explained away as 'nostalgie de la boot' " (p. 20).

6. Tsvetkov's *Eden* (Ann Arbor, Mich.: Ardis, 1985) contains a self-Englished version of one of his earlier Russian poems. Loseff, whose English is quite good, despite his disclaimers, already uses it for "rough drafts" of scholarly papers and the like, but then he has Anglophones edit them. For his poetry, he collaborates closely with a translator, discussing his text line by line.

7. Nor should one forget such major practitioners of bilingual writing earlier in the century as Yvan Goll, Stefan George, Sholom Aleichem, Gabriel Preil, Semën Frug, Emmanuil Kazakevich, Bruno Jasienski, and Karen Blixen—Isak Dinesen as well as others such as Rilke and Arp, whom we have already mentioned.

8. The Jungians make much of "meaningful coincidences," a concept they trace to classical Chinese texts: "The classical Chinese texts did not ask what *causes* what, but, rather, what 'likes' to *occur with* what" (M.-L. von Franz, "The Process of Individuation," in Carl C. Jung, *Man and His Symbols* [New York: Dell, 1968], 227).

9. Samuel Beckett, *Proust*, (New York, Grove Press, Evergreen, 1931), 64.

10. Nabokov speaks several times of his sense of this function as "transmitter." For example: "After the first shock of recognition—a sudden sense of '*this* is what I am going to write'—the novel starts to breed by itself; the process goes on solely in the mind, not on paper; and to be aware of the stage it has reached at any given moment, I do not have to be conscious of every exact phrase. I feel a kind of gentle development, an uncurling inside, and I know that the details are there already, that in fact I would see them plainly if I looked closer, if I stopped the machine and opened its inner compartment; but I prefer to wait until what is loosely called inspiration has completed the task for me. There comes a moment when I am informed from within that the entire structure is finished. All I have to do now is take it down in pencil or pen. Since this entire structure, dimly illumined in one's mind, can be compared to a painting, and since you do not have to work gradually from left to right for its proper perception, I may direct my flashlight at any part or particle of the picture when setting it down in writing" (*Strong Opinions* [New York: McGraw-Hill, 1973], 31–32).

Appendix. Samuel Beckett

1. Harry Cockerham, "Bilingual Playwright," in Katherine Worth, ed., *Beckett the Shape Changer* (London: Routledge & Kegan Paul, 1975), 143.

2. Raymond Federman has quite rightly observed that "little critical attention has been paid to Beckett's bilingualism and his unique activity as a self trans-lator" ("The Writer as Self-Translator," in Allan Warren Friedman, Charles Rossman, and Dina Sherzer, eds., *Beckett Translating/Translating Beckett* [University Park: The Pennsylvania State University Press, 1987], 7). The first section of *Beckett Translating/Translating Beckett* begins to fill in this critical gap.

3. Martin Esslin, "Samuel Beckett: The Search for Self," in *The Theatre of the Absurd* (New York: Doubleday, Anchor, 1961), 1.

4. Even the most peculiar of all exiled aristocrats, Charles Kinbote, is sure that, behind the beaver beard of his alias, he still is, as he always was, Charles the Beloved, King of Zembla. If he is not, then we are dealing with delusion, not with the normal trauma of exile.

5. It is probably significant in this regard that the only Russian bilingual writer in whose works one *does* briefly see the Beckett syndrome is Elsa Trio-let, whose exile was initially the result of her own choice and who, at the time she was writing *Zashchitnyi tsvet* as well as thereafter, made frequent visits back to the Soviet Union—to which she could have returned permanently, had she so desired.

6. Deirdre Bair, *Samuel Beckett: A Biography* (New York: Harcourt Brace Jovanovich, Harvest, 1978), 38.

7. During his Trinity College period, Beckett even succumbed to the beret syndrome: "Following his two trips to the continent, Beckett began to wear a French beret, to pepper his speech with gallicisms his parents couldn't under-stand—actually becoming a bit of a snob, as undergraduates often are before parents who might not have enjoyed the same educational advantages" (ibid., 55). It is amusing that such "undergraduates" never seem to realize that the beret is almost exclusively either a lower-class or a military headgear, except for men who are old enough to have fought in World War I. One suspects that Beckett put his away in a closet when he settled in at the École normale su-périeure.

8. Of course, proper English had already been loosened up considerably by Joyce's Private Carr, who had bawled: "I'll wring the neck of any fucking bas-tard says a word against my bleeding fucking king. . . . I'll do him in, so help me fucking Christ! I'll wring the bastard fucker's bleeding blasted fucking windpipe. . . . God fuck old Bennett. He's a whitearsed bugger. I don't give a shit for him" (*Ulysses*, pp. 597, 600, 603 of the 1934 1st American ed.).

9. Cockerham, "Bilingual Playwright," 155: "Although Beckett is often said to be fully bilingual, it is important to remember that he is not bilingual in the sense of having possessed two languages since childhood. His French was learnt at a comparatively late stage and as a foreign language, so that in the acquiring of it, the order of events was for him the opposite of what it would have been for a native speaker: first the formal study, then, to the extent that this happens when a language is thus acquired, the unconscious imbibing of everyday patterns of speech, vocabulary and idiom."

10. Nabokov maintained that Beckett's French always showed traces of its

having been acquired formally: "Beckett's French is a schoolmaster's French, a preserved French, but in English you feel the moisture of verbal association and of the spreading live roots of his prose" (*Strong Opinions* [New York: McGraw-Hill, 1973], 172). Many studies have painstakingly documented the vulgarisms of the first prose works that Beckett wrote in French (e.g., Ruby Cohn, "The First Burst into French," in *Samuel Beckett: The Comic Gamut* [New Brunswick, N.J.: Rutgers University Press, 1962]) as well as the vulgarisms of the French translation of the erstwhile "stylistically elegant Murphy" (Ruby Cohn, "Samuel Beckett, Self-translator," in *The Comic Gamut*). See also Vivian Mercier, *Beckett/Beckett* (New York: Oxford University Press, 1977); Hugh Kenner, *Samuel Beckett: A Critical Study* (New York: Grove Press, 1961); and Lawrence Harvey, *Samuel Beckett: Poet and Critic* (Princeton: Princeton University Press, 1970).

11. Erika Ostrovsky, "Le silence de Babel" [The silence of Babel], in the Cahier de l'Herne, *Samuel Beckett* (Paris: L'Herne, 1976), 206–211; 206. Vivian Mercier has remarked that although "Joyce's hoard of Irish knowledge and feeling was virtually inexhaustible, Beckett had brought little that was usable and durable from his insulated Irish community" (*Beckett/Beckett*, 37). The fact that there was not that much to throw overboard may be a clue to the whole process.

12. At the time of the publication of "Assumption," *transition*, the important Paris review published by Eugene and Maria Jolas, identified Beckett (with or without his assent) as "an Irish poet and essayist teaching at the École normale supérieure" (*transition*, 16–17 [June 1929], 268–271; 268).

13. These were translations of poems and prose by Eugenio Montale, Raffaello Franchi, and Giovanni Comisso, published in *This Quarter* 2 (April-June 1930), 630, 672, 675–683, respectively.

14. Ralph Ellison, "The World and the Jug," in *Shadow and Act* (New York: Random House, 1964), 140.

15. It is curious that Beckett's involvement with Joyce (which partook both of a family and a literary relationship) resembles quite closely the links between some of Beckett's later "odd couples"—in particular, Hamm and Clov in *Fin de partie* [Endgame].

16. Beckett's translations of poems by Paul Eluard, André Breton, and René Crevel were published in *This Quarter* 5 (September 1932).

17. Bair, *Samuel Beckett*, 288. These poems were not published until 1946 in *Les temps modernes* [Modern times], no. 14 (November 1946).

18. T. S. Eliot, "Le directeur" [The director]; "Mélange adultère de tout" [An adulterous mixture of everything]; "Lune de miel" [Honeymoon]; and "Dans le restaurant" [In the restaurant]. Other cases of English-language writers who wrote in another language would include William Beckford, *Vathek* (late eighteenth century); Bruce Lowery, "La Cicatrice" [The scar], which he subsequently self-translated into English; and, of course, Oscar Wilde.

19. Letter to Thomas McGreevy, April 3, 1938, quoted in Bair, *Samuel Beckett*, 288.

20. Bair, *Samuel Beckett*, 288.

21. It is perhaps primarily to these early poems in French that Beckett's famous comment that it is easier to write "sans style" in French really applies.

22. Bair, *Samuel Beckett*, 329.

23. Cohn, *The Comic Gamut*, 261.

24. Ibid., 262.

25. Cockerham, "Bilingual Playwright," 151.

26. Olga Bernal, "Le glissement hors du langage" [Slipping out of language], in *Samuel Beckett* (L'Herne), 219–220.

27. E.g., Gérard Durozoi, in *Beckett: Quatre commentaires* [Beckett: Four commentaries] (Paris: Bordas, 1972), 135–137.

28. Furthermore, *Mercier et Camier* still belongs to the series of texts that Ludovic Janvier categorizes as "récits lointains" [distanced narratives]. See his useful table in "Lieu dire" [Naming places], *Samuel Beckett* (L'Herne), 195.

29. It is true that Beckett never became "French" in this way, despite the fact that an intimate knowledge of French culture is evident in his choices of variants for English idioms in the French translation. In our sense, Nabokov was no longer a particularly "American" novelist in *Look at the Harlequins!* or *Transparent Things* or even, perhaps, in *Ada*.

30. Samuel Beckett, *Proust* (New York: Grove Press, Evergreen, 1931), 46–47.

31. Beckett made this comment in "Hommage à Jack B. Yeats," quoted in Mercier, *Beckett/Beckett*, 112.

32. Beckett, *L'innommable* (Paris: Editions de minuit, 1953), 63. While elsewhere in the present book the English translation always precedes the original language, in the case of Beckett, to avoid possible confusion, the original language, whether French or English, is cited first. Hereafter, references to *L'innommable* will appear in parentheses in the text.

33. The English translation is, of course, Beckett's: *The Unnamable*, in Samuel Beckett, *Three Novels* (New York: Grove, Evergreen, 1955), 324. Hereafter, references to *The Unnamable* will be to this edition and will appear in parentheses in the text.

34. Mercier, *Beckett/Beckett*, 37.

35. Beckett, *Not I* (1972), in Samuel Beckett, *I Can't Go On, I'll Go On*, ed. Richard W. Seaver (New York: Grove Press, 1977).

36. Beckett, *Proust*, 16–17.

37. Mercier, *Beckett/Beckett*, 4.

38. Beckett, *Not I*, 604.

39. It is interesting that, in the later period, Beckett also experimented with combining two systems of expression in a single work, as did Triolet. In Beckett's case, the combination is words and music: e.g., the carefully supervised operatic version of *Krapp's Last Tape* with music by Marcel Mihalovici, who commented, "I composed the music of *Krapp* under his constant supervision . . . showing him each fragment as it was completed: he would approve or disapprove, and I complied meticulously with his suggestions" (Pierre Melèse, *Samuel Beckett* [Paris: Seghers, 1966], 155). Mihalovici's remarks resemble

those of Beckett's translators, Patrick Bowles and Ludovic Janvier. The process seems to have been quite similar. There were also radio plays with music, such as *Cascando,* with music by Mihalovici, and *Words and Music* with music by John Beckett. In the latter two works, the music functioned as a character.

40. This remark to Shenker is widely quoted, as in John Fletcher's article "Ecrivain bilingue" [Bilingual writer], in *Samuel Beckett* (L'Herne), 212–218; 213.

41. In talking to Lawrence Harvey, Beckett said that his first French poems had been written in a "period of lostness, drifting around, seeing a few friends—a period of apathy and lethargy" (Harvey, *Poet and Critic,* 193). For comments on the later period, see Fletcher, "Ecrivain bilingue," 216.

42. If, for example, the BBC asked for something, Beckett naturally wrote in English. This is not exactly comparable to his early ambidexterity in cricket. There he *always* batted left-handed, but bowled right-handed (Bair, *Samuel Beckett,* 29). He was therefore *not* a switch-hitter in cricket: one function, one dominant hand.

43. Ibid., 625–626; 622–623.

44. For example, see Beckett's comments to Alan Schneider: "I have nothing but wastes and wilds of self-translation before me for many miserable months to come" (quoted ibid., 485–486).

45. Mercier, *Beckett/Beckett,* 4.

46. Beckett, *Proust,* 8.

47. Ostrovsky, "Le silence de Babel," 211.

48. A good example of the way in which the text passes—and where it sticks—is Hugh Kenner's documentary "Beckett Translating Beckett: *Comment c'est,*" *Delos* 5 (1970), 194–211. Many other articles treat this same problem. One of the worst is Martina Von Essen's "Samuel Beckett, traducteur de lui-même" [Samuel Beckett, self-translator], *Neuphilologische Mitteilungen* 73 (1972), 866–892. Despite, or because of, her critical jargon, Von Essen manages to slide by some of the most interesting word play, as though she did not even see it.

49. Steiner says: "It is as if the initial job of invention was done in a crypto-language, compounded equally of French, English, Anglo-Irish and totally private phonemes" ("Extraterritorial," *Triquarterly* 17 [1970], 121–122).

Index

This book forms part of the
STUDIES OF THE HARRIMAN INSTITUTE,
successor to:

STUDIES OF THE RUSSIAN INSTITUTE

Abram Bergson, *Soviet National Income in 1937* (1953)

Ernest J. Simmons, Jr., ed., *Through the Glass of Soviet Literature: Views of Russian Society* (1953)

Thad Paul Alton, *Polish Postwar Economy* (1954)

David Granick, *Management of the Industrial Firm in the USSR: A Study in Soviet Economic Planning* (1954)

Allen S. Whiting, *Soviet Policies in China, 1917–1924* (1954)

George S. N. Luckyj, *Literary Politics in the Soviet Ukraine, 1917–1934* (1956)

Michael Boro Petrovich, *The Emergence of Russian Panslavism, 1856–1870* (1956)

Thomas Taylor Hammond, *Lenon on Trade Unions and Revolution, 1893–1917* (1956)

David Marshall Lang, *The Last Years of the Georgian Monarchy, 1658–1832* (1957)

James William Morley, *The Japanese Thrust into Siberia, 1918* (1957)

Alexander G. Park, *Bolshevism in Turkestan, 1917–1927* (1957)

Herbert Marcuse, *Soviet Marxism: A Critical Analysis* (1958)

Charles B. McLane, *Soviet Policy and the Chinese Communists, 1931–1946* (1958)

Oliver H. Radkey, *The Agrarian Foes of Bolshevism: Promise and Defeat of the Russian Socialist Revolutionaries, February to October 1917* (1958)

Ralph Talcott Fisher, Jr., *Pattern for Soviet Youth: A Study of the Congresses of the Komsomol, 1918–1954* (1959)

Alfred Erich Senn, *The Emergence of Modern Lithuania* (1959)

Elliot R. Goodman, *The Soviet Design for a World State* (1960)

John N. Hazard, *Settling Disputes in Soviet Society: The Formative Years of Legal Institutions* (1960)

David Joravsky, *Soviet Marxism and Natural Science, 1917–1932* (1961)

Maurice Friedberg, *Russian Classics in Soviet Jackets* (1962)

Alfred J. Rieber, *Stalin and the French Communist Party, 1941–1947* (1962)

Theodore K. Von Laue, *Sergei Witte and the Industrialization of Russia* (1962)

John A. Armstrong, *Ukrainian Nationalism* (1963)

Oliver H. Radkey, *The Sickle under the Hammer: The Russian Socialist Revolutionaries in the Early Months of Soviet Rule* (1963)

Kermit E. McKenzie, *Comintern and World Revolution, 1928–1943: The Shaping of Doctrine* (1964)

Harvey L. Dyck, *Weimar Germany and Soviet Russia, 1926–1933: A Study in Diplomatic Instability* (1966)
      (Above titles published by Columbia University Press.)

Harold J. Noah, *Financing Soviet Schools* (Teachers College, 1966)

John M. Thompson, *Russia, Bolshevism, and the Versailles Peace* (Princeton, 1966)

Paul Avrich, *The Russian Anarchists* (Princeton, 1967)

Loren R. Graham, *The Soviet Academy of Sciences and the Communist Party, 1927–1932* (Princeton, 1967)

Robert A. Maguire, *Red Virgin Soil: Soviet Literature in the 1920s* (Princeton, 1968; Cornell, 1987)

T. H. Rigby, *Communist Party Membership in the U.S.S.R, 1917–1967* (Princeton, 1968)

Richard T. DeGeorge, *Soviet Ethics and Morality* (University of Michigan, 1969)

Jonathan Frankel, *Vladimir Akimov on the Dilemmas of Russian Marxism, 1895–1903* (Cambridge, 1969)

William Zimmerman, *Soviet Perspectives on International Relations, 1956–1967* (Princeton, 1969)

Paul Avrich, *Kronstadt, 1921* (Princeton, 1970)

Ezra Mendelsohn, *Class Struggle in the Pale: The Formative Years of the Jewish Workers' Movement in Tsarist Russia* (Cambridge, 1970)

Edward J. Brown, *The Proletarian Episode in Russian Literature* (Columbia, 1971)

Reginald E. Zelnik, *Labor and Society in Tsarist Russia: The Factory Workers of St. Petersburg, 1855–1870* (Stanford, 1971)

Patricia K. Grimsted, *Archives and Manuscript Repositories in the USSR: Moscow and Leningrad* (Princeton, 1972)

Ronald G. Suny, *The Baku Commune, 1917–1918* (Princeton, 1972)

Edward J. Brown, *Mayakovsky: A Poet in the Revolution* (Princeton, 1973)

Milton Ehre, *Oblomov and His Creator: The Life and Art of Ivan Goncharov* (Princeton, 1973)

Henry Krisch, *German Politics under Soviet Occupation* (Columbia, 1974)

Henry W. Morton and Rudolph L. Tökés, eds., *Soviet Politics and Society in the 1970s* (Free Press, 1974)

William G. Rosenberg, *Liberals in the Russian Revolution* (Princeton, 1974)

Richard G. Robbins, Jr., *Famine in Russia, 1891–1892* (Columbia, 1975)

Vera Dunham, *In Stalin's Time: Middle-class Values in Soviet Fiction* (Cambridge, 1976)

Walter Sablinsky, *The Road to Bloody Sunday* (Princeton, 1976)

William Mills Todd III, *The Familiar Letter as a Literary Genre in the Age of Pushkin* (Princeton, 1976)

Elizabeth Valkenier, *Russian Realist Art, The State and Society: The Peredvizhniki and Their Tradition* (Ardis, 1977)

Susan Solomon, *The Soviet Agrarian Debate* (Westview, 1978)

Sheila Fitzpatrick, ed., *Cultural Revolution in Russia, 1928–1931* (Indiana, 1978)

Peter Solomon, *Soviet Criminologists and Criminal Policy: Specialists in Policy-Making* (Columbia, 1978)

Kendall E. Bailes, *Technology and Society under Lenin and Stalin: Origins of the Soviet Technical Intelligentsia, 1917–1941* (Princeton, 1978)

Leopold H. Haimson, ed., *The Politics of Rural Russia, 1905–1914* (Indiana, 1979)

Theodore H. Friedgut, *Political Participation in the USSR* (Princeton, 1979)

Sheila Fitzpatrick, *Education and Social Mobility in the Soviet Union, 1921–1934* (Cambridge, 1979)

Wesley Andrew Fisher, *The Soviet Marriage Market: Mate-Selection in Russia and the USSR* (Praeger, 1980)

Jonathan Frankel, *Prophecy and Politics: Socialism, Nationalism, and the Russian Jews, 1862–1917* (Cambridge, 1981)

Robin Feuer Miller, *Dostoevsky and "The Idiot": Author, Narrator, and Reader* (Harvard, 1981)

Diane Koenker, *Moscow Workers and the 1917 Revolution* (Princeton, 1981)

Patricia K. Grimsted, *Archives and Manuscript Repositories in the USSR: Estonia, Latvia, Lithuania, and Belorussia* (Princeton, 1981)

Ezra Mendelsohn, *Zionism in Poland: The Formative Years, 1915–1926* (Yale, 1982)

Hannes Adomeit, *Soviet Risk-Taking and Crisis Behavior* (George Allen & Unwin, 1982)

Seweryn Bialer and Thane Gustafson, eds., *Russia at the Crossroads: The 26th Congress of the CPSU* (George Allen & Unwin, 1982)

Roberta Thompson Manning, *The Crisis of the Old Order in Russia: Gentry and Government* (Princeton, 1983)

Andrew A. Durkin, *Sergei Aksakov and Russian Pastoral* (Rutgers, 1983)

Bruce Parrott, *Politics and Technology in the Soviet Union* (MIT Press, 1983)

Sarah Pratt, *Russian Metaphysical Romanticism: The Poetry of Tiutchev and Boratynskii* (Stanford, 1984)

STUDIES OF THE HARRIMAN INSTITUTE

Elizabeth Kridl Valkenier, *The Soviet Union and the Third World: An Economic Bind* (Praeger, 1983)

John LeDonne, *Ruling Russia: Politics and Administration in the Age of Absolutism, 1762–1796* (Princeton, 1984)

Diane Greene, *Insidious Intent: A Structural Analysis of Fedor Sologub's Petty Demon* (Slavica, 1986)

Richard F. Gustafson, *Leo Tolstoy: Resident and Stranger* (Princeton, 1986)

William Chase, *Workers, Society and the State: Labor and Life in Moscow, 1918–1929* (Illinois, 1987)

John E. Malmstad, ed., *Andrey Bely: Spirit of Symbolism* (Cornell, 1987)

Zenovia A. Sochor, *Revolution and Culture: The Bogdanov-Lenin Controversy* (Cornell, 1988)

Marcus C. Levitt, *Russian Literary Politics and the Pushkin Celebration of 1880* (Cornell, 1989)

Elizabeth Klosty Beaujour, *Alien Tongues: Bilingual Russian Writers of the "First Emigration"* (Cornell, 1989)

Library of Congress Cataloging-in-Publication Data

Beaujour, Elizabeth Klosty.
  Alien tongues.

  (Studies of the Harriman Institute)
  Bibliography: p.
  Includes index.
  1. Authorship. 2. Bilingualism and literature. 3. Multilingualism and litera-
ture. 4. Authors, Exiled—France—Paris—History and criticism. 5. Authors,
Russian—France—Paris—History and criticism. 6. Literature—Exiled au-
thors—History and criticism. 7. Neurolinguistics. I. Title. II. Series.
PN137.B43 1989   809'.889'171044361   88–43287
ISBN 0–8014–2251–5 (alk. paper)